Mismanaged Money
in American Healthcare

THREE BOOKS BY COLLEEN AYCOCK
AND MARK SCOTT
AND FROM MCFARLAND

*The First Black Boxing Champions:
Essays on Fighters of the 1800s to the 1920s*
(Edited by Colleen Aycock and Mark Scott 2021 [2011])

Tex Rickard: Boxing's Greatest Promoter
(Colleen Aycock and Mark Scott 2012)

*Joe Gans: A Biography of the First
African American World Boxing Champion*
(Colleen Aycock and Mark Scott 2008)

Mismanaged Money in American Healthcare
Problems and Solutions

LISA FAMIGLIETTI
AND MARK SCOTT

McFarland & Company, Inc., Publishers
Jefferson, North Carolina

LIBRARY OF CONGRESS CATALOGUING-IN-PUBLICATION DATA

Names: Famiglietti, Lisa, 1954– author. | Scott, Mark, 1962– author.
Title: Mismanaged money in American healthcare : problems and solutions / Lisa Famiglietti and Mark Scott.
Description: Jefferson, North Carolina : McFarland & Company, Inc., Publishers, 2023 | Includes bibliographical references and index.
Identifiers: LCCN 2023027964 | ISBN 9781476687452 (paperback : acid free paper) ∞
ISBN 9781476649931 (ebook)
Subjects: LCSH: Medical care, Cost of—United States. | Medical care—United States—Cost effectiveness. | Medical care—United States—Finance.
Classification: LCC RA410.53 .F36 2023 | DDC 338.4/33621—dc23/eng/20230628
LC record available at https://lccn.loc.gov/2023027964

BRITISH LIBRARY CATALOGUING DATA ARE AVAILABLE

ISBN (print) 978-1-4766-8745-2
ISBN (ebook) 978-1-4766-4993-1

© 2023 Lisa Famiglietti and Mark Scott. All rights reserved

No part of this book may be reproduced or transmitted in any form or by any means, electronic or mechanical, including photocopying or recording, or by any information storage and retrieval system, without permission in writing from the publisher.

Front cover: Health care costs imagery
(Shutterstock/AnemStyle)

Printed in the United States of America

*McFarland & Company, Inc., Publishers
Box 611, Jefferson, North Carolina 28640
www.mcfarlandpub.com*

Table of Contents

Tables, Charts and Maps	vii
Introduction by Lisa Famiglietti	1
1. Death Rode a Pale Horse in 2020	5
2. The Medicaid Cluster	14
3. Where Does the Drug Money Go?	25
4. Money, Politics, and Data	34
5. Required Profits and MCOs	41
6. Coding and Billing	59
7. The Curious Case of CPT Code 92507	76
8. Curiouser and Curiouser	93
9. Managed Care Organizations: Down the Rabbit Hole	111
10. Regulations and Estimates	127
11. Regulation Failures: Third-Party Recovery and Site-Neutral Requirements	133
12. Cost-Shifting and the Flip and Roll	150
13. Scams with Teeth, Regulations without Teeth	156
14. Solutions for Unauditable Hospital Costs	169
15. Unnecessary Surgeries and Tests	183
16. Ethics in Healthcare Billing	189
17. Adding Up the Costs	199
Chapter Notes	205
Bibliography	217
Index	219

Tables, Charts, Images and Maps

Tables

Table 1. "Are State Managed Care Medicaid Programs Fertile Ground for Fraud?"	16–17
Table 2. Poverty Level, Medicaid Eligibility, and Income Limits for Texas	17
Table 3. Internal Rate of Return for $100 Million for 20 Years at 3 Percent Interest Rate	42–43
Table 4. Internal Rate of Return for $100 Million for 20 Years at 15 Percent Interest Rate	43
Table 5. 2016 Texas Health and Human Services Commission (30 Minutes of Direct Contact) Fee for Service Rates, CPT 92507	105
Table 6. Texas Medicaid Managed Care Organization Rate for CPT 92507 by Provider Type Compared with Texas Health and Human Services Commission Fee-for-Service and Medicare Rates	113
Table 7. Third Party Liability Example	144
Table 8. Examples of Dental Support Organizations and Dentist Payment Structures	157

Charts

Chart 1. Major U.S. Wars' Death Tolls vs. Death Toll for COVID-19	10
Chart 2. Cumulative Data for COVID-19 Through May 10, 2022	11
Chart 3. Federal Expenditures for Texas vs. Total of Federal and State Medicaid Expenditures, 2002–2019	19
Chart 4. MaxROI Market Cap Period from Mid–2014 Through July 2021	44
Chart 5. U.S. Spending on Healthcare in 2019	77
Chart 6. HHSC Consolidated Budget by Fiscal Years, Combined Amounts	79
Chart 7. Texas Health and Human Services Commission Consolidated Budget by Fiscal Years	81

Tables, Charts, Images and Maps

Chart 8. Comparison of Maximum Payment from Texas Medicaid vs Maximum Payment from Medicare (2016) — 82
Chart 9. 15-Minute Units Maximum Texas Medicaid Payment, CPT 92507 — 82
Chart 10. 30-Minute Session Maximum Texas Medicaid Payment, CPT 92507 — 83
Chart 11. 45-Minute Session Maximum Texas Medicaid Payment, CPT 92507 — 83
Chart 12. 60-Minute Session Maximum Texas Medicaid Payment, CPT 92507 — 84
Chart 13. HHSC FFS Rates vs Medicare/Commercial Rate, CPT 92507, 2019 Texas Medicaid — 92
Chart 14. Percentage Increase in Therapy Provided by a HHA Compared to Increase in Total National Health Expenditures Based Upon Data from KFF, 2010–2020 — 94
Chart 15. Comparison of Medicaid Spending for Texas Medicaid Beneficiaries Based on Location — 95
Chart 16. HHSC Adopted Rates 2019 for CPT 92507 vs Medicare Rate — 106
Chart 17. HHSC Rates (Adopted 12/01/2017) CPT 92507 — 107
Chart 18. Texas HHSC Rates for Fully Licensed SLPs — 109
Chart 19. HHSC Rates for Fully Licensed SLPs vs SLP-Assistants for Years 2017 and 2019 — 109
Chart 20. CPT Code 92507, MCO Rates for Provider Type HHA — 114
Chart 21. CPT Code 92507, MCO Rates for Provider Type CORF/ORF — 114
Chart 22. CPT Code 92507, MCO Rates for Provider Type Independent (Place of Service—Office) — 115
Chart 23. CPT Code 92507, MCO Rates for Provider Type Independent (Place of Service—Home) — 115
Chart 24. HHSC Fee for Service, CPT 92507 Billed with GN Modifier, Comparison Year 2014 — 134
Chart 25. TX HHSC Units Paid by Provider Type, Same Licensed Professionals, Same Coverage Guidelines and Limitations, Comparison Year 2014 — 134
Chart 26. Texas HHSC Utilization Summary for 2014 — 135
Chart 27. Change in Utilization of CPT 92507 by Provider Type 2014–2016 Based Upon HHSC Utilization Summaries — 136
Chart 28. Texas HHSC Rates CPT 92507, 2019 FFS — 138
Chart 29. Medicare Rates for All Provider Types vs Texas Medicaid Office and Home POS Rates for CPT 92507, 2019 — 138
Chart 30. Loss of Third-Party Payment, CPT 92507, CORF/ORF — 147

Chart 31. HHSC Adopted Rates Effective 09/01/2019 Comparing Licensed Assistant Rates to Medicare Rate for Fully Licensed SLP ... 148

Chart 32. Percentage Difference Between Texas Medicaid Rate for SLP Assistants and Medicare Rate for Fully Licensed SLP, 09/01/2019 ... 148

Chart 33. Texas Dentist Participation in Medicaid and DSO Affliation, Fall 2015 ... 158

Chart 34. Dental Care Use 2011 and 2016 ... 162

Chart 35. Dental Care Utilization 2016 ... 163

Images

Image 1. Sample Diagnosis Codes on HCFA 1500 Claim Form ... 66
Image 2. Sample Components of HCFA 1500 Claim Form ... 72
Image 3. MaxROI Rates for Speech Therapy ... 108

Maps

Map 1. Dr. John Snow's Map Shows Wide Area of Investigation for the 1854 London Cholera Epidemic ... 62

Map 2. The Location of the Broad Street Pump on Dr. John Snow's Map of the 1854 London Cholera Epidemic ... 78

Map 3. Service Delivery Areas for Texas Medicaid Managed-Care Organization ... 118

Graphic

Graphic 1. Comparison of Real-World Consequences of Inflated Payments by Texas Managed-Care Organizations ... 146

Introduction

Lisa Famiglietti

There are countless studies, theories, and investigations into what drives healthcare costs. Most reflect percentage increases in millions and billions of dollars related to technological innovation, prescription drug use, overuse of care, hospital ownership of physician groups, administrative cost—mandated care, unit price increases—the list is endless. Warren Buffett likened the increases in U.S. healthcare cost to the economy's tapeworm.

All of these views point to a variety of causes. All are from a 30,000-foot perspective. Perhaps we need a new perspective: from the ground up. To do this, one would need to look at specific costs and perhaps follow one healthcare plan and one code using the ground-up approach.

I am a licensed and certified speech-language pathologist (SLP). I have been in private practice, offering habilitative and rehabilitative services to those with communication disorders and swallowing disorders, for more than 38 years.

Through the years, the variability between Medicaid and other public plans and commercial insurance has always been something of a mystery to me.

Unlike commercial insurance, Medicaid coverage and reimbursement is dictated by law and is paid by the taxpayer. As a provider, I have had a bird's-eye view of implementation of mandated coverage and rate development guidelines as it applies to my scope of practice. The lack of adherence to standardized practices and prescribed guidelines and the potential impact on cost was and remains bewildering.

A few years ago I ran into an old friend, Mark Scott. I told him about a Medicaid payment issue I was having, and he mentioned that he had once been in charge of various Medicaid audits.

Later we had lunch and ended up discussing the enigmas of the healthcare system. Why did America have so many uninsured when the country spends approximately a fifth of its gross national product on healthcare? Why was the country so unprepared for the COVID-19 pandemic?

It turned out that Mark and I had a lot in common as far as knowledge of Medicaid. We decided that it would be a service to the public if we could help lift the veil from healthcare finance in the United States. How does the government interact with corporate America? Are government agencies partners with the corporations in providing cost-effective solutions to Americans? Does government provide oversight of corporations? Do these two forces inadvertently behave in any ways that are tantamount to acting as coconspirators?

How well did the world's most expensive healthcare system do in containing the COVID-19 pandemic? Where does the money for the so-called "Medicaid Cluster" go? We discuss these questions in Chapters 1 and 2.

Why do pharmaceuticals cost so much? We discuss this in Chapter 3. What is the history of information systems and what sway do they and their builders have today? We discuss this in Chapter 4. In Chapters 7 through 9 we focus on one specific therapy code for which one state overpaid approximately $630 million in one two-year period. By looking at the specific code, we can provide a detailed look at how costs can spiral out of control.

In subsequent chapters we use our extensive knowledge and experience to delve into the multitude of factors that influence healthcare costs and prices. How do regulatory activities affect healthcare costs? We address this issue throughout the book, and especially in Chapters 10 through 12.

In Chapter 13 we "bite off" for discussion some of the problems with dental care costs. In Chapter 14, we address the elephant in the room, hospital costs, along with suggestions for accounting for and auditing those costs based on practices from other segments of the economy. Finally, we provide a brief treatise on the ethical framework, which, in the best of worlds, can help rein in healthcare costs.

Since healthcare costs eat up around one-fifth of the world's largest economy, that of the United States, solutions to runaway costs merit analysis from every means and angle available. This book is unique in its examination of implementation of public healthcare policies at the national, state and provider levels. The impact of policy—or, more to the point, the impact of not adhering to funding accountability requirements and national standards—will be illustrated throughout the book.

Recently, in the course of writing this book, I realized in a very personal way how critical the healthcare system is. I have the best possible insurance and, as a healthcare provider, I know almost every detail as to how to access healthcare. I will recount my experience of healthcare working at its best here, in part to throw into relief some of the less fortunate situations described later in the book.

On a Sunday morning, I awoke with stomach and back pain, gastric bloating, and indigestion. I first thought these symptoms reflected an endocrine imbalance, as I do not consistently produce some of the pituitary hormones because I had a noncancerous tumor of the pituitary removed. After attempting to deal with my symptoms, which I believed were associated with hypocortisol, I felt better. I ate a bit, partially dressed myself, straightened up the kitchen, and called my brother, who resides in the Balkans. After an initial hello, my breathing became labored and my speech was halting due to a sharp, acute, right-sided pain. I hastily indicated that I was unable to talk and would call back later. No doubt this caused my brother some significant angst. I rifled through the closet to find the one pair of pants I thought would allow for the girth of my bloating. I told my husband that I needed to be taken to the ER. That was all I said: "I need to go to the ER," an utterance that is understood by all indications that a healthcare crisis needs immediate and skilled intervention. My husband got his coat and we went to the nearest ER.

On the way there, the pain worsened and was focused on the right side. Upon arrival at the hospital, the symptoms were reviewed, labs were ordered, I was started on an IV including pain management, and a CT was ordered. Within the hour, tests confirmed appendicitis, with elevation of white blood count and other markers of infection. Shortly thereafter, an internist magically appeared and carefully reviewed my medical history, which was not conducive to the current situation; I had had a patent foramen ovale closure, a device that closes a hole between the right and left chambers of the heart, approximately six weeks prior to this event and was taking short-term blood thinners as a precautionary measure. If this was not enough for the internist, and the surgeon who appeared very shortly thereafter, I also required precautionary treatment with IV cortisol due to the stress of a surgery due to my endocrine status.

I entered surgery just over 90 minutes after arrival at the ER. In the operating room prior to being anesthetized, my health history was reviewed, as well as the risk factors of my medical history.

Sometime later, I awoke in a room on another floor of the hospital on IV antibiotics. I was then informed by the internist, and later the surgeon, that my appendix had ruptured, but they were able to do a laparoscopic procedure to clear the infection. I would remain in the hospital for some time due to the need for IV antibiotics. I would be able to be discharged on oral antibiotics when certain lab values had been achieved.

Ten weeks prior to this, I was sitting at work, and my chest felt extremely full, which usually indicates a pre-ventricular contraction that resolves if I can cough or clear my throat. However, this time, the fullness did not resolve and the vision in my left eye became chaotic. I have no other way to describe the instability of visual imprecision. This was accompanied by the feeling that I would faint. These symptoms quickly passed but were so alarming that I made an appointment with the cardiologist because of the fullness in the chest and my medical history.

After listing the symptoms, an atrial septal deficit was suspected, and tests were ordered. Literature indicates that everybody is born with a "hole in their heart" but that the communication between the two chambers closes in most people between 10 and 12 months of age; however, 25 percent carry this defect their entire life, and some individuals experience difficulties as they age.

I needed healthcare when I needed it. It is not something that can be inventoried or put on layaway. We need the full range of healthcare, including hospitals, doctors, nurses, technicians, imaging departments, pharmacists, rehabilitation therapists, etc. The list is endless. This book is an effort to look at the cost of healthcare in the hopes of sustaining it.

From Mark's and my combined experience in providing healthcare and auditing healthcare systems, we have made an effort to investigate the cost and to answer the question: "Where does the money go?"

Our sampling reveals an undeniable fact: quality of healthcare costs cannot be examined without data collected from macro- and micro-level investigation or without examination of healthcare policies and governmental mandates.

Some of the anecdotes in this book are from Lisa Famiglietti's (LF) experience as a healthcare provider and some are from Mark Scott's (MS) experience as an auditor of healthcare programs. For these anecdotes we have designated the speaker with either LF or MS.

1

Death Rode a Pale Horse in 2020

Nothing New Under the Sun

The world had ample warning of the 2020 COVID-19 pandemic. This "novel" coronavirus was new only in that humans had not previously been infected by the specific virus, or "exposed to precisely that configuration of surface antigens,"[1] and therefore had not developed antigen-specific antibodies to recognize and combat it. However, public officials had been put on notice many times of the likelihood of such a pandemic. By the middle of 2022, COVID-19 had killed over one million Americans.

During 2020, a 2014 speech by former President Barack Obama was often quoted. He had warned that America must prepare for the danger of a pathogen that would be both airborne and deadly.[2] In 2005, former President George W. Bush had warned, "If we wait for a pandemic to appear, it will be too late to prepare."[3] In 2020, the United States was not prepared for the COVID-19 pandemic, even though, as the richest country in history, the U.S. spends approximately one-fifth of its gross national product on healthcare.

This book is about where the money goes in the huge and massively expensive United States healthcare industry. The money is spent "in many cases, for conditions that could have been prevented or better managed with public health interventions."[4]

In 1976, the U.S. Secretary of Health, Education, and Welfare, F. David Mathews, told the nation, "There is evidence there will be a major flu epidemic this coming fall. The indication is that we will see a return of the 1918 flu virus that is the most virulent form of the flu. In 1918 a half million people died. The projections are that this virus will kill one million Americans in 1976."[5]

Apprised of the dire situation, President Gerald Ford told a national television audience on the night of March 24, 1976, "I am asking the

Congress to appropriate $135 million, prior to the April recess, for the production of sufficient vaccine to inoculate every man, woman and child in the United States."[6] The situation was brought under control.

In 1982, Dr. Richard Krause of the U.S. National Institute of Health, when asked why there were so many new infectious diseases, told Congress, "Nothing new has happened. Plagues are as certain as death and taxes."[7]

Nothing new indeed. In fact, the miseries of pandemics were known at least as far back in time as the writing of Revelations, where Pestilence "rode a pale horse." We cite history that should have informed public policy to emphasize the magnitude of the healthcare failure in 2020. Plagues had visited Europe throughout the centuries. They were well documented and challenged every assumption on which societies were built. Mother Nature taught medieval kings how tenuous their so-called divine rights actually were. The bubonic plague killed up to half of Europe's population from 1347 to 1351.

Europeans brought various plagues to the Americas. In 1617 the Great Epidemic in North America wiped out much of the Native population. According to historian Edward T. O'Donnell, "historians estimate that 90 percent of the population from Connecticut to Maine was wiped out." In Boston, "so many had died so suddenly, countless bodies were left unburied. The woods were so full of bones and skulls that it seemed 'a newfound Golgotha.'"[8]

In 1804, in lands newly acquired under the Louisiana Purchase, Americans died in the multitudes in New Orleans and the surrounding territory from yellow fever, a disease brought by an Asian mosquito. The disease had a 50 percent mortality rate. Mosquito eradication in the mid–20th century and a vaccine finally rendered the yellow fever epidemic a relic of the past. Of the 19th-century tuberculosis pandemic, Edgar Allan Poe wrote that "Darkness and Decay and the Red Death held illimitable dominion over all."[9] Tuberculosis is still with us today, though it is not nearly as deadly as when it was referred to as "The White Plague," thus named because of the pallor it caused in its victims. Public health measures taken in the 20th century finally contained the disease in the United States.[10]

These and other pandemics were addressed during eras without mass communication, computers, or the trillions of dollars that are spent on healthcare in twenty-first-century America.

In his book, *The Great Influenza*, John M. Barry wrote in 2004 of how RNA viruses multiply and spread at astounding speed. "So, viruses that use RNA to carry their genetic information mutate much faster—from 10,000 to 1 million times faster than any DNA virus."[11] Influenza is an RNA virus. So are HIV and the coronavirus.

In his 1995 book *The Hot Zone*, Richard Preston described how rapidly multiplying and highly infectious "hot viruses" attack. The virus tries to take possession of its human host, and in so doing damages or destroys the lungs and other organs. A hot virus often attacks the victim's brain. Of one Marburg virus victim Preston writes, "His personality is being wiped away by brain damage."[12] Of course, in 1995 Preston was not familiar with the "COVID-brain" or brain-fog syndrome that became commonplace in 2020, eventually showing up in America's children.[13]

Preston wrote, "The more one contemplates the hot viruses, the less they look like parasites and the more they begin to look like predators." He described how viruses hide during the incubation period, like a lion in the savanna grass during the "lengthy stalk that precedes an explosive attack."[14] Preston added, "Some of the predators that feed on humans have lived on the earth for a long time, far longer than the human race, and their origins go back, it seems, almost to the formation of the planet."[15]

In her 1993 book about emerging viruses, *A Dancing Matrix: How Science Confronts Emerging Viruses*, Robin Marantz Henig wrote, "The next major emerging virus, according to many experts, will probably not be a bizarre one at all: It will probably be influenza." She quoted John La Montagne, then the chief of infectious diseases at the National Institute of Allergy and Infectious Diseases: "Influenza is a horrible, fulminant, and rampant disease." In just the month of October 1918, influenza killed 196,000 people in the United States.[16]

Henig also wrote of the critical need for "close contact with public health officials internationally, especially in China, where pandemic strains have historically originated."[17] In the years just prior to 2020, "The Trump administration cut staff by more than two-thirds at a key U.S. public health agency operating inside China, as part of a larger rollback of U.S.-funded health and science experts on the ground there leading up to the coronavirus outbreak."[18]

Lots of Dollars, Little Sense

The COVID-19 crisis would point out disparities, waste, windfalls, profiteering, and economic inequities in the U.S. healthcare system, by far the most expensive in world history. According to the U.S. Center for Medicare and Medicaid Services, usually referred to as CMS, the United States spent $3.8 trillion on healthcare in 2019. Yet when COVID-19 began filling up the nation's hospitals in the spring of 2020, basic personal protective equipment (PPE) supplies such as face masks were in such low supply that healthcare providers had to re-wear masks for weeks.[19] The rest of the world already knew the importance of PPE in fighting pandemics. Approximately 32 million people died worldwide from contracting the HIV virus. PPE played a major part in combating the spread of HIV so that it did not kill more. Everyone from dentists to boxing referees, who were exposed to blood, took up wearing protective gloves. Yet during the early months of COVID-19 in 2020, PPE was chronically in short supply.

The United States spends nearly 20 percent of its gross domestic product on healthcare—more than twice the average percentage of other developed countries. The U.S., with a population of 330 million, spends over $10,000 per person on healthcare. Luxembourg spends the second highest per-capita amount, $8,000 per person. Yet the fundamental problem of stemming a pandemic seemed beyond the U.S.'s abilities and resources. Where does all the healthcare money go?

America watched with vague interest while reports came out of China in December 2019 about a virus that probably originated in a "wet market," where all kinds of exotic animals are sold for human consumption. This was "déjà vu all over again," in the immortal words of Yogi Berra. The swine flu had come from the same source in 2009. Yet the United States (and several other developed countries) did not have competent plans or equipment to confront COVID-19. "Sadly, America faced similar national stockpile distribution shortages regarding personal protective equipment (PPE) as with ventilators."[20]

The German chancellor, Angela Merkel, understood something immediately. This new virus had a long gestation period and was contagious before and after the victim showed any symptoms. Using basic statistical models that any business school graduate should understand, Merkel stated in early March 2020 that Germany should expect at least 75 percent of their population to contract the virus unless proper measures were taken immediately,[21] while Former President Donald Trump said on February 27, 2020, in regard to the virus, "It's going to disappear. One day it's like a miracle—it will disappear."[22]

If competent public health policy had been in place, that miracle might have occurred sooner and saved many more lives. By spring of 2020, the lack of preparedness became painfully clear, as states began competing against one another to obtain the limited amounts of needed pandemic equipment. Federal assistance to the states came slowly, if at all. The budgets of state and local governments were stretched to the breaking point. As 2020 proceeded, it was clear that the United States, the country that spent by far the most on healthcare, did not have an effective public health policy in place. Again, where does the money go?

Ignorance, Disease, and Death

The COVID-19 pandemic will be a placeholder in the collective memory of Americans, much like the Cuban Missile Crisis or the assassination of John F. Kennedy. In retrospect it will seem odd that there was such rancor about policies designed to save lives. One basic complaint about the stay-at-home orders was "This is unconstitutional! If I want to get sick it's my choice." By summer of 2020, the United States had more COVID-19 cases than any other nation. Would this have occurred if an adequate public health policy had been in place?

There was considerable controversy over having citizens wear a basic face mask to protect themselves and others against the virus, and which type of mask would be effective. The virus could be transmitted by one person's coughing or even speaking within six feet of another person. Doctors and hospital personnel have worn such masks for years to prevent infecting their patients, and to prevent contracting infections. The masks reportedly do not protect the wearer so much as they might protect those with whom the wearer comes into contact. However, the public was flying blind to some extent because of the relative paucity of accepted public health information during the initial months of the outbreak.

"The masks cause you to inhale carbon dioxide" was one reason cited for not wearing them. One congressman claimed he contracted the disease because he wore a mask.[23] The scientific community easily repudiated this argument. People screaming at the top of their lungs that they could not wear masks because of their breathing problems caused raised eyebrows among those who had no breathing problems, who nonetheless could never imagine being able to yell at that volume.

The lack of public health awareness and a lack of well-developed public health policy over several decades enabled the country to drift into the realm of gallows humor. A Florida woman earned her 15 minutes of fame when she said, "I don't wear a mask for the same reason I don't wear underwear. Things got to breathe!"[24] For the first several months of the pandemic in the United States, masks were in very short supply.

In early July 2020, Arizona hospitals issued a "reverse triage" policy,[25] just like in war where only those who have a good chance of living are treated. In Texas, mayors began preparing stadiums to be used as hospitals to handle the flood of cases. Mortuaries were at capacity, most notably in New York City. On July 10, the city of Austin, Texas, announced it was bringing in "mobile morgues,"[26] refrigerated trucks, to store the overflow of dead people caused by the out-of-control coronavirus. Waiting lines for crematoriums and "drive-by funerals" became part of the American landscape.

Oddly, many "success stories" were presented, of virus victims who had survived being intubated. In this process, the patient is put into an induced coma, and a tube is placed into their lungs to oxygenate the body. Grisly photos of tubes being extracted, bloody and with little chunks of tissue, were shown on the networks with appropriate warnings about graphic content. During the pandemic, intubation was not a guarantee of survival.[27]

A Wartime President

President Donald Trump was quoted in *Time* magazine, referring to himself as a "wartime president"[28] in relation to the fight against COVID-19. But preparedness for this war was not present, due to a lack of an adequate and generally accepted public health plan. Contingency planning for war has meant the difference between survival or extinction of nations for centuries, and the United States has had excellent military preparedness since the end of World War II. Yet contingency planning for control of the disease proved lacking, and by 2022, nearly a million U.S. citizens had died of COVID.

An effective wartime leader, Winston Churchill was wont to use, in various combinations, the metaphors of pestilence, war, and politics. Churchill once referred to Bolshevism as the "Lenin virus" and said that Germany had injected the Bolshevik revolutionary into Russia "like a vial of typhus."[29] Churchill had held many posts in the British government before his famous tenure as prime minister. He had been First Lord of the

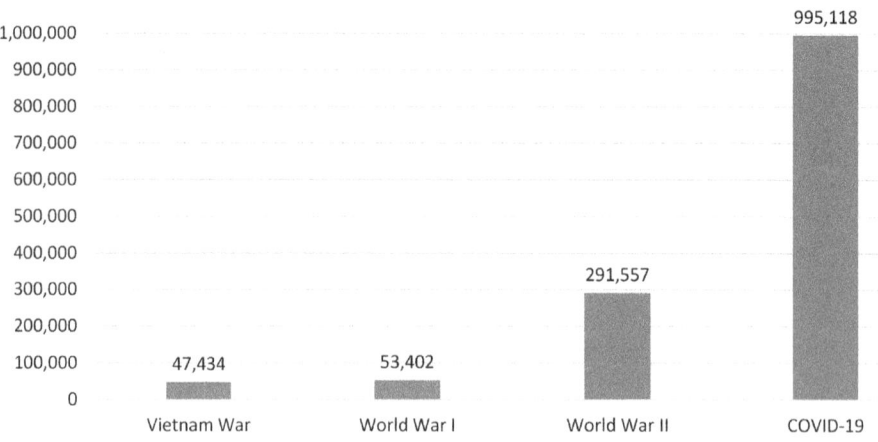

Chart 1. Major U.S. Wars' Death Tolls vs. Death Toll for COVID-19

1. Death Rode a Pale Horse in 2020

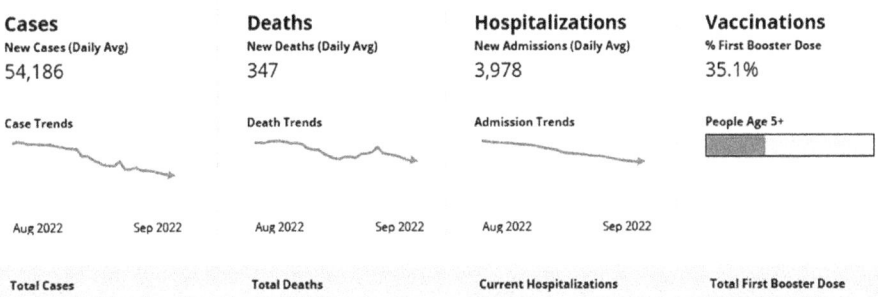

Chart 2. Cumulative Data for COVID-19 Through May 10, 2022

Admiralty when World War I broke out and later was head of the War Munitions department in that war. Churchill was a master of logistics and supply chains, as well as a great writer and orator. "In war," Churchill had famously noted, "Truth is so precious that she must be accompanied by a bodyguard of lies." In this regard, the pandemic of 2020 definitely resembled war.

Fighting efforts to close down some aspects of the American economy, public officials said that if the economic shutdown continued, deaths by suicide "definitely would be in far greater numbers than the numbers that we're talking about"[30] for COVID-19 deaths. Talk like this resonated with out-of-work Americans who began to equate shutdowns with Communist tyranny. On July 6, Trump tweeted, "We now have the lowest Fatality (Mortality) Rate in the World."[31]

In fact, the U.S. had the world's ninth-worst mortality rate, with 41.33 deaths per 100,000 people, according to Johns Hopkins University. Public health officials fought an uphill battle throughout 2020 in trying to get the U.S. to follow basic precautionary measures because of the lack of generally accepted public health policy. The claim was made that "99 percent" of COVID-19 cases are "totally harmless." This played on the assumption that healthy people would rather avoid inconvenience than worry about the vulnerable one percent. But in fact, the COVID-19 death rate held stubbornly at around 1.6 percent throughout the year and was much larger in subcategories of the population. For the 98.4 percent who survived, the virus was often very harmful indeed.

The casualties of the COVID-19 war proved very real. By the end of 2020, U.S. daily death tolls would climb on some days to over 3,000, and in January 2021 were over 4,000 on many days.

Lung damage, heart problems, and "brain-fog" were among the

long-term effects for surviving COVID-19 "long-haulers." One study found that "even a month after being discharged, more than 70% were reporting shortness of breath and 13.5% were still using oxygen at home."[32]

Studies continue as to the impact of long-term effects.

America's healthcare workers have shown heroic grit throughout the pandemic, despite lack of sufficient PPE and serious staff shortages. The trauma of the "battlefield" was brought home to television viewers as overworked hospital staff were shown struggling to save lives while trying to keep themselves safe with inadequate supplies.

Wendy Dean and Simon G. Talbot, cofounders of the nonprofit Moral Injury of Healthcare, wrote a November 2020 article about the challenge to healthcare worker morale: "Long before the pandemic emerged, the relationships between health care organizations and their staffs were already strained by years of cost cutting that trimmed staffing levels, supplies, and space to the bone. Driven by changes in health care reimbursement structures, systems were 'optimized' to the point that they were continually running at what felt like full capacity, with precious little slack to accommodate minor surges, much less one the magnitude of a global pandemic."[33]

On the "home front" of the war in 2020, local politicians dealt with the constant dueling priorities of trying to keep people safe and at the same time enable them to pay their bills. Parents dealt with homeschooling, while many Americans lost their jobs and businesses.

During the long summer of 2020, school personnel were often terrified that they would be sent back into unsafe classrooms. The stress of doing administrative work and conducting high-tech webinars while having children at home was considerable. The joke circulated that if the government lacked the will to cure the pandemic, then parents around the country would surely mobilize and be up to the task, after enduring a few months at home with their children with the schools shut down. Perhaps a positive effect of the pandemic was that Americans gained more respect for teaching as a profession.

As summer turned to fall, the number of COVID-19 cases and the death toll mounted. Instead of Death riding the red horse of war, a situation that seemed imminent on several occasions prior to 2020,[34] Death rode the pale horse of pestilence, faster and faster.

When October 2020 rolled in, COVID-19 was so infectious that even the famously germophobic Trump contracted it. The virus spread through the White House and the Senate like wildfire. Apparently cured a few days later, prematurely declaring victory in the war, Trump said "You don't need to be afraid" of the virus. Of course, the president did not really experience the virus in the same way as millions of other Americans.

In November 2020, the situation went from bad to worse. Caitlin Rivers, an epidemiologist at the Johns Hopkins Center for Health Security, stated, "Unfortunately, we are entering what I think will be the worst stretch that we have experienced so far. We're seeing hot spots all across the country and new highs for the number of cases and hospitalizations."[35] On December 15, Speaker of the House Nancy Pelosi stood beside a chart showing how COVID deaths had exceeded total U.S. combat deaths in World War II. On December 17, the *Journal of the American Medical Association* noted that COVID-19 had become the nation's leading cause of death.[36]

Another effect was a shortage of labor that continued after the COVID shutdowns ended. This was followed by upward pressure on wages, a good thing for the millions of Americans struggling from paycheck to paycheck. During the so-called Black Death, or bubonic plague of the mid-14th century, "So many peasants died during the plague that fields lay abandoned." Lords became desperate for workers. Taking advantage of the scarcity of people, the survivors demanded higher wages—in cash and fair treatment. It was like the origins of a labor union—for the first time, *they* dictated the conditions of their labor. As one nobleman put it, "Servants are now masters, and masters are servants."[37]

Many cultural transformations resulted from the Black Death period. Giovanni Boccaccio became one of the greatest European prose writers of all time, cementing his fame with his writing of *The Decameron*, a series of stories set during the plague years. He wrote critically and in a way that would have seen him accused of heresy in earlier medieval years.

"And who can doubt that there are still others who will say I have an evil and venomous tongue because in certain places I have told the truth about friars there is no question but that they are moved by the best of motives seen how friars are good men who flee hardship for the love of God do their grinding when the mill pond is full and never blab about it afterward."[38]

In a similar way, the COVID-19 pandemic brought out rancor in public discourse that would have seemed unacceptable before. A "Herman Cain Award" was unofficially instituted to (dis)honor people who publicly denied the severity of COVID and then died from it. This descent into the abyss of incivility might have been avoided if there had been accepted and effective public health policy in place. The trillions of dollars the U.S. spends on healthcare each year did not effectively go to stem the tide of death and disinformation in 2020. In the chapters that follow we will describe where the healthcare money does go.

2

The Medicaid Cluster

Breaking Down Large Numbers

Of the trillions of dollars spent on healthcare in the United States, a large proportion can be attributed to fraud, waste and abuse, according to the U.S. Government Accountability Office (GAO). GAO reports provide periodic analyses and estimates of improper payments in Medicaid and Medicare. In one report, GAO-18-598T, published in 2018, the GAO estimated improper Medicaid payments of $36.7 billion during 2018. In another report, GAO-18-660T, the GAO estimated that improper payments were about $52 billion in 2018. To quote the colorful 1960s Senator Everett Dirksen: "A billion here, a billion there, and soon you're talking real money."

One problem with citing these large dollar amounts is that the aggregation of the numbers makes them so large that they all but lose meaning. Medicaid and Medicare, especially their financing, are considered to be among the most complex topics in government. The financial trickery in the programs can also be complex, to the extent that it overwhelms and fatigues even those who are interested. However, we can start our inquiry into these arenas with a simple example from another field.

In 1990, I (MS) had been given my first auditing assignment. (Audits are systematic reviews of accounting, information systems, work processes, and other aspects of business and government.) I was setting up my new office when a hurried country voice twanged, "C'mon! Get your stuff. We gotta be in East Texas by noon." That was Billy, who would be training me to conduct audits. After having worked a couple of years in movie finance and distribution, I had wanted a calmer job. In five minutes, we were in a pickup truck, burning rubber as we headed to the Piney Woods of East Texas to interview a saloon owner.

The place we were auditing was a bar and dance hall. The owners lived in a nearby house with an office, and we met there. They had a bloodhound dog that gave us a skeptical look. We were "revenuers" after all. Billy explained to the owners the sales numbers and the calculations, which had been derived from purchase information that the state obtained from licensed distributors, and "pour" information, which determined the expected number of drinks from a given bottle. "Ma'am," Billy said, "In the bar business a fifty percent cost of goods sold is kinda high."

The woman who owned the saloon said, "Are you trying to say I'm stealing?"

"Naw! Nope! I'm just saying that fifty percent cost of goods sold is kinda high." At that time a bottle of vodka, bought wholesale, cost a bar about $4. The bottle would yield about 20 drinks on average. An individual drink would sell for around $4. So, if the bottle yielded 20 × $4, or $80 in revenue, then the cost of goods sold for that product would be $4/$80, or 5 percent. Thus, 50 percent was kind of high, as Billy said.

Billy showed her one of the sales printouts as the bloodhound by the door gave a snarl. "I'll leave some calculations for you to look over. You need to send in a check payable to the state for thirty thousand." We headed toward his truck.

"Ya see," Billy said when we were in his flatbed truck. "She prolly skimmed a lot more than what we found. So, she'll go on and send in the check." He nodded approvingly. "Ya just gotta be real polite like I was." This was, I gathered, the proper comportment in this situation. Sure enough, the saloon owner paid the extra taxes without much more grumbling.

This tax-man delivery of bad news became an important part of my job for the next few years. At that time, the state of Texas charged a high and well-audited gross-receipts tax of 14 percent on all alcoholic beverages sold in bars and restaurants. There was a huge incentive to cheat. Every now and then the state would file a complaint against a saloon owner for "falsafyin' a gummint record," but mostly they just collected the unpaid taxes.

When it comes to rendering unto Caesar, sales and other revenues are often underreported, while expenses are overreported in order to lower reported profits and thereby reduce taxes. I have pointed out this situation as an example of what would become clearer to me over the years: When things seem "kinda high" they usually are more than kind of high.

But where does the healthcare money go? That is the question we will return to throughout this book. We start with Medicaid because it has been for years the payor for the most varied groups of citizens. Also, Medicaid is public health insurance, and the program is funded by a combination of federal and state dollars. It provides medical care to millions of Americans who would otherwise not receive care. It is worthy of close scrutiny. In this chapter we will tell you some very dry facts about Medicaid spending, which once they are digested will establish the magnitude of certain problems in healthcare finance.

According to the Centers for Medicare and Medicaid Services, usually referred to as CMS, national health expenditures, or NHE, amounted to $3.8 trillion in 2018. Medicaid spending was $613.5 billion, or 16.1 percent of total NHE.[1] Medicaid was established in 1965 as Title XIX of the Social Security Act. Over the years it has become the primary payor of healthcare for low-income Americans and the disabled.[2]

Medicaid is a complex group of healthcare programs, which for organizational and accounting purposes is referred to in government as "the Medicaid Cluster." Medicaid is means-tested, and eligibility is based upon the national poverty level. Under the Affordable Care Act, often referred to as "Obamacare," Medicaid was expanded in most states to include other populations.

Are Medicaid Dollars Spent Fraudulently?

As a prelude to our discussion of where the Medicaid money goes, we can reference other reports from the federal government's watchdog agency, the GAO. In 2018 the GAO reported in their understated way that CMS and the states were not "well positioned" to identify improper payments to or by managed care organizations; the GAO reported this because CMS had delegated managed care program integrity to the oversight of the state programs. The states had previously focused primarily on fee-for-service programs and were not consistently conducting audits of payments to and from Medicaid managed care organizations.[3]

The American Bar Association stated that there were systemic problems in the Medicaid managed care and thought the managed care organization was vulnerable to fraud, including "payment for services and treatment not covered by the program, payments for service not medically necessary, payments for services billed but not provided or misbilled." They predicted the projected fraud to be at $17.5 billion in 2004.[4] In particular, they thought the managed care program included the following susceptibilities:

American Bar Association Perceived Risks of Managed Care	American Bar Association's List of Prevalent Areas of Fraud
Contract procurement fraud	Falsification of healthcare provider qualifications
Marketing enrollment fraud	Falsification of financial solvency
Underutilization fraud	Falsification of inadequate provider network
Claims submitted and billing procedures fraud	Fraudulent subcontract

2. The Medicaid Cluster

American Bar Association Perceived Risks of Managed Care	American Bar Association's List of Prevalent Areas of Fraud
Compliance fraud	Fraudulent subcontractor
Fee-for-service fraud in Medicaid managed care	Bid rigging or self-dealing
Embezzlement, threat, or related fee-for-service fraud	Collusion among providers
Misrepresentation or fraud	Contracts with related parties
False advertising of health maintenance contracts	Illegal tying agreements
False information and advertising generally	
False statement as entities	
False claim settlements	
Misrepresentation in home and managed care organization applications	

Table 1. *"Are State Managed Care Medicaid Programs Fertile Ground for Fraud?"* American Bar Association. Pages 23 and 25.

Reduced Percentage of People Receiving Medicaid in Some States

Medicaid was expanded under the Affordable Care Act so that, based on 2020 Medicaid eligibility requirements, a household that makes less than 138 percent of the federal poverty level qualifies for Medicaid. The 2020 poverty levels and corresponding Medicaid eligibility requirements for Texas were:

Family Size	Texas Poverty Level	Medicaid Eligibility Level	Income Limit for Receiving Medicaid
1	$12,760	$17,609	$25,265
2	$17,240	$23,791	$34,136
3	$21,720	$29,974	$43,006
4	$26,200	$36,156	$51,876
5	$30,680	$42,338	$60,747
6	$35,160	$48,521	$69,617
7	$39,640	$54,703	$78,488
8	$44,120	$60,886	$87,358

Table 2. **Poverty Level, Medicaid Eligibility, and Income Limits for Texas.** Benefits.gov

Medicaid is paid completely by state and federal funds—that is, by the taxpayers—and so transparency is paramount for this program. Other states will be chosen for analysis of other aspects of the healthcare system. Texas has a balanced budget amendment, which means that the state can only spend the funds that the legislature appropriates each biennium (two-year period). Medicaid is the largest portion of the state of Texas's budget.[5]

To be eligible for Medicaid in Texas, you must have income under the limits cited above, and also be one of the following:

1. pregnant
2. responsible for a child 18 or younger
3. blind
4. have a disability or a family member of your household with a disability
5. be 65 years of age or older[6]

It is clear that most single individuals do not qualify for Medicaid in Texas.

Medicaid has a matching requirement, such that for most of the Medicaid programs, the state has to provide $0.40 for every $0.60 that the state receives from federal funds. Medicaid is an entitlement program, so that once a state accepts funding for a covered group of the population, it must pay the covered expenses for those groups. So, when accepting Medicaid, each state is earmarking a big slice of its own state budget. There is also the risk that the utilization of Medicaid could exceed projections, leaving the state vulnerable to cost overruns.

Despite not accepting the expansion of Medicaid during the Obama administration, Texas federal Medicaid expenditures have risen almost 15 percent per year for the last two decades.[7] Texas has the highest number of uninsured people of any state, not only in absolute numbers but also as a percentage. In 2019 Texas had an 18.4 percent rate of uninsured residents, as compared to 9.2 percent for the rest of the United States.[8] About five million Texans do not have health insurance of any kind.[9]

Texas implemented a consolidation of health-related agencies in 2003 and 2004. The goal was to economize on administrative costs by taking 11 agencies and whittling them down to five. The head of the health agencies, and the one that would administer Medicaid, was the Health and Human Services Commission, or HHSC.

Medicaid expenditures in Texas have in fact increased substantially over the past 20 years, as shown below in figures from Texas's annual schedules of federal financial assistance. (These schedules are posted on the State of Texas State Auditor's Office's website.) Costs for federal programs are aggregated under the federal categorization system: the Catalogue of Federal Domestic Assistance. The federal expenditures are

2. The Medicaid Cluster

matched in various ratios by the states. The most common match, and the match for Texas, is 40 percent.

The federal government has a well-established method of tracking assistance payments to states. Medicaid expenditures are included in a category called the "Medicaid Cluster." This cluster of federal funds does not include all Medicaid expenditures; however, the annual numbers are a good gauge of the rise of expenditures. The federal expenditures for Texas, taken from state financial records, from 2002 to 2019 and the totals of federal and state Medicaid expenditures, and Children's Health Insurance Plan (CHIP), taken from other federal records, are shown in the chart at page bottom. (The totals for CHIP and state match are taken from un-audited records.)

From 2009 to 2011, the Texas Medicaid program received additional funding from the American Recovery and Reinvestment Act of 2009. Texas did not otherwise expand Medicaid as a result of Obama administration policies, yet Texas Medicaid spending increased from 2002 to 2019

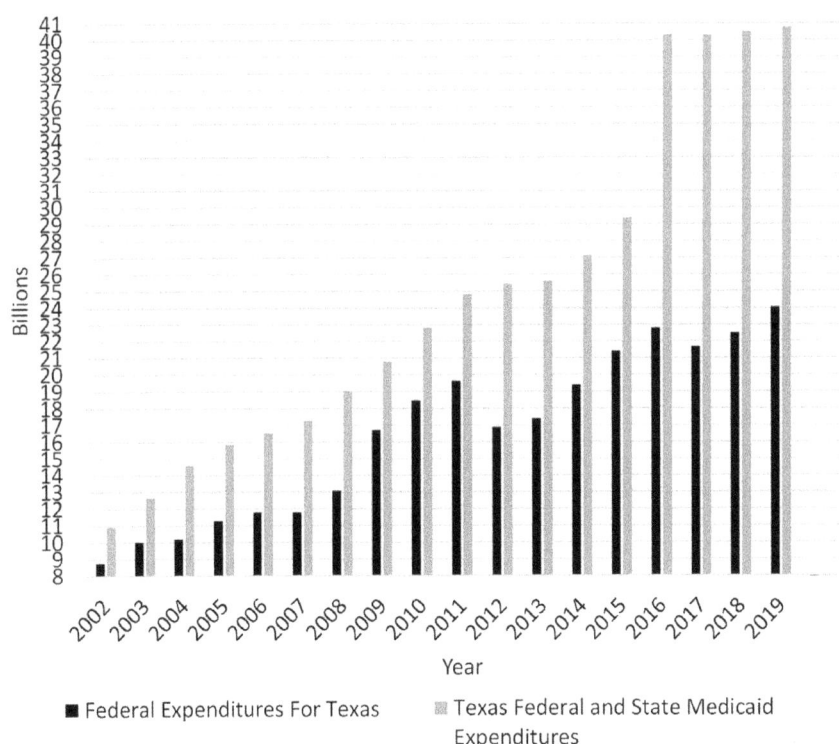

Chart 3. Federal Expenditures for Texas vs. Total of Federal and State Medicaid Expenditures, 2002–2019

at an average rate of 14.3 percent. This by far exceeds the overall inflation in the United States for that period, which averaged 1.98 percent.[10]

When Things Seem High

The GAO and Bar Association reports cited earlier provide a bird's-eye view of the probability of fraudulent or improper expenditures. Some may say, well, these are only probabilities and estimates, so what is the concern? In this regard we can offer certain specific situations from experience.

Before becoming an auditor, I (MS) had worked in the movie/finance business. We spent much of our time trying to raise money. As noted, for reporting to the tax man, the idea is to show low sales and high expenses. When reporting for investors, often a different game is afoot. The other side of a sales transaction, or "debit" is an account receivable. The accounts receivable ledger, or A/R, is a pesky commodity in the accounting world. That is partly because when it comes to sales and debts, the tendency to lie is omnipresent.

It was A/R that had foretold the demise of the movie company where I worked before becoming an auditor. The product the company sold, movies, would fly around the world via satellite to far-flung and exotic-sounding foreign companies. However, payment for said product was very unreliable. The accountants wanted letters of credit or large deposits before booking sales. But the accounting department was shouted down by the sales department and salesmen who got paid based on "sales," not on cash received. This inconvenient truth showed up and loomed large in the A/R account.

Around this time (it was the late 1980s), there was much discussion of "moral hazard" in the financial markets. This meant a separation of risk from rewards. The savings and loans companies did not bear the risk of many of the risky investments they made, because their deposits were insured by the federal government. This moral hazard was obviously occurring with respect to the collection risk on the movie sales. The salesmen reaped the reward of the sales without any regard to the collection risk. I would see many moral hazard situations later in the realm of healthcare finance.

As for the movie company, when the investment bankers and everyone else caught on to the dubious A/R accounts, the company's stock took a dive. The company's explanations to the underwriters, as to why the A/R was "kind of high," were not sufficient.

I moved on to the audit profession, and I worked my way up. Several years after leaving the dubious pleasures of auditing bars in Texas towns where the bar owners were also often the sheriff and/or chief of police, I went to work auditing health programs. In 1999 I was appointed as a director of Medicaid audits for the state of Texas Health Department.

On my first day on the job, the woman who was to prove my indispensable deputy told me, "There's a very contentious issue with the accounts receivable."

My mind raced. How could there be bogus sales in Medicaid? Then I remembered "pay and chase." I said, "There shouldn't be too much A/R if they are recouping the overpayments every billing cycle."

She said, "There's a pretty big balance. They want us to approve writing it off."

Medicaid had long been set up on the "pay and chase" system. The providers/doctors had complained that it took the state too long to process their payments. The solution was to err on the side of paying most claims, and then later, if the payment was deemed to be erroneous, it would be deducted from future payments to the same provider.

It seemed fair enough. But how could A/R of that nature linger on the books very long, unless doctors quit filing claims? An overpayment should be recouped in the next billing cycle. For this reason, I thought the A/R that ended up being nearly $300 million was "kinda high."

The trick was that many of the providers for Texas Medicaid held numerous billing numbers under which they submitted claims. Providers need a Tax Identification Number (TIN) (issued by the IRS for tax returns and business formation) and a National Provider Identifier (NPI) when enrolling in all health plans and to enroll in the Texas Medicaid program. Once enrolled, the provider is given a Texas Provider Identifier number (TPI) that is only used for billing Texas Medicaid for services provided. Some providers who are enrolled in multiple programs within Texas Medicaid are given separate and distinct TPIs for each program. However, the provider's Tax Identification Number (unless the business closes) and NPI will remain unchanged. It is these two identifying numbers that should have been used for any tracking and subsequent "edits and audits" in the system, not the TPIs. In general, an edit tells whether a service is allowable; an audit tells whether there is any reason to withhold the payment from the provider who filed the claim.

What often happened was that when one TPI was flagged with a disallowed payment, the provider would just use another TPI next time or close the healthcare entity. If the individual/entity is no longer billing under a distinct TPI, the state is unable to recoup from future reimbursement. The amounts in question then became accounts receivable, and the A/R balances grew quite large. I wrote the audit report—there was little argument about the detailed descriptions of what had happened. But who was to blame for the situation? Eventually it was settled in court. But the problem with provider billing numbers lingered.

Moral Hazard in Healthcare

After a while I became the audit director for all of the programs under the old health department. When I started in my new position, I asked around and learned that there was widespread concern over the Vendor Drug Program (VDP), as it was then called. The costs of the program were skyrocketing. The program worked like this:

1. If a drug company wanted their drugs to be provided through the program, the company had to apply for it to be included in the state's Vendor Drug Formulary.
2. The drug company would describe the benefits and price of the drug and submit the information in an affidavit to the state.
3. The state would review the information, and if the drug was approved, the drug and price information were entered into the formulary.
4. Pharmacies contracted with the state to dispense doctor-prescribed drugs that were in the formulary.
5. The state paid the pharmacies based on the units that the pharmacies had dispensed and on the prices that were in the formulary, which came from affidavits submitted by the drug companies.

This was a recipe for unaccountability. In the tradition of moral hazard, the price risk had been separated from the entity receiving the benefit, i.e., the pharmacy. Around this time (the year was 2000), a marketing strategy whereby drug companies taught their "spread" to pharmacies came to light. The setup worked like this:

A drug manufacturer would sign up with a third-party payor like the Texas Medicaid program. The manufacturers would fill out an affidavit stating that the drug price was, for example, $5. This set the price that the state would pay. The real price that the drug company charged the pharmacy was $4.

This created a 25 percent "spread" for the pharmacy. The pharmacy pays $4 to the manufacturer, then receives $5 from the state. The pharmacy reaps the reward of 25 percent profit on the drug in question. But they can say quite correctly that *they* did not charge a price to the state—they only reported the quantity of the drugs they dispensed. The price that the state paid came from the manufacturer's affidavit. All of these spreads can add up quickly, and often the spread was more than 25 percent.

What does the drug manufacturer get? Market share. The higher the price that they can get into the formulary, the greater the spread and the more likely that the pharmacies will buy from this manufacturer.

At one point I was promoted to a position that directed pharmacy audits. There was an established audit function of the pharmacies. During these audits, the paid prescriptions were audited in terms of the validity of the prescription and the quantities dispensed. The pharmacy prices had not been audited before, because the pharmacies could accurately claim that they did not have any contract with the state related to the prices, since the state dealt with the manufacturers.

It seemed to me, and I was not alone in this perception, that the yearly increases in the costs of the VDP were "kinda high," as my mentor Billy had put it on that clear day so far out in East Texas. I had the audit staff review the invoices that the pharmacies paid to the manufacturers, and compare them to the prices in the formulary. Indeed, the audits disclosed large "spreads" for many drugs. Prices in the formulary were adjusted, and many years later the manufacturers paid large settlements to the state for having overstated the prices on their affidavits.

The year after these audits were completed, the VDP was moved from the health department to the HHSC, the state's designated Medicaid administration agency.

I moved on to auditing in fields other than healthcare, but I would continue to find that the larger the sums I audited, the more likely I was to find that someone had been able to offload responsibility, or risk to the public, for the profits they were making at public expense. The drug manufacturers remained adamant that they did not bill the state and only filled out some paperwork about the drugs. They created a perfect "moral hazard" situation where the risk and reward were separated.

Scams with Teeth

It is said that "Everything's Bigger in Texas." However, one thing in Texas that historically was not big was the amount of money spent on indigent healthcare.

As a result of a 1996 case, *Frew et al v. Phillips et al*, wherein the courts ruled that Texas did not adequately fund dental care for poor children, Texas provided millions in funds for such dental care.[11] The Texas legislature, in response to the lawsuit, increased budgeted funds for children's dental services. The amounts spent on these services grew to the point where Texas spent $424 million on orthodontics under Medicaid between 2008 and 2010.[12]

In 2012 stories started to appear about the funds being used for cosmetic and other non-essential purposes, which were not allowed under Medicaid rules.

One dental clinic, All Smiles Dental & Orthodontics, billed Medicaid for at least $15 million in a two-year period, which was twice the amount the entire state of Illinois billed Medicaid for such services over the same period.[13]

In the years to come, numerous allegations of fraudulent practices in the dental arena were made against dentists and Xerox, the state of Texas claims administrator at the time. The state and federal governments launched investigations, which a later chapter will show were somewhat inconclusive. Often moral hazard was more to blame than fraudulent intent.

Eventually, the State of Texas Supreme Court ruled in 2018 that Xerox was responsible for $1 billion in fraudulent Medicaid payments.[14] Xerox settled the case for $235.9 million, and the taxpayer was left holding the bag for the rest, another case of moral hazard.[15]

3

Where Does the Drug Money Go?

The Spread

As noted in Chapter 2, moral hazard arises in financial matters when the risk is separated from the reward—the cost from the benefit. In a one-on-one transaction, Party One knows that the other Party's profits are likely to come at Party One's expense. This is not the case for most transactions in healthcare, where there are so many parties to a transaction.

The way that pharmaceuticals are paid for provides a case in point. How much of the approximately $4 trillion per year that the U.S. spends on healthcare goes to prescription drugs? In 2019, Senator Amy Klobuchar caused a stir when she stated that prescription drugs "are nearly 20 percent of our health care costs now when you include hospital prescription drugs." PolitiFact, a publication that evaluates the veracity of politicians' claims, rated her statement as "mostly true," though they thought 15 percent to 17 percent would be a better estimate.[1]

How are drug costs determined? According to federal law, "State Medicaid programs reimburse pharmacies for prescription drugs based on the ingredient costs for the drug and a dispensing fee for filling the prescription."[2] This delightfully minimalist expression does not take into account rebates that are paid, which we will discuss later in this chapter.

The word "ingredient" brings to mind an alchemist crushing herbs, stirring potions, and then mixing up the pills. Either by intent or by chance, the term provides some obfuscation benefit when prices are under scrutiny. The "ingredient costs" are generally a per-dose price, for which there has been considerable gaming of the system for decades, primarily through a system called "the spread," discussed below and in the previous chapter. According to a 2021 Rand Corporation report, prescription drug prices in the United States are 2.56 times those in other countries.[3] The U.S. spent $539 billion on pharmaceuticals in 2020.[4]

So, what are the ingredients that cost so much? Generally, they are drugs that have been included in a formulary administered by a third-party payor, where the pricing information is provided by the drug manufacturers. A pharmacist will send a claim to a third-party payor, stating how many pills he or she has dispensed, and the third-party payor will pay the pharmacist based on the cost information provided by the manufacturer. The pharmacist does not submit anything related to the price but is the one who receives the money. What could possibly go wrong? We audited to find out.

When the audits were complete, it turned out that for chain pharmacies, for 12 National Drug Codes (NDCs), the Estimated Acquisition Cost (EAC) to invoice percentages ranged from 200 percent to 668 percent; for 15 NDCs, 110–199 percent; and for 79 NDCs, less than 110 percent.

For special pharmacies, for 16 NDCs the EAC to invoice percentages were 200 percent to 691 percent. For 28 NDCs, the EAC to invoice percentages were 110 percent to 199 percent; and for 51 NDCs the EAC to invoice percentage was less than 110 percent.[5]

When we finished the audits, we had enough evidence of overpricing to have the VDP reduce prices for numerous drugs, with projections of millions of dollars in savings. The VDP made appropriate adjustments to the prices, and we forwarded the audit results to the Office of Attorney General (OAG), where there were staff to pursue possible fraud.

During the audits, a humorous and useful anecdote filtered back to me. In a different state, a sales representative for one of the drug companies had apparently gotten confused as to the difference between a third-party payor and the pharmacies to which he was selling drugs.

The salesman had asked Medicaid personnel, "What kind of spread does your supplier give you?"

The Medicaid staff were perplexed. "What's a spread?"

"That's when for example you tell a third-party payor the drug costs $5. Then you pay only $4. You get to keep the $1 spread."

"But we *are* the third-party payor."

There were varied reports on how the rest of the conversation went, most indicating that the salesman was not at all dismayed or embarrassed by his gaffe, just doing business as usual.

Around the time we were conducting the pharmacy invoice audits at the old health department, efforts were being made to consolidate health and human service agencies into the Texas HHSC. The Medicaid VDP and the related audit functions were moved from the health department to HHSC. During 2002, I had little contact with the pharmacy programs. The consolidation of agencies had been proceeding at a slow pace for several years. In 2003 the Texas legislature passed House Bill 2292, which

3. Where Does the Drug Money Go?

dramatically speeded up the consolidation. The old health department was abolished along with its board.

Several of the Medicaid audit functions were moved to the HHSC Office of Inspector General (OIG). I was eventually appointed to lead one of the audit groups. This was around 2005. During the interim of 2002 to 2004, the auditing of the pharmacies had been changed.

When I arrived at OIG, I was happy to see many of my colleagues from Medicaid. I soon learned that since the consolidations had begun, little audit work had been done in the Medicaid areas, other than audits by outside entities. The OIG was more law enforcement oriented and concentrated more on investigations of fraud than on auditing.

The investigations had stirred up the wrath of the pharmacists by constantly alleging fraud and by the auditors/investigators' use of "extrapolation" of audit samples. For example, a 10 percent sample with $500 in errors would be projected onto the whole population of transactions, resulting in a $5,000 audit exception. There was much arguing back and forth between the state and the audited entities. The pharmacy audits had come to a standstill.

The Office of Inspector General was supposed to be funded in part by identification and recovery of fraud, waste, and abuse, and so their processes had changed from basic auditing and moved more toward the area of fraud investigation with the intention of recovering money. Also, the OIG auditors had aggressively used extrapolations and pursued recoveries of the resulting projected amounts. At one hearing there was testimony from the pharmacists about the unfairness of statistical sampling, extrapolations and/or projections, and claims that some of the state officials had become overly bureaucratic or even imperious in their dealings with industry. One witness said, "I have been 'extrapolated' and it's a very unpleasant experience!" There was a pause and expectation that he was going to show his extrapolation wounds, but he moved on with his presentation.

When I moved over to OIG, I was asked whether there was anything that could be done about the deteriorating pharmacy-audit situation. I said that yes, we could do the audits the way we had been doing them before the consolidations. I wrote up a lengthy memorandum on how to proceed, describing the methodology we had used.

This was presented to the HHSC Legislative Oversight Committee. They asked what was needed to proceed. I said, "Quintilius Varus, give me back my legions!"[6] or something to that effect. In other words, I would need the FTEs (full-time equivalents, as people are accounted for in government budgeting), which had been taken during the consolidations, to be restored.

While I waited for my legions (staff), I was told I first had to meet with a group of drug company and pharmacy lobbyists. A few days later I received an offer for a higher-paying job in another field of auditing, which I took. I did not work in healthcare auditing after that.

A few years later, I was working at my desk when I received a phone call from the attorney general's office, telling me to expect a subpoena related to my tenure as audit director of the old health department.

I called back and asked what it was about. I was told that I would have to testify for up to three weeks. I said I was not sure if I had the time. An hour later a letter was sent via email to me and all the board members to whom I reported. The letter said that I had no choice but to testify, and that I was to be given time off to do so. They could not tell me what it was about—only that it had to do with audits I had done at the health department. I learned later that this was to avoid any appearance of coaching a witness.

It turned out that the proceeding was about the audits I had done of the pharmacy invoices. When I arrived to provide testimony, there were the state lawyers, lawyers for the drug companies, and lawyers representing various other parties. The drug company lawyers asked me if the pharmacy invoice audit had been a standard audit. I said that we audited pharmacies regularly, but that this was the first time we had audited the prices. I said further that since the VDP formulary was a state information system, it could be audited under the Internal Auditing Act. The lawyers representing the drug companies had boxes of reports that I had signed over the years, and even handwritten notes I had jotted down.

"Is this your handwriting?"

"Yes," I said.

"Do you remember a Ms. —?"

"Yes, how is she doing?"

"Objection!"

It went on like that for a while as they asked me about general aspects of the drug programs. The lawyers for the state pulled me out of the room a couple of times to tell me that I was being "too helpful," meaning talking too much. After lunch the head drug company lawyer came back on the attack. She asked how I put the drug prices in the formula. I said I did not put them there.

"But you audited the prices in the formulary?"

"Yes."

"Which prices did you audit?"

"The ones that were there." For a while the back-and-forth sounded like the "Who's on First" skit.

"When you spoke to the pharmacists—"

"I never spoke to the pharmacists."

I did not know exactly where they were headed, but I recognized the age-old trick of trying to implicate the auditor.

"What prices did you tell your staff to put into the formulary?"

I said, "They audited the prices that were already there."

"So, you don't know how they got there?"

I drew a blank, and they thought that they had drawn blood.

"I think the VDP staff did the data entry."

"And what prices did they use?"

At that point I remembered something. It was true that we did business with the pharmacists and not the drug makers. But in order to have the drugs included in the state drug formulary, the manufacturers had to provide affidavits to the state, attesting to the prices of their drugs.

"Now I remember," I said. "The prices came from the affidavits that the drug manufacturers provided to the VDP staff."

The lawyers for the drug manufacturers at this point asked for a recess. The state lawyers seemed almost gleeful. We resumed and the drug company lawyer asked me a few more perfunctory questions, then said that was all the questions they had. The potentially three weeks of testimony was over in less than a day.

In a few months there was an announcement that several drug companies had settled cases relating to "the spread," and that the state would get back hundreds of millions of dollars.

Except for the affidavits, it was almost the perfect flimflam. The pharmacies made a windfall without having to falsify documents. The manufacturers got a lot more business by giving larger spreads, and to audit the whole mess took a lot of staff and man hours. Today, almost two decades later, "the spread" is still a known practice in the pharmaceutical business, and that is where a good portion of the drug money goes.[7]

Drug Rebates

A standard component of the pricing structure for pharmaceuticals consists of rebates. A rebate is a return of part of the purchase price by the buyer to the seller. The Medicaid rebate amount for brand-name drugs is 23.1 percent[8] of the average manufacturer price. Other plans specify different rebate amounts for different drugs. The obvious question is why not just reduce the initial price by 23.1 percent?

When the subject of rebates is taught in business schools, the reason given as to why they are preferable to lower prices is that the manufacturer wants to be sure that the discount goes to the ultimate consumer, who is the decision-maker. So when a car is purchased, sending the rebate directly from the manufacturer to the buyer ensures that the decision-maker obtains the benefit and that the manufacturer benefits from the goodwill. In the pharmacy business, the decision-makers are the Pharmacy Benefit Managers (PBMs), and they are the ones who receive the rebates from drug manufacturers.

PBMs administer prescription drug plans for more than 266 million Americans who have health insurance from a variety of sponsors including commercial health plans, self-insured employer plans, union plans, Medicare Part D plans, the Federal Employees Health Benefits Program (FEHBP), state government employee plans, managed Medicaid plans, and others.[9]

PBMs enter into rebate agreements with drug manufacturers, whereby the manufacturer pays a percentage of the drug price back to the PBM as a rebate. The higher the drug price, the higher the rebate back to the PBM. The patient also has to pay a higher deductible.

If this sounds like a kickback to the PBM, others have thought so as well. The law that allows these rebates is an exemption to federal law called the Anti-Kickback Statue, or AKS.[10]

Currently, the AKS discount safe harbor set forth at 42 CFR § 1001.952(h) enables a pharmaceutical manufacturer to provide rebates to health plans and PBMs so long as the rebate is disclosed to the buyer, and the buyer takes certain actions to disclose the rebate to Health and Human Services (HHS) on its annual cost report.[11]

Rebates as a percentage of total spending increased from 22 to 24 percent for brand drugs, while for specialty drugs it increased from 10 to 13 percent between 2017 and 2019.[12]

The reason for the growth of rebates is the desire of PBMs to increase their profits, and also to be in the driver's seat when it comes to controlling the market. The consumers (patients) are out of the loop when it comes to rebates. The pharmaceutical companies pay the rebates in order to gain preferential treatment of the drugs on the PMBs' formularies. In 2018 pharmaceutical companies paid roughly 40 percent of their gross revenues back to PBMs, suppliers, and providers in rebates and chargebacks.[13]

Rebates have been a feature in Medicare Part D since the program began in 2006. They are projected to reach 26.7 percent of Medicare drug costs when the final numbers for 2020 are calculated.[14]

Medicaid and private insurance also use drug rebates. This has created a lack of transparency in drug pricing because the rebate agreements are proprietary. Back to our question at the beginning of the book: "Where does the money go?" A large portion of the costs of pharmaceuticals is camouflaged in the rebates.

Do consumers benefit from pharmacy rebates? Part of the money that goes to rebates can and should be "clawed back" by Medicare and other PBMs. Audits that I (MS) conducted in 2001 indicated that PBMs could recoup more money from rebates by more frequent reconciliations and collections of rebates from drug manufacturers. However, it does require hard work, and here again the corporations rely on moral hazard. Since it is somebody else's money, there is not much appetite among regulators to be strict in this area.

Advertising and R&D

While we are discussing where the money goes, we should also discuss how and why the money goes there. In 2020, pharmacy advertising in the United States topped $6.58 billion.[15] An obvious question is whether these ads are addressing existing needs, or trying to create new needs for drugs. Some of the conditions for which the drugs are advertised are quite vague. Once while I was watching television with some friends, an advertisement came on showing a couple ballroom dancing. The voice-over said, "Ask your doctor about —."

One of the ladies present remarked, "I always wanted to dance. I think I'll get me some of that drug." There were laughs all around. It was a mystery what malady the drug was supposed to cure. Do you have some vague malaise? If you have good insurance, there is no reason to suffer! By next month you too can be dancing with the lady or man of your dreams.

Do drug ads work? According to Harvard Health Publishing on Direct to Consumer (DTC) advertisements,[16] "Estimates suggest drug sales rise by $4 for every dollar spent on advertising. At health care visits, up to a third of patients ask about a drug ad they've seen. The ads have been shown to increase the number of prescriptions written for those products."

The advertisements usually include a long recitation of side effects. You may have bloating, head throbs, death, low birth weight, the veins above your eyes may pop, and so forth. However, studies show that consumers "tune out" the side-effect information. A paper published in the journal *Nature Human Behavior* shows that "the long recitation of side effects actually serves to diminish or blunt negative perceptions of the drugs."[17] The United States and New Zealand are the only countries to permit direct-to-consumer advertising of prescription drugs.[18]

One of the pharmaceutical industry's arguments in favor of high returns is that they should be reimbursed and rewarded for the high cost and risks of their research and development expenditures. In 2019, the pharmaceutical industry spent $83 billion on R&D. Adjusted for inflation, that amount is about 10 times what the industry spent per year in the 1980s.

However, more than 60 percent of drugs listed on the World Health Organization's drug lists are "me-too" drugs.[19] These are drugs that are not actually new, but are marketed in a new way, or slightly modified to cure some new malady. Marcia Angell, the former editor of the *New England Journal of Medicine*, said, "It's expensive to produce an innovative drug. On average, the bill runs to more than $400 million. So drug companies often take a less costly route to create a new product. They chemically re-jigger an oldie but goody, craft a new name, mount a massive advertising campaign and sell the retread as the latest innovative breakthrough."[20]

In her book *The Truth About Drug Companies*, Angell notes that "in the five years 1998 through 2002, 415 new drugs were approved by the Food and Drug Administration (FDA), of which only 14 percent were truly innovative."[21] The drug companies use existing drugs and make slight modifications. Furthermore, for me-too drugs, "Researchers supported by the National Institutes of Health (NIH) usually do the initial work of drug discovery. Then the drug companies keep stringing out and exploiting those discoveries."[22]

Lobbyists

So the next question might be, "Why do the American people put up with this? Are they stupid?" Certainly not. Distracted and uninformed, yes, but not stupid. Corporations spend a lot of money to keep them distracted and uninformed. According to physician Robert Yoho, "US pharmaceutical companies spent $4 billion on lobbying from 1998 through 2018, more than aero-space, defense, and oil/gas combined."[23]

What do they get for their money?

The law that established the Medicare Part D benefit, which covers retail prescription drugs for those 65 and over, includes a provision known as the "non-interference clause," which states that the Health and Human Services Secretary "may not interfere with the negotiations between drug manufacturers and pharmacies and may not require a particular formulary or institute a price structure for the reimbursement of covered part D drugs."[24]

In his book *Pharma: Greed, Lies, and the Poisoning of America*, Gerald Posner describes how the non-interference clause and the utilization of rebates resulted in steadily increasing drug prices: "What resulted was a complex and obscure scheme of rebates by which drug manufacturers paid PMBs to get their drugs on the formularies. The costlier the brand-name medication, the larger the rebate demanded by the PMB."[25] The manufacturers are incentivized to raise prices to get their products included in the formularies.

Medicare must pay providers 106 percent of the average sales price, which is the average price to all non-federal purchasers in the U.S., inclusive of rebates. We saw earlier in this chapter how average prices can be manipulated and overstated. Because the drug companies are making so much money off the government, of course they do not want the government interfering. The non-interference clause is under congressional review as this book is being written, but whatever may happen to the clause, it is nonetheless part of the story of where the money goes.

Since Medicare Part D was implemented, along with the non-interference clause, it pays on average 73 percent more than Medicaid and 80 percent more than the VA for brand-name drugs. If it paid the same, the federal government could save between $15.2 and $16 billion a year.[26]

4

Money, Politics, and Data

The Messiah of Efficiency

Ross Perot, who ran for president in 1992 and famously remarked that NAFTA would result in "a large sucking sound" of jobs being outsourced to foreign countries, started his fabled entrepreneurial career by founding and running Electronic Data Systems (EDS) in Dallas, Texas, in the 1960s. He had been a top salesman at IBM and would usually meet his sales quota early in the year and would not be able to increase his income after that.[1] Later he said, "If I stayed, I would have become a gray middle-management problem."[2]

One day while Perot was waiting to get his hair cut, he looked through an issue of *Reader's Digest*, where he saw a quote from Henry David Thoreau: "The mass of men lead lives of quiet desperation." Perot at that moment identified with the quote, deciding to take his life in a different direction.[3] Soon his company EDS would make history.

From his own hard work Perot knew well how the data processing programs worked. With his restless energy, he began doing data processing for other companies at night. He came up with the idea of time sharing, after viewing what he considered a waste of computer hardware capacity.

Perot had ambition and a work ethic that were "bigger than Dallas," to use a Texas phrase from the sixties. He lived in North Dallas, near the intersection of Preston Road and LBJ Freeway. In the first few years after he started EDS, his wife Margo would hold bridge parties, where the ladies would see an exhausted Perot come home late after working long hours on his quixotic quest that for a while seemed doomed to failure. "If it was easy, everyone would be doing it," was an oft-heard refrain from him in those years.

Perot's electronic ship, so to speak, came in with the passage of the Medicare Act in 1965. Medicare is so well established today that it seems forgotten how hard it was to pass. One of the battlefields of the Medicare war was in the difficulty of providing initial cost estimates from available data.

In a conversation between Bill Moyers and President Lyndon B. Johnson in April 1964, Johnson became frustrated about a statistic that had been repeated several times but was inaccurate.[4] The statement was that Medicare would cost "about $1 per month per worker," which was subsequently proven wrong. Johnson feared the American Medical Association would use it as political fodder against the passage of Medicare. The conversation ended with Johnson saying, in reference to the cost estimates, "I don't know what to put on this average though." LBJ was voicing a concern that would grow in America over the years: how to obtain accurate information on healthcare costs.

In 1964, leading up to the passage of Medicare, the legislation seemed unlikely to pass. Various LBJ strategy sessions were recorded and show the strength of the pushback. They also show that from the start, obtaining current, correct data and information was both paramount and problematic.

On July 30, 1965, President Johnson made Medicare the law of the land by signing HR 6675 in Independence, Missouri. Former President Harry S. Truman was issued the very first Medicare card during the ceremony. In 1965, the budget for Medicare was about $10 billion.[5]

According to EDS's LinkedIn profile, "The creation of Medicare in 1965 gave EDS an opportunity to enter government contracting, and by 1968 Medicare and Medicaid contracts provided about 25 percent of EDS revenues. By 1977, healthcare-claims processing accounted for nearly 40 percent of EDS revenues."[6]

The Social Security Amendments of 1965 created Medicaid by adding Title XIX to the Social Security Act.[7] Ross Perot and EDS were well positioned to profit and grow by contracting with Medicare and Medicaid. By 1979, EDS had annual revenues of $270 million and 8,000 employees. In 1980 EDS had a shock when they lost the Texas Medicaid contract bid to Bradford National Corporation. Perot successfully lobbied state officials to overturn the selection. EDS, and later its subsidiary, National Heritage Insurance Company (NHIC), developed a reputation for playing hardball on state contracts.

In 1999, I (MS) took a job as a director of Medicaid audits. When I received the offer and started telling other people around the state, the response was more of condolence than of congratulations. In fact, when I first applied, the hiring manager had a puzzled look. He said, "You *want* that job?"

I had heard tales of the politics that permeated the program, that there were old grudges among the contractors, and that the staff were eccentric in some cases, obnoxious in others. The job involved auditing Medicaid financial operations, mainly the large contract between the state and NHIC. NHIC was the State of Texas' contracted subsidiary of EDS, which operated the Medicaid program.

One person who would report to me was an army veteran who managed the information technology audits. He had an impressive resume. He also had a string of complaints filed against him for offensive remarks and not wanting to use the latest audit methods. I read through the complaints and thought they were vague. I met with him and at first asked him to tell me about his experience.

He said, "Mark, I learned this auditing business from the ground floor in the '60s when I was in 'Nam. I had 20 coders working for me. I also had five local women living with me." I had probably inadvertently raised an eyebrow when he added, "Because, you know, the dollar was *real* strong back then."

Of course! He missed the days of the strong dollar and what it could buy. After I got him and some of the other staff calmed down, we turned our attention to the snake pit of computer transactions we were responsible for auditing. Various parties in the state were worried that the Medicaid auditors were not testing dummy claims—that is, making up false claims and then seeing if the system caught them.

The IT auditor who now reported to me said, "That's like looking for a needle in a damn haystack!" He did not want to perform dummy claim testing. Indeed, he had developed a different, pretty good system for making sure proper edits, or payment-blocking mechanisms, were in place. Then he would test every month to make sure that the contractors were not turning off the edits to speed up the process, lessen their workload, and increase their profits. The system was based on provider codes and procedure codes, as we will discuss in a later chapter.

The edits were designed to test Medicaid claims for various attributes to determine whether the service was payable under Medicaid. If it was, then the claim would go through "audits" to determine if the provider was eligible to be paid. One audit that would cause a payment to be withheld was if the provider owed money to the Medicaid program.

I was told of a burgeoning problem with accounts receivable and that the contractors wanted to meet with me ASAP. The only time executives in charge of huge pots of money want to meet immediately with an auditor is when they want some waiver or sign-off that will benefit them at someone else's expense. (The very essence of moral hazard.)

I asked the Deputy Director how the doctors/providers usually paid back receivables.

"They are recouped in the next payment cycle. Like the IRS withholds tax refunds."

4. Money, Politics, and Data

"Oh well," I said. "Then there shouldn't be a big balance unless there was suddenly a lot of bankrupt or deceased providers."

"It's gotten bad," she said.

Indeed it had. The amounts on the books that year, including IRS liens, turned out to be $86 million, and the purpose of the meetings was to ask for my permission to "write them off." I refused; the situation eventually ended in litigation and a state settlement with the contractor.

The problem had to do in large part with a "pay and chase" system that had developed in Medicaid. Providers had complained that it took too long to get paid. So the state began a system whereby the claims that required more analysis before being finalized would be paid, and then if later deemed improper they would be "chased," i.e., recouped from the provider.

The way the system was set up in 1999 is instructive, although many changes have been made since. After the claims had been processed through the edits and audits, the "gray area" payments would be paid subject to further analysis. If a claim was later flagged as improper because the service was ineligible, or the provider was not qualified, etc., a receivable was set up, to be recouped against the next claim filed by the provider. The receivable would be offset from the next payment to the provider, and the accounts would be squared.

The problem in many cases was that by the time the state was ready to recoup the payments, the provider might have started billing and receiving payment under a different provider number. A subsequent nationwide improvement was the National Provider Identifier (NPI) coding system, which made it easier to identify and recoup overpayments from providers, because bills could be linked to one common number without the laborious after-the-fact work that I and my IT auditor had done.

During the creation of the Texas financial budget in 1999, when George W. Bush was the Texas governor, there was a desire among some politicians to show Texas as a beacon of fiscal conservatism. One result of this was that Medicaid was underfunded, to make the Texas budget for 2000–2001 look leaner. Politics and data accuracy were once again at odds. The actuarial projections for what Medicaid would cost Texas in the coming biennium were approximately $600 million more than what the Texas legislature appropriated. (The state has to pony up a "match" for Medicaid, typically around 40 cents to every 60 cents of a Medicaid dollar, and so the Medicaid budget is a considerable liability and cost to the state.)

Whatever arm-twisting went into developing the final numbers during the 1999 session, it was general knowledge that the state projections were significantly lower than those of the professional actuaries. In 2000, the shortfall caused by the low budget projections started to manifest itself. Old resentments against EDS and NHIC came to the fore. At the time NHIC was building a new software system, Compass-21, to handle claims processing for Medicaid in Texas. It seemed they were constantly behind on their deliverables. There was a system of financial penalties in place, and NHIC was consistently incurring penalties and then asking the state to waive the penalty amounts.

There was also consistent acrimony over how they managed their two large concurrent contracts with the state. One was the Compass-21 contract, and the other was the claims-processing contract. On the Compass-21 contract, there were expense ceilings; NHIC would have to absorb cost overruns. The claims-processing contract had more leeway. There were complaints, not least of which were from NHIC's competitors, that NHIC had underbid the Compass-21 contract and was now shifting costs to the claims-processing contract. The same staff at NHIC worked on both contracts, so the cost-shifting was not easy to detect.

Because of EDS's history of always getting the Medicaid contracts ("by hook or by crook" was the term often used), EDS's competitors and even some state officials felt none too sorry for the company as their contract problems piled up. Also, although there was no connection, in some quarters insinuations were made that the Medicaid shortfall had something to do with EDS's management of the Medicaid claims processing.

At that time, the claims-processing contract was an "insured arrangement" whereby EDS/NHIC was paid premiums based on Medicaid-covered populations. The state offered NHIC incentives to control costs, subject to the requirement that all eligible Medicaid claims had to be paid.

NHIC was paid under a formula whereby they received the lesser of an amount based on the number of claims processed, versus a cost formula from the federal acquisitions regulations (FAR). The FAR formula was more in line with defense contractor costs than Medicaid processing. A few years before I (MS) became the Medicaid audit director, my predecessor had insisted that NHIC use the FAR formula.

This was done because at the time the use of the FAR formula lowered the indirect cost rate that NHIC could charge to the state. The formula used payroll, revenue, and assets to allocate indirect costs such as office expense. Unlike a defense contractor, NHIC did not have heavy capital items devoted to their contract. They used the FAR under protest.

NHIC had an account for processing state Medicaid claims, the balance of which averaged between $200 million and $300 million. They also set up a separate capital account "buffer" which they claimed in the use of the FAR formula, that was also between $200 million and $300 million. Eventually they would claim this latter amount as a "capital account" for the FAR formula.

4. Money, Politics, and Data

The buffer amount increased the indirect costs NHIC could charge, in the event that the FAR formula resulted in a lower amount due to NHIC for processing the claims. The similarity of the amount of the buffer to the claims-processing amounts made some state officials think NHIC had fraudulently used state funds to prop up their formula. This was easily disproved; however, the situation created suspicion and ill will toward NHIC and their parent company, EDS.

These formulas all had to do with the processing fees that NHIC earned. It turned out that the FAR formula did not come into account the first year of the contract, and it changed the amount due by between $1 million and $2 million the second year of the contract. The FAR calculations had nothing to do with the billions of dollars in Medicaid claims that were paid, or with the $600 million Medicaid shortfall.

However, the pressure on EDS/NHIC had mounted to such an extent that their hold on the Texas Medicaid Administrative Systems (TMAS) contracts was finally broken. The long saga of the EDS domination of Medicaid and Medicare contracting came to an end. However, the memory of Ross Perot's striking it rich with a Medicare/Medicaid information system lived on. Over the past two decades many entrepreneurs have attempted to emulate Perot's road to riches. Some of these attempts have resulted in more infamy than fame.

After the passage of HB 2292, the health agency consolidation, there were no oversight boards for the Texas health and welfare agencies that were consolidated into HHSC (although there were various "councils" with ambiguous authority). The power of the TMAS contractors grew with the lack of oversight. Various software vendors did quite well, selling computer systems, software, and consulting services to the state.

During the middle stages of the consolidations, when the duties and responsibilities of auditors were in a state of flux, I was given a file to "look into." A software consultant was getting paid around $20,000 per month, and nobody was quite sure why.

When I reviewed the invoices, they were filed with a state employee job summary which listed activities like "participate in meetings," "lead discussions" and other general activities. It turned out that someone had employed the simple expedient of stapling a partial state employee job description to the purchase order, and paid based on that.

I brought the issue up with one of the staff lawyers. He said, "We can get away with that. It's enough to make the payment." Such payments for vague deliverables grew more commonplace.

Lax contracting practices among the Texas health agencies would eventually lead to the 2015 contracting scandal over the HHSC-21CT contract,[8] which resulted in the resignations of the top managers of the Texas

Office of Inspector General at HHSC. The fallout from the scandal caused the Texas legislature to write an overhaul bill for state contracting.[9]

The business of managing data for government health programs has grown enormously from the early days of Ross Perot and EDS. The Centers for Medicare and Medicaid Services (CMS) has reimbursed billions of dollars to states for the development, operation, and maintenance of claims processing and information retrieval systems—the Medicaid Management Information Systems (MMIS) and Eligibility and Enrollment (E&E) systems. Specifically, from fiscal year 2008 through fiscal year 2018, states spent a total of $44.1 billion on their MMIS and E&E systems.[10] A proper MMIS system is now an engrained requirement for Medicaid programs.

States receive 90 percent federal financial participation (FFP) for approved design development and installation projects. They also receive 75 percent FFP for operation of state and mechanized claim processing and information retrieval systems.[11] If Ross Perot were alive today, he might render judgment that the industry he created has itself become a large sucking sound, the sound of diverted healthcare dollars.

5

Required Profits and MCOs

In the 1997 movie *Fierce Creatures*, about outrageously ruthless financiers, John Cleese's character states to a group of employees that his corporate-gangster boss "*requires* a 20 percent return on his investments." This is after we have seen the boss robbing pension funds, closing whole companies, firing all the employees, and generally terrifying anyone in his realm.

Michael Palin's character asks in his famously irreverent way, "Why 20 percent? It seems pretty arbitrary."

Cleese responds belligerently, "Because that is what he *requires*." The rest of the movie is a hilarious satire of how ruthless corporations had become. The management team of a zoo decides that they will only keep deadly animals, "fierce creatures," because that has always been the ticket, since the times of the Circus Maximus and the gladiators, for entertainment. The fierce creatures referred to in the movie title are, in reality, the corporate gangsters who are running the show.

Managed Care Organizations (MCOs), it turns out, only *require* a 15 percent return. Most MCOs make higher returns, but they will magnanimously accept 15 percent in a pinch.

This is documented in a Society of Actuaries publication.[1] The basic claim made on behalf of the MCOs is that there is a risk-free rate of 3 percent. The risk premium for MCOs, according to their literature, including "beta," market risk, etc., is around 12 percent. Thus, the required 15 percent.

We are examining this in the context of the overall inquiry of this book: "Where Does the Healthcare Money Go?"

The *required profit* of a corporation goes by various names: Cost of Capital, Return on Investment (ROI), internal rate of return, etc., and can be determined on a pre-tax or after-tax basis, with various nuances. It is a rational way of allocating capital in a *pure* market economy, but the usual assumptions do not hold up when government guarantees and other factors affecting risk are brought into play.

The cost-of-capital metric is used by companies internally to judge whether a capital project is worth the expenditure of resources, and by investors who use it to determine whether an investment is worth the risk compared to the return. The cost of capital depends on the mode of financing used. It refers to the cost of equity if the business is financed solely through equity, or to the cost of debt if it is financed solely through debt.[2]

The MCOs, it seems, require 15 percent on their investment because their business is risky; otherwise, they would put their money into a safer, more profitable venture. (Lobbying, perhaps?)

What constitutes the risk? Does an MCO face uncertainty as to market demand? No. There is virtually no risk that healthcare will no longer be needed. Does the MCO face geopolitical risk? No. There is no risk of having assets appropriated by a hostile foreign government. Is there any credit risk that the government will not pay them? No.

This 15 percent is in addition to the "overhead" and indirect costs that are paid by all healthcare providers. It is after the nurses, janitors, and everyone's salaries have been paid. It is after the CEOs and all their executives have been paid. It is also after high administrative costs have been paid. "Private insurance companies' administrative costs—time and money spent solely on paperwork and bureaucracy in order to determine eligibility and approve or deny claims—can be as high as one-third of their expenditures, depending on the type of plan."[3]

The 15 percent rate of return required by MCOs is pure profit to the shareholders. How much does this presumption of a 15 percent required return, as over and above the risk-free rate of 3 percent, add to healthcare costs?

Let us look at how required ROI translates into required profits. The simple example below of a project that costs $100 million will show the cost differential. At 3 percent ROI, the required annual profits are $6.72 million. Using the same cost scenario, the required profits in order to earn an ROI of 15 percent are $15.97 million.

Interest Rate	Discount Factors	Discount Factors	Discount Factor	Yield
3%	1	1.806111	0.553675754	
3%	1	0.553676	0.4463224246	
3%	0.446324246	0.03	14.87747486	

Calculation of Required Profit

5. Required Profits and MCOs

Interest Rate	Discount Factors	Discount Factors	Discount Factor	Yield
$100,000,000.00	14.87747			$6,721,570.76 required profit per year

Table 3. **Internal Rate of Return for $100 Million for 20 Years at 3 Percent Interest Rate**, example created by author (MS)

Interest Rate	Discount Factors	Discount Factors	Discount Factor	Yield
15%	1	16.36654	0.061100279	
15%	1	0.0611	0.938899721	
15%	0.938899721	0.15	6.259331474	
Calculation of Required Profit				
$100,000,000.00	6.259331			$15,976.147.04 required profit per year

Table 4. **Internal Rate of Return for $100 Million for 20 Years at 15 Percent Interest Rate**, example created by author (MS)

What are the required ROIs in other industries, ones with real financial risks?

For the grocery industry, a standard ROI is 5.5 percent.[4] For small grocery stores, "one to four percent is more typical."[5]

The oil industry has a weighted average cost of capital of 10 percent.[6] This industry is affected by risks related to huge shifts in supply and demand, foreign competition, and sometimes geopolitical risks.

If it seems like MCOs are making out like bandits, they are. The largest MCO in Texas, with the largest government contracts, in five years went from a "market cap" of $12 billion in November 2016 to a market cap of $44.24 billion in November 2021.[7] The market cap nearly quadrupled in five years. Market cap is an estimation of the value of a company's equity (outstanding shares of stock). Clearly, a large amount of healthcare money finds its way to corporate coffers. The chart on the following page tells a story of profitability stretching toward the sky.

Rate Setting: From Simple Cost Recovery to Elaborate Profit Strategy

When it comes to paying for medical services, there are certain basic concepts that need to be kept in mind. The federal Medicaid and Medicare

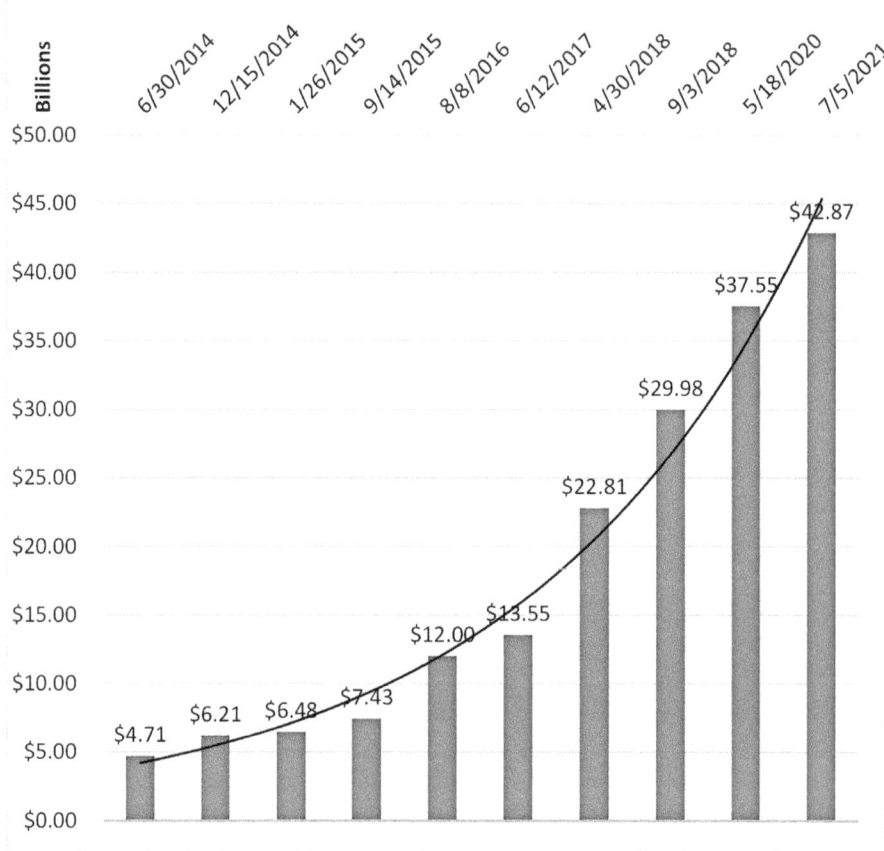

Chart 4. MaxROI Market Cap Period from Mid-2014 Through July 2021

regulations refer to "reimbursement" for medical services. This seems straightforward, but it is not. There are various ways that the cost of services, "reimbursements," are calculated, which will be discussed in this chapter.

We can analyze the reimbursement rates, based on costs including salaries, bonuses, and even contractual profits, and do so separately from the consideration of the source of payments. The purpose of this analysis is to liberate us from the notion that rates are too complicated to control.

The Government Accountability Office (GAO) has for decades issued reports on the need for improved controls over Medicare and Medicaid rate setting. In 1994 it stated that "issues concerning appropriate rate setting and risk adjustment are central to the current efforts to reform the nation's health care system. The Medicare risk contract program shares several features with those systems proposed under health care reform—for example, the use of capitated payments and the need for risk adjustments."[8]

"Capitated payments" refers to the billing of healthcare on a per-patient basis, rather than on a fee-for-service basis. "Risk adjustments" refers to the numerous variables that would affect how much the healthcare will cost on a per-person basis, such as patient age, health history, costs in different geographic areas, inflation, etc.

Almost a decade before the 1994 initiatives on healthcare reform, the GAO had written, "Accurate base cost data are essential in setting prospective payment rates."[9]

What constitutes cost data in the context of rate setting?

Most health services, including Medicaid and Medicare, are paid for under a system of reimbursement rates, based on cost data, and not according to the free-market concept of "what the market will bear." Cosmetic surgery, and some retail healthcare services, are priced on a market basis, but most payments for healthcare services are based on cost reimbursement. The basic elements in determining proper reimbursement rates are an accurate cost pool and an accurate unit of service. But these basic elements can become very complex indeed.

We can analyze what seems like a simple example. Let us say that there is a clinic in a small town that performs various healthcare services. The clinic serves a group of people covered by Medicaid, and a group covered by Medicare. Let us also say that the clinic performs various cosmetic procedures for private-pay individuals.

There are 200 Medicaid patients, 200 Medicare patients, and 50 patients who receive cosmetic procedures. There are three doctors performing different services. This example is designed to illustrate rate-setting math, and so we are not for the moment concerned about the propriety of pediatricians, orthopedic surgeons, and cosmetic surgeons working under the same roof.

To keep it simple, the costs of the clinic include building rental, salaries, supplies, utilities, and insurance. If there were no established rates from Medicaid or Medicare, and the clinic was directed to determine proper rates in accordance with standard rate-setting practices, how would their accountant proceed on determining rates? The examples below are for the purpose of demonstrating basic calculations. They are overly simplified to show the basic elements of costs; however, the layout of the methodology is to show that rate setting is understandable. It will be apparent from the examples how, if unqualified expenses get included in the cost pools, the resulting rates will be inflated.

The costs would be placed in three categories:

1. Direct costs
2. Allocated costs
3. Indirect costs

The pediatrician performs checkups and tonsillectomies. The orthopedic doctor performs knee surgeries and hip surgeries for elderly patients with Medicare. The cosmetic surgeon would be paid directly from the revenues from cosmetic surgery, and his salary is not included in the Medicaid/Medicare cost pool. (Our example will illustrate the importance of excluding non-allocable costs.)

The monthly salaries and other expenses for the clinic:

Orthopedic Surgeon: $16,000
Pediatrician: $18,000
Cosmetic Surgeon: $20,000
Four nurses: $33,000
Rent: $5,000
Utilities: $1,000
Insurance: $5,000
Supplies: $2,000
Total Costs: $100,000 per month

How do we determine the cost pools attributable to Medicaid and Medicare patients? From the $100,000 total costs, we must deduct the amounts allocable to the cosmetic surgeon. His salary is $20,000 and his insurance is $2,000. So that leaves a balance of $78,000 attributable to Medicaid and Medicare.

Of the nurses, one works only on orthopedic patients. Her salary is $10,000 per month, and this is a direct charge to the orthopedic surgery pool. The remaining $23,000 of nurses' salaries is divided by three, so $7,667 is allocated to the cosmetic surgeon, with the balance to allocate to Medicaid and Medicare is ($78,000 minus $7,667, or $70,333).

We must also allocate part of the overhead, or indirect costs, to the cosmetic surgery. The rent, utilities and supplies total $8,000. One-third of that is $2,666.67. The remaining balance for the Medicaid/Medicare cost pool is $70,333 minus $2,666,67, or $67,666.

The resulting orthopedic costs are:

Direct Costs
Orthopedic doctor $16,000
One nurse $10,000

Allocated Costs
Nurses' salaries $7,667
Insurance $1,500

Indirect Costs
$2,667

Total orthopedic cost pool per month
$37,834

Pediatrician Costs
Direct Costs
Pediatrician's salary $18,000

Allocated Costs
Nurses' salaries $7,667
Insurance $1,500

Indirect Costs
$2,667

Total pediatrician cost pool per month
$29,834

The Medicare cost pool, $37,834, plus the Medicaid cost pool, $29,834, equal the amount of total costs not allocated to the private-pay cosmetic surgery.

So now that we have the cost bases, we can proceed to the utilization data for this simple example. Even in this example, it was important to remove the legitimate, but not allocable, private-pay services from the cost base to avoid inflating the base. The cost bases that are used in rate determinations for millions of Medicare and Medicaid recipients can also quickly become inflated by fraudulent and erroneous costs.

To compute a capitated rate for the orthopedic clients in the clinic example, we need basic estimates of utilization. The annual cost allocated to orthopedic patients in the clinic example is $37,834 per month, times 12, or $454,008 per year, based on prior years' data. If each of the 200 orthopedic clients goes to the clinic four times per year, then the per-visit cost would be $454,008 divided by 800, or $567.51 per visit. To smooth out the billing, the clinic would bill a monthly rate of $189.17 per person. So, the monthly billing for 200 patients would be 200 times $189.17, or $37,834. The per-visit cost amount is computed here just to demonstrate the math. We could increase the hypothetical number of clients to lower the computed per-visit cost.

For the pediatrician clients, the annual cost is $29,834 times 12, or $358,008. If each of the 200 Medicaid clients goes to the clinic six times per year, then the per-visit rate would be $358,008 divided by 1,200, or $298.34 per visit; The monthly per-person rate would be $149.17, and the monthly bill to Medicaid would be 200 times $149.17, or $29,834. For both Medicare and Medicaid, the monthly billing compensates the clinic for all costs including salaries and overhead.

As we look at the audited cost pools later in this chapter, we should keep in mind two dichotomies related to contracts for processing healthcare claims. First, there are two basic ways to pay providers: capitated, or per-person rates, and fee-for-service (FFS) rates. Both rely on historical cost data; the difference is that the cost numerator would be divided by a different denominator. For capitated rates the costs are divided by the number of patients served; in FFS, the costs are divided by the number of services provided.

The second dichotomy is between a straight claims-processing contract and a risk-based contract. Under a claims-processing contract, the processing firm is paid per claim. Under a risk-based or "insured arrangement," the claims administrator is paid according to risk groups, and there are incentives for the administrator to contain costs. We will discuss this in a later example. In any scenario, accurate cost numbers are needed for determining proper reimbursement rates.

Fee for Service

Providers receiving fee-for-service payments are also, conceptually, being reimbursed for cost. The reimbursement rates are based on a cost pool, which is the numerator, divided by a denominator defined by the expected units of service. Both the cost and the units of service are adjusted for geographic cost differences and variations in utilization.

Using the same small clinic example, what if the pediatrician and orthopedic doctors were replaced by an eye surgeon, who performed only routine surgery, and by an ear, nose, and throat (ENT) doctor, who only performed nasal surgeries?

In this case they might be paid on a fee-for-service basis. To compute the rate, the same cost base could be used in the numerator. The denominator would be the anticipated number of surgeries.

The amount to allocate after subtracting the direct charges to the cosmetic surgery income would still be $67,667. Let us say that the nurse who just worked on orthopedic now works only for the eye surgeon.

Eye Surgery Cost Pool
Direct Costs
Eye surgeon's salary: $18,000
Eye surgery nurse: $10,000

Allocated Costs
Nurses' salaries $7,667
Insurance $1,500

Indirect Costs
$2,667

Total eye surgery cost per month
$39,834

ENT Cost Pool
Direct Costs
ENT doctor's salary: $16,000

Allocated Costs
Nurses' salaries $7,667
Insurance $1,500

Indirect Costs
$2,666

Total ENT cost per month
$27,833

The eye surgeon's cost and the ENT's cost, $39,834 plus $27,833, add up to the $67,667 of clinic's total costs not charged to the cosmetic surgery, whose procedures are not covered by Medicaid or Medicare. If the eye surgeon performed 30 surgeries per month, then the FFS rate would be $39,834 divided by 30, or $1,328. If the ENT also performed 30 procedures per month, the FFS rate would be $928.

Both the capitated rates and the fee-for-service rates can be computed so that all costs, including salaries and overhead, are paid in full. Medicare follows a methodology like our example of the clinic, though clearly with complicating factors depending on what services are covered, cost differences for different geographic areas, health risks of patients, etc. Medicare is paid for from funds that are deducted from everyone's wages, self-employment income, etc. Medicare recipients are generally happy with their insurance, and there is generally no hue and cry from providers that they are not paid enough. The "rub" is that a person generally must be 65 or older to be eligible, which makes sense in the context of wanting it to be a program covered by the person's prior years of working and paying into the fund. We are not taking a position for or against Medicare for all, but we are going to point out the success of the Medicare rate-setting process, as compared to Medicaid and various MCOs.

To compute a capitated rate in the real world, our clinic example would have to be adjusted for variations in costs and utilization. The

Medicaid and CHIP Payment and Access Commission (MACPAC) is the legislative agency that provides policy and data analysis to govern healthcare reimbursement rates. According to MACPAC, for inpatient services, "some States use payment methods that reimburse hospitals based on the reported costs, while others pay for the number of days that a patient is in the hospital."[10]

For outpatient services, "methods include payment based on reported cause, payment based on the volume of services provided, and in a few cases, payment based on the bundle of services commonly associated with a particular patient condition."[11]

Payments to physicians are "based on the concept of relative value, whereby physician services or procedures have different values based on the resources involved in performing a procedure or service. Resources include physician work, practice expense, and liability insurance. Other States tie physician payments directly to Medicare by basing their fee schedules on a fixed percentage of the Medicare fee schedule. The amount Medicaid pays typically is less than 100% of the Medicare amount."[12]

According to MACPAC, "States often apply a variety of adjustments and incentives to the base payment rates." This is consistent with Section 1902 (a) 30 (A) of the Social Security Act, to "pay for all Medicaid covered services and safeguard against unnecessary utilization in" being "consistent with efficiency economy and quality of care," and that the rates be "sufficient to enlist enough providers so that care and services are available under the plan at least to the extent that such care and services are available to the general population in the geographic area."

MACPAC requires that rates be "actuarially sound," that is, set in a way that probabilistic estimates of future outlays will be both adequate and not so high as to break the bank. Rate setters are required to consider medical trend inflation, utilization trends, disability, ongoing healthcare needs, catastrophic claims, and other factors that require actuarial expertise.[13]

If these simple calculations included additional costs such as an administrative fee for an MCO for managing the care, perhaps 10 percent or whatever seemed an accurate cost or market rate, it would still not create the situation in the U.S. today where we spend so much more than other countries, and for less healthcare.

So, what is the reason for our situation?

Obfuscation and Other Problems with Rate Setting

Medicaid is taxpayer funded, approximately 60 percent by the federal government and 40 percent by the individual states. These dollars come

5. Required Profits and MCOs

from general revenue, not a dedicated fund, as in the case of Medicare. Private insurance is not paid from taxpayer dollars. Since Medicaid affects all taxpayers, Medicaid rates, and how they are determined, should be of interest to all American taxpayers.

Medicaid administrators encounter two horns in an ongoing dilemma. First, a reimbursement rate must be high enough that the covered population has enough providers to furnish healthcare services. Second, the Medicaid program requires that all eligible services for eligible populations be paid for by the states, unless a particular waiver is in place. Budgeting for Medicaid thus requires careful actuarial analysis to avoid breaking the bank. One of the waivers available is the Section 1915 B waiver, which permits states to utilize managed care plans, or MCOs.

The cost pools in the real world can get very murky. Well-intentioned groups contribute to the muddle in various ways. The audit profession itself can contribute to the muddle.

In 2003, House Bill 2292 was passed in Texas, which consolidated the administrative functions of numerous health and welfare agencies into one agency, the HHSC. The audit functions were a topic of some debate during the consolidation process. Several of the audit functions ended up at the Office of Inspector General (OIG). Part of the funding for OIG was supposed to come from cost savings and recoveries from fraud, waste, and abuse.

Hospital cost audits were put under the OIG, even though it was more of an accounting function. The cost pools needed to be consistently monitored so that inappropriate or non-allocable costs could be removed. (We can think of the cosmetic surgeon in our clinic example.)

The agency where I (MS) had been the audit director was abolished along with its board. Under the new organization of agencies, I managed the audits of pharmacies and other functions at OIG for a short time. I soon found a different job in a field unrelated to healthcare. But while I was at OIG, I heard complaints from the rate setters that they were not receiving the cost audits they had been accustomed to receiving.

The problem was that one of the agency officials had decided to turn a basic accounting function into a long and tedious audit process. The OIG wanted the cost report function to be included under them, so that they could claim the routine rate adjustments as savings attributable to fraud, waste and abuse. One of the officials, who was a CPA, did not want to sign the "audits" (which were in reality just accounting adjustments based on cost testing) unless a thorough audit process (which was not applicable) was followed. The result was months, perhaps years, of delays generating reports, and of cost rates that were not properly adjusted.

Medicaid in Texas provides a fertile ground for analysis of rising costs and rates. Texas was one of the few states to not expand Medicaid eligibility categories. Therefore, rapidly rising costs are not attributable to covering more people. Medicaid spending in Texas rose at a rate of 14.3 percent per year from 2002 to 2018, while the general inflation rate was 1.9 percent. Where did all the money go?

In the realm of MCOs, several corporations whose primary business is managing Medicaid are Fortune 500 companies. Bluntly stated, this means that the corporations get rich from the funds that are designed to provide healthcare for poor people. How do they accomplish this?

A basic system of carrot, stick, moral hazard, and obfuscation is in place. Government employees might look forward to retiring, and then working for or consulting for the industry that they regulate. Within the government agencies, administrators won't be told outright, in most cases, to do anything blatantly illegal. Rather, they will be given vague directives to "show some leadership," i.e., not do anything to upset important officials, campaign donors, etc. Those who show such "leadership" will be promoted, for the most part. That is the carrot to encourage obfuscation, to encourage government employees to follow the agendas that enrich corporate interests.

One of the sticks used to ensure obfuscation of rates is basic ridicule. During hearings, board meetings, and other opportunities for oversight, obfuscators can count on the reluctance of people to ask what might seem to be a stupid question. A simple roll of the eyes is often enough to discourage questions. This is one obfuscation stick.

The moral hazard is that the taxpayer, not the MCO or the government officials, pays for the risks and profits.

Our point in this book is not to make accusations, but rather to describe the factors that increase costs. If a chief financial officer for an MCO presented to his corporate board that he had figured out a way that healthcare providers could be paid fairly, that nobody would be denied proper healthcare services, that no excessive profits would be made, and that all the corporate officials could sleep with a clear conscience in the certitude of heaven's applause, that CFO would likely be heard from no more. He would most likely be conducted out of the building by security, or it would be reported that he had decided to retire in order "spend more time with his family."

With that caveat against assigning blame, let us look at an actual case of a cost pool used for rate setting. As noted, several MCOs have done very well indeed by managing Medicaid. One MCO that operates in Texas is a subsidiary of a Fortune 500 Fortune 25 corporation. According to a state audit report, corporate officers' bonuses and other unallowable costs were included in the cost bases used to compute capitation rates.

5. Required Profits and MCOs

In their report of January 2018, SAO report number 18-015, the State Auditor's Office (SAO) reported questioned costs, including "$29.6 million in bonus and incentive payments paid to affiliate employees that were unallowable under the contract" with the corporation.[14]

The corporation also was given permission by the state Medicaid agency to "report affiliate profits as cost without following the approval process outlined in its contract with" the corporation.

The SAO also reported other questioned costs based on sample testing, noting that the corporation had "exceeded the limitation on executive compensation by 6.9 million" for five individuals.

Wow! The salaries of five individuals, who had been paid $6.9 million *too much*, were included in the cost pools. It sounds at the very least "kinda high," to echo the anecdote from Chapter 2. The questioned costs were probably just the tip of the iceberg, since they came up in sampling and there was no projection of the sample to the entire payment "universe," as is sometimes done by auditors. Unallowable expenses, when not properly removed from cost pools, can greatly inflate the rates that are charged. (Think of our clinic example, where the cosmetic surgery would have greatly inflated the amounts charged to Medicare and Medicaid if they were not removed from the cost pool.)

The corporation disagreed with the auditor's findings and wrote a mind-numbing retort, the gist of which related to "the auditor's interpretation of cost principles regarding performance-based compensation and incentive payments," while also touting "a level of simplicity for the holding company system in which Corporation is a wholly owned subsidiary." Although the Texas Medicaid payment structure is more complex than our example, the payments are still conceptually based on costs. The corporation was trying (and apparently succeeding) to include various bonuses, profits, and other hidden corporate gains in the costs for paying for the healthcare of low-income populations.

These MCO rates are known to be the subject of intense scrutiny. It is not a large leap in logic to say that unallowable costs loom large in MCO rates that are not so well scrutinized. MCOs have become the primary vehicle for delivering healthcare within the Medicaid program (94% in Texas).

When it comes to the rates charged for healthcare, our goal in this chapter has been to clear away some of the fog. Medicaid is in fact run by corporations, so the constant fearmongering about "socialized medicine" is just part of the mystification of economics by those who profit from the status quo. Costs can and must be analyzed dispassionately.

Now let us review some background on MCOs and the federal Medicaid program. The federal government funds the largest share of healthcare services, including Medicaid. The United States Census Bureau indicated that 17.8 percent of the U.S. population was covered by Medicaid in 2019. Texas, ranked second in population, is among the few states that have not expanded its Medicaid program but ranks third in Medicaid spending. According to the Kaiser Family Foundation (KFF) in 2019, Texas spent 22 percent of its "state general funds" on Medicaid while the state with the largest population, California, spent 16 percent. The 2020 Texas HHSC publication, *Texas Medicaid and CHIP Guide 13th Edition*, reports that 4.3 million (15 percent) Texans are enrolled in Texas Medicaid, including 43 percent of Texas children. Historical data published by Texas HHSC indicates that children comprised 76 percent of Texans covered by Medicaid and CHIP in February 2020. Ninety-four percent of all Texans enrolled in Texas Medicaid and CHIP were enrolled in a Medicaid MCO.

What Are Medicaid MCOs and Why Are a Large Percentage of Medicaid Recipients Enrolled in Them?

A large portion of the sum spent on healthcare is reimbursed through healthcare plans. There are several types of public and private healthcare plans. Managed care organizations (MCOs) are groups, organizations, or companies that are developed to "increase the efficiency of healthcare services." The managed care plans often require that the insured only receive services if they seek healthcare through a specific network of providers defined by the health maintenance organization (HMO). The MCO often requires the use of primary care physicians, who act as "gatekeepers" who must evaluate your need for a specialist and make any referrals to a specialist. You must agree to go to a specialist within the MCO's provider network for the services to be covered.

- Preferred Provider Organization (PPO), is a type of organization-based insurance that often requires a lesser coinsurance or copayment if services are provided by a preferred provider within the PPO's network.
- Point-of-Service, which runs very much like an HMO. Most of the medical needs must be met by in-network providers, but beneficiaries are allowed to go out of network for a higher fee.

Most private insurances require that the subscriber pay a premium. Premiums are usually paid by an employer on behalf of an employee; however, individuals can also pay premiums for themselves or their dependents. This could be considered a subscription fee for the service.

5. Required Profits and MCOs

Medicare is a federal healthcare plan for adults 65 years and older, adults with disabilities, and individuals of any age, including children, with end-stage renal disease.

Medicare is funded by two trust funds: the hospital insurance (HI) trust fund and the supplementary medical insurance (SMI) trust funds. The monies to fund the trust funds are authorized by the enactment of the Federal Insurance Contributions Act (FICA) of 1935. Funds are also derived from premiums from those insured by Medicare and from investment income.

Those covered by Medicare, like most with private health plans, have:

- Deductibles, which is a monetary amount after which the health insurance begins to pay for services.
- Copayment or coinsurance, which is a fixed sum to be paid before any medical service is rendered. An important caveat is that copayments are not subject to maximum out-of-pocket limits, and they do not count against the deductible. For instance, one may have a $5,000 deductible, which must be paid before the insurance begins to participate in the payment of healthcare services for the insured. Once the deductible is paid, however, one may also have a coinsurance for a particular procedure.
- Annual insurance maximum. is the maximum amount that a health plan will pay on behalf of the insured.

Medicaid is paid by state and federal taxpayer funds, as Medicaid is a joint venture between the states and the federal government. While states can charge limited premiums and fees for selected groups of Medicaid recipients, vulnerable groups like children and pregnant women are exempted from most healthcare costs.

Due to the rapidly rising cost of Medicaid costs to the federal and state governments, the concept of "managed care" was an optional service delivery model adopted by Congress in 1973. The MCOs were intended to decrease the cost of Medicaid and increase the quality of care provided to the low-income children, disabled children, pregnant women, and the elderly disabled population.

A May 2011 Pugh Trust publication touted the expansion of managed care and described an MCO as not "a traditional fee-for-service plan." Fee-for-service is when a healthcare plan or the state, acting as a health plan, directly pays providers for services. For many years, fee-for-service models were criticized as "overly expensive" secondary to a lack of coordinated care, unnecessary tests, and treatments. Some believe the FFS model incentivizes overuse.

Congress allowed states to sign contracts with MCOs (State Plan authority [Section 1932 {a}] waiver authority Section 1915 [a] and [b]). These MCOs work as a health plan, very much like an HMO; however, these HMOs would be exclusive to Medicaid recipients. The MCO model is generally based upon a fixed per-person cost or capitated rate. The state pays the MCO a capitated rate rather than paying providers directly.

Private insurance began a model of the HMO in the 1970s. In many of the HMO models, the patient, for whom the employer paid the premium, had centralized care through a primary care provider and were required to receive a referral for specialty services to be covered by the health plan. Without the referral and preauthorization of the insurance company, services were not covered by the plan. These plans, in some cases, paid incentives to primary care physicians to curtail the use of specialists.

The pursuit of the Medicaid managed care concept was driven by the fact that Medicaid budgets were exceeding the cost of public education in some states. It was thought MCOs' costs, based upon a fixed rate, would allow the state to properly budget. Under the FFS model, the state cost was whatever was paid out to providers during that year. MCOs had a set rate for each person covered, a capitated rate. These are often referred to as "risk" contracts, as the MCO that takes the contract "risks" underestimating cost and not receiving enough money from the state to provide the adequate access to quality healthcare.

Under the MCO plan, each individual Medicaid MCO has to recruit its own physicians and hospitals and negotiate rates with these entities. Some states made participation in MCOs mandatory, requiring individuals to choose between different contracted Medicaid MCOs or receive no services.

The use of MCOs has been controversial as to whether or not it provides the economic savings that states anticipated. As reported by the Stateline, by the Lewin Group, managed care savings were "greater when applied to disabled populations." The report states that 40 percent of Medicaid savings over an eight-year period in Arizona came from this high-cost population. A Georgetown University Health Policy Institute report indicated that their research, based on a five-county pilot program in Florida, "yielded little in the way of concrete evidence of either efficiencies or cost reductions."[15]

Fast forward to 2020. In October, Kaiser Family Foundation reported that "Sixty-nine percent of Medicaid beneficiaries were enrolled in comprehensive managed care plans nationally" and reviewed and highlighted some risk-based managed care trends:

- A member per month payment is the dominant form of Medicaid MCOs throughout the nation. These are considered risk-based contracts.

5. Required Profits and MCOs

- Federal law requires that payments made to MCOs must have actuarial soundness., meaning payments must be based on accurate probabilistic estimates. These types of arrangements are different from fee-for-service, as the capitation rate establishes fixed payment for the plan for expected utilization, administrative cost, and profit. According to KFF, all risk plans are generally for a duration of one year and must be approved by Center for Medicare and Medicaid Services (CMS) to "ensure that payments are not too low; and include risk sharing agreements, risk and acuity adjustments, medical loss ratios (MLR) incentive, and withhold arrangements."
- As of July 2018, two-thirds of the nation's Medicaid beneficiaries received the Medicaid-covered care through comprehensive risk-based MCOs.
- Children and adults without disabilities are more likely to be enrolled than seniors of low income or individuals with disability. However, some states are increasing the use of MCOs for this population.
- In 2019, payments to comprehensive risk-based MCOs accounted for the largest portion of Medicaid spending.
- A number of commercial carriers have a significant stake in the Medicaid and Medicare market. MCOs represent a mix of private, for-profit, private nonprofit, and government plans. Six private companies have MCOs in ten or more states. All six of the for-profit companies are publicly traded companies ranked in the Fortune 500.
- Broad federal and state rules increase the discretion of the MCOs to ensure access of care, to enroll and pay providers, and to recruit specialists to participate in the Medicaid program. Medicaid MCOs have greater difficulty recruiting specialty providers to their plans than primary care providers. However, the plans themselves indicate these challenges are likely due to a provider shortage and not lack of desire for providers to participate in the Medicaid program.

A Georgetown University publication dated February 23, 2021, indicates that five of the largest Medicaid MCOs are included in the Fortune 500. In 2020, four ranked in the top 100.[16]

The fourth ranked healthcare company in the Fortune 500 has 22.7 million Medicaid enrollees, which comprised 12 percent of its total enrollment of 23.4 million. The seventh ranked company in the Fortune 500 has 6.6 million Medicaid enrollees accounting for 14 percent of their total enrollment of 48.4 million. The 29th ranked healthcare company in the Fortune 500 listing had Medicaid enrollment of 8.8 million or 21 percent of its total enrollment of 42.9 million. The 42nd rated company had Medicaid enrollment of 13.6 million, which represented *over 50 percent* of its total enrollment of 25.5 million, making this particular plan dependent on its Medicaid enrollment and funding.

The Georgetown University Health Policy Institute Center for Children and Families indicated that its review of these companies' earnings relative to the Medicaid program and enrollment was difficult due to the fragmented or lacking information available regarding these companies, noting that little transparency exists due to the lack of public policy.

The value of the addition of the Medicaid MCOs to the private companies reviewed by Georgetown is clear from the ranking of many in the Fortune 500, the annual listing of public companies in the U.S. ranked by revenue. The ranking is often of great interest to financial groups, particularly investors.

In this book, we have focused on the Texas Medicaid program because Texas ranks third in Medicaid funding nationally, is the second most populous state, and has not participated in Medicaid expansion, which means the data can be analyzed and compared over time without the artificial influx of expanded enrollment and spending resulting from the expansion of the Affordable Care Act.

Does the federal government provide oversight of the Medicaid MCOs?

MCOs are required to offer the same level of service as "traditional" Medicaid with the same provider qualifications. Qualifications of providers and those served must align with federal guidelines and state guidelines.

Medicaid MCOs do not fall under the authority of the federal government, as they are contractors of the sole Medicaid agency designated by the state. Oversight of MCOs falls to the sole state Medicaid agency, not the federal government (Section 1932 of the Social Security Act).

6

Coding and Billing

In this chapter we will begin to delve into the "nuts and bolts" of healthcare costs: the sophisticated coding and billing systems that are common to all of the payment methodologies in the business of healthcare. We will discuss the powerful electronic data-gathering tools and how they can be utilized to inform public policy. Later we will concentrate on a specific healthcare service code to illustrate many of the problems that can arise in these sophisticated systems.

When you seek healthcare services, you must complete numerous forms that gather demographic information, health history information, current health concerns, consent for treatment and consent for your provider to file claims with your insurance company. Some of this information is used to disclose potential costs to you. For example, if you have a deductible, your healthcare provider will estimate your total due and will collect that amount from you during your visit.

The moment the forms are completed, the coding and billing process begins; that process ends after your visit and/or consultation. The process comes to a close with payment received by your healthcare provider.

Insurance plans and others require providers to submit claims to receive payment. "Clean claims" are claims that contain all regulatory required data. The claims data is generally submitted electronically for processing and payment.

The use of front-end analytics and "big data analytics" to assess the legitimacy of claims prior to payment is touted as an effective means to mitigate waste, fraud and abuse at the practice site as coding is standardized. Claims can yield information about the cost of healthcare. Information derived from electronically generated claims can be used by researchers because electronic claims allow for easy collection of data from a large number of patients.

Coding is the process of selecting codes that reflect what is "wrong" with you; what procedures and/or services were used to diagnose/treat what is "wrong" with you; in what amount were the procedures/services provided to diagnose/treat what is "wrong" with you; and where the procedures/services were provided to you.

Billing is the process of filing claims to be reimbursed for the procedures/services that were provided and to identify the professional/facility/institution that provided the service, the professional who rendered the service/procedure, the qualifications of the professional/facility/institution that provided the service, what entity was to receive the reimbursement for the service, who received the service and when they received it, and what the professional/facility/institution charged for the procedure or service.

Ross Perot's claims-processing systems, discussed in Chapter 4, grew in sophistication over the years and are now quite powerful and capable. The reason that the systems are still more part of the problem than a solution is that they are not properly utilized. Along with the rise of Medicare and Medicaid, powerful billing, authorization, and classification methodologies have been developed and automated.

Claims analyses are completed to assist in forming public policies, research, and insurance plans, both public and private. Analyses often lead to startling findings. In a letter of concern to the Center of Medicare and Medicaid Services (CMS), Texas's state Medicaid agency indicated that claims data revealed "Overbilling through an established practice and pattern, or an epidemiological event of such magnitude that its lack of identification would roughly equate to overlooking the disappearances of the dinosaurs."[1]

Coding, Epidemiology, and Healthcare Costs

What constitutes an epidemiological event? What is epidemiology? The father of epidemiology is generally identified as a Dr. John Snow of England. Dr. Snow was an obstetrician who had an interest in anesthesiology and was anesthesiologist to Britain's Queen Victoria. His participation in the history of English medicine is portrayed in the PBS series *Victoria*.

Dr. Snow is considered the father of epidemiology based on his development of investigative methods he used in 1854 when an epidemic of cholera erupted in London's so-called Golden Square area. Dr. Snow, who had interests in many fields of medicine, had published an article in 1849. He theorized the origin of cholera was not caused by breathing vapors or a "miasma in the atmosphere," as was widely believed at the time. To prove his theory, Dr. Snow's 1854 investigation centered around a geographical grid, which he used to chart deaths from the outbreak of cholera and commonalities between those who died. He believed the source of the epidemic was waterborne and came from a pump located in the Golden Square area. To prove his point, he investigated and charted all deaths on what is now referred to as a "spot" map. He determined that the majority of those who contracted cholera as well as those who died of it lived and worked around the well. He also investigated those who were stricken who did not live near the well. Most of the evidence that Dr. Snow gathered suggested the outbreak was related to the Golden Square pump; however, this theory did not account for those who did not have access to the pump nor those who did not live near the Golden Square during the cholera outbreak of 1854 but had perished from it nonetheless. Dr. Snow interviewed those people and determined that most had a link to the pump at the square. He also examined why many of those who resided in Golden Square did not contract cholera. He particularly observed that those who worked for a brewery and those who drank the brewery's product did not contract cholera. Further investigation revealed that the brewery had its own well.

Dr. Snow's investigation additionally addressed those who lived outside the area and did not rely on the well but nonetheless contracted cholera. In one case, death was related to water that was taken from the Golden Square pump to another area of London. The water was taken by someone who enjoyed the water when they resided in the area, and therefore sought water from the Golden Square pump. After careful investigation, Dr. Snow identified the source of the cholera outbreak but did not know how the water became contaminated. Subsequently, the outbreak was attributed to a mother who had washed, at the Golden Square well, a diaper of a cholera-infected child who had contracted it through another source.

Dr. Snow conducted a second investigation based upon data collected in the 1854 cholera outbreak. He examined the rates of deaths associated with two water companies, the Lambert Company and the Southworth and Vauxl Company, over a seven-week period in the summer of 1854, comparing the mortality rates and ultimately determining that there was less mortality associated with the company that brought water from sources uncontaminated by the sewer release in London.

Dr. Snow established an organized, systematic manner to collect data from which assumptions on transmission and cause could be identified.[2] The use of epidemiology continues to this day, including in the tracking of the pandemic data, and is based on fact-finding analysis.

Systematic review of data can be useful in many aspects of healthcare, including data mining relative to reimbursement via claims review that directly focuses on possible overutilization/underutilization.

Map 1. Dr. John Snow's Map Shows Wide Area of Investigation for the 1854 London Cholera Epidemic

Texas Medicaid as a Case Study

Texas Medicaid is a fertile area for studying healthcare costs because:

- Texas Medicaid is a significant source of healthcare coverage for children and disabled individuals in Texas, covering at least one in five Texans.[3]
- Texas Medicaid is publicly funded; therefore, its policies, procedures, and costs are transparent.
- Texas did not opt to expand Medicaid services via the Affordable Care Act, so data can be followed for multiple years without the impact of expansion.[4]
- Texas is the second most populous state.
- Texas ranks third in the United States in its Medicaid spending, with 19.1 percent of the state's healthcare dollars spent on Medicaid. California, which expanded Medicaid, is more populous by more than 10 million people and only spends 19 percent of its healthcare spending on Medicaid.[5]
- Texas Medicaid claims requirements themselves provide information.

6. Coding and Billing

The Texas Administrative Code Title 1, Part 15, Chapter 354, Subchapter A. Division 1. Rule 354.1001 claims information requirements (effective 01/01/2015): "(a) Eligible providers are required to provide separate claims information for each eligible recipient. Claims must be complete, accurate, and as specified by the Texas Health and Human Services Commission (HHSC) or its designee; (b) Required information included in the following: (1) name, address, and appropriate Texas provider identification number of the provider service or supplier of both. (2) the date of the claim; (3) the name, address, identification number, and date of birth of the individual who received the services or supplies or both; (4) the type of service or supplies or both provided; (5) the date(s) each service or supplies or both were provided; (6) the amount of each charge for various types of services or supplies or both; (7) the total charge for services or supplies or both; (8) credits for any payments made at the time of submission, including payments by private insurance or Medicare; (9) indication that the eligible recipient has health, accident or other insurance policies, or is covered by private or governmental benefit systems, or other third-party liability, when reported, known or suspected; (10) the date of the eligible recipient's death, if applicable; and (11) the name and associated national provider of: (A) the eligible billing provider; (B) the ordering referring provider and other professional, if services, supplies or both are ordered or rendered."

Healthcare Coding and Billing Processes Are Standardized. What Components Are Regulatorily Required?

As Texas Medicaid had already realized suspected overutilization of speech therapy services, our example will reflect the most frequently billed speech therapy service code, 92507.

For illustration, we will examine paper claims because we cannot demonstrate electronic claims in this book. Electronic claims contain the same information as paper claims, only in electronic format. There are two types of claims:

- Medical professional services, including physician and non-physician practitioners' claims, are filed on the CMS 1500 Form.
- Hospital inpatient, outpatient, skilled nursing, and emergency room services are filed on the CMS UB04 Form.

Most claims are submitted electronically. This is highly encouraged as the health insurance plans indicate electronic transmission allows for faster processing and payment of claims, eliminates the cost of sending paper claims, allows tracking for each claim sent, and minimizes clerical data entry errors.

All claim information used for payment, whether on paper or

electronic forms, is the same information that is then directed to the payor source. In the case of Texas Medicaid, the claim information is sent to the Texas HHSC or to a Texas Medicaid MCO contracted by the Texas HHSC.

Let us concentrate on the form for medical and healthcare professional services. These include physicians as well as non-physician practitioners such as physical therapists, occupational therapists, and speech-language pathologists.

For electronic claims, a practice management system vendor or clearinghouse can be used to initiate electronic claim submissions. Electronic claims are reviewed and validated for HIPAA compliance and then are forwarded directly to the health insurance plan from which payment is requested.

Current Procedure Terminology (CPT) Code 92507 comprises 95 percent of speech therapy claims; our claims tracking will reference only that one code.[6]

Definition of CPT 92507

Speech/hearing treatment (CPT 92507) The treatment/intervention, (e.g., prevention, restoration, amelioration, and compensation) and follow-up services for disorders of speech, articulation, fluency and voice, language skills and the cognitive aspects of communication.[7]

All electronic claims should align with correct coding initiatives, national benchmarks, and industry standards, which are established by:

- Center for Medicare and Medicaid Services (CMS)
- The American Medical Association (AMA) Current Procedure Terminology (CPT) ®
- Healthcare Common Procedure Coding System (HCPCS)
- International Classification of Diseases, 10th Edition (ICD-10), as of October 1, 2015
- International Classification of Diseases, 9th Edition (ICD-9), before October 1, 2015

There are many components of a claim that are valuable in the tracking of services and payments for the services and must be present for claims to be eligible for payment.

Providers, including physicians and non-physicians and facility/institutions, must be enrolled first in Texas Medicaid and also enrolled in specific Medicaid MCOs if they are providing services to those enrolled in a Medicaid MCO. Once enrolled, Texas Medicaid, until very recently, issued a Texas Provider Identifier (TPI) as well. Exclusive use of the National Provider Identifier (NPI) and elimination of local identifiers like the TPI was adopted by HHSC as of September 1, 2021.[8]

Just as Dr. Snow analyzed and plotted data he collected through observation and interviews, auditors can systematically conduct data analysis from healthcare claims submissions, including:

- Who received the service? (patient identification information)
- What service was rendered? (CPT code)
- Where was the service provided? (place of service [POS])
- How was the service provided? (modifiers)
- How much service was provided? (NCCI edits)
- For what reason? (ICD-10 diagnosis code[s])
- Who ordered the service? (NPI of the ordering healthcare provider)
- Who rendered the service? (NPI of the rendering provider; NPI of facility that rendered the services)
- Was the rendering provider qualified? (taxonomy)
- What entity billed for the service? (NPI and taxonomy of the billing provider)
- Was the entity billing the service qualified to bill for the service? (taxonomy of billing provider)

Requests for authorizations and documentation of services are maintained by the provider and are not submitted with claims; however, authorization numbers issued by Texas Medicaid or a Texas Medicaid MCO must be entered on the claim form. Health plans, including Medicaid and Medicare, can at any time ask for copies of such records.

What is required on a claim? The short answer is ICD-10, Place of Service (POS), Current Procedure Terminology (CPT) code with modifier and units of service, NPI, and taxonomy, as well as compliance with National Correct Coding Initiative (NCCI) edits. All of these terms will be explained in this chapter. Without this information, the claim will be rejected by an electronic claim clearinghouse, or the health plan and payment denied.

What Is ICD-10?

ICD-10 is the International Classification of Diseases and Related Problems (ICD). The classification list is maintained by the World Health Organization (WHO). It contains codes for diseases, signs/symptoms, abnormal findings, complaints, social circumstances, and external causes of injury or disease.

ICD-10, the tenth revision of the ICD, was endorsed by the 43rd World Health Assembly in 1990 and first used by member states in 1994.

The WHO manages and publishes the base version of the ICD. The current version contains 14,000 different codes. Through use of the optional subclassifications, ICD-10 allows specificity regarding the case, manifestation, location, severity, and type of illness or injury. Approximately 27 countries use ICD-10 for reimbursement and resource allocation in their health systems, and some member states have made modifications to accommodate their own needs. The unchanged international version of ICD-10 is used in 117 countries for reporting cause of death and other statistics. The United States uses its own national variant of the ICD-10 called the ICD-10 Clinical Modifications (ICD-10-CM). The ICD-10 Procedural Coding System (ICD-10-PCS) was adopted for capturing inpatient procedures. The ICD-10-CM and ICD-10-PCS were developed by the Centers for Medicare and Medicaid Services (CMS) and the National Center for Health Services (NCHS).

The adoption of the ICD-10-CM was quite controversial when first proposed. Providers were concerned about the vast number of codes being added, the complexity of the new coding system, and the cost associated with the transition from the former version. CMS weighed the concerns against the benefits and adopted its use. CMS required use by all healthcare providers by October 2015.

Two common complaints voiced of the United States regarding ICD-10-CM were related to the long list of potential relevant codes for a given condition, such as rheumatoid arthritis, as well as the assigned codes for seldom seen conditions (e.g., W55.22XA, Struck by a Cow—Initial Encounter, and V91.07XA, Burn Due to Water Skis on Fire—Initial Encounter).

The ICD code contains a diagnostic description which supports the provision of healthcare services. The ICD diagnostic codes are relevant for tracking and for payment, as these codes indicate why the procedures were provided.

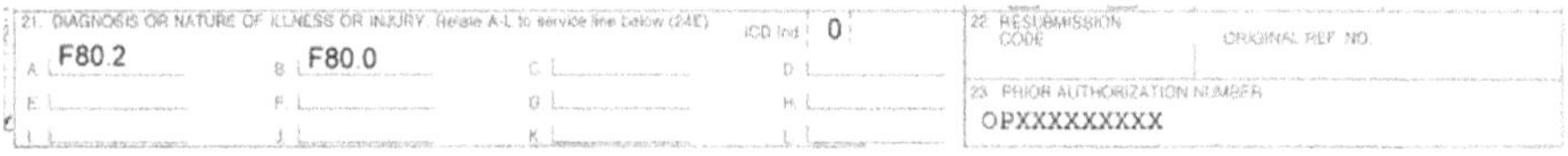
21. DIAGNOSIS OR NATURE OF ILLNESS OR INJURY Relate A-L to service line below (24E) ICD Ind 0
A. F80.2 B. F80.0 C. D.
E. F. G. H.
I. J. K. L.
22. RESUBMISSION CODE ORIGINAL REF. NO.
23. PRIOR AUTHORIZATION NUMBER
OPXXXXXXXXX

Image 1. Sample Diagnosis Codes on HCFA 1500 Claim Form

What Is Place of Service (POS)?

POS codes are used on professional claims to specify where services were provided. POS codes are two-digit codes maintained by CMS.

Standard POS code use was required by provisions of the Health Insurance Portability and Accountability Act (HIPAA) of 1996. All health plans and providers of healthcare services are required to use the POS code set maintained by CMS on all electronic transactions.

What Is a CPT Code?

The Current Procedural Terminology (CPT) system was developed by the American Medical Association (AMA) and is used for the purposes of identifying the professional services provided in a way that can be universally understood by institutions, private and governmental payors, researchers, and other interested parties. CPT is a registered trademark of the AMA. CPT codes help track healthcare utilization, identify service for payment, and gather statistical healthcare information about populations.

In 1966, the AMA Current Procedural Terminology Standard Codes and Terms were developed mainly for surgical procedures to be contained in medical records, insurance claims, and information for statistical purposes.

In 1970, the AMA broadened the system of terms and classification codes to include diagnostic and therapeutic procedures in surgery, medicine, and specialties as well as procedures related to internal medicine. In 1977, the AMA introduced a system for periodic updating of codes to keep up with the ever-changing medical environment.

In 1983, the CPT coding system was adopted by CMS as part of the the Health Care Common Procedural Codes System. HCPCS is divided into two principal subsystems: HCPCS Level I, comprised of CPT codes which describes services and procedures, and HCPCS Level II, specifically developed by CMS to identify medical supplies, durable medical equipment, prostheses, and orthotics used in medical procedures.

Level I CPT codes are numerical codes used primarily to identify medical services and procedures provided by qualified healthcare professionals. In 1983, CMS mandated that CPT codes be used to report services for Part B of the Medicare Program, and in 1986 required state Medicaid programs to use the CPT codes. As part of the Ombudsman Reconciliation Act of 1987, CMS mandated the use of CPT codes for reporting outpatient hospital surgical procedures. As part of HIPAA in 1996, the Department of Health and Human Services (HHS) designated the HCPCS, including Level I CPT code sets, as the national standards for electronic transmission for all healthcare information. The CPT code is used by federal programs, Medicare and Medicaid, and throughout the United States by private insurers and providers of healthcare.

CMS was granted a "royalty-free license" for use of the CPT codes in both print and electronic CMS publications. The license granted restricts the use of the CPT codes by CMS. The restrictions require that CMS and its agencies notice the use of AMA coding, indicating to all using the CPT code system that CPT codes are copyrighted. The copyright statement must be published on each succeeding page of a publication when "CPT or HCPCS Level 1 content appears."[9] In all publications, notice must indicate that the user of the publication, frequently a health plan manual, agrees to the terms of the licensing agreement. The licensing agreement must state that the CPT codes cannot be altered in their definition. To alter the code description would violate the licensing agreement with the AMA.

The *Texas Medicaid Provider Procedures Manual* (*TMPPM*) contains a web user and licensing agreement, and one must attest to the content before using the online version of the provider manual, as the manual identifies which CPT codes are covered by the program and which providers can provide the service described by the CPT codes. All versions of the manual follow the AMA requirement for notification and end user agreement consistent with the AMA licensing agreement.

What Is a Code Modifier?

Modifiers are two-digit codes that further describe/provide more specific information on a service/procedure. There are two categories of modifiers:

Level I CPT modifiers contain two numeric digits and are updated by the AMA annually.

Level II HCPCS modifiers contain two alphanumeric characters and are updated by CMS annually.

What Is an NPI?

The National Provider Identifier is a ten-digit number. The NPI is supposed to be an intelligence-free numeric identifier. It does not carry personal information about healthcare providers, either professionals or healthcare organizations or healthcare plans. The NPI only reveals pertinent information for the public, including where the provider is located and the healthcare specialty.

The NPI is issued only to those healthcare professionals/organizations and facilities defined by 45 CFR 160.103. The application for the NPI can only be completed by defined providers or on behalf of defined healthcare providers. By filling out the NPI application, one allows the NPI enumerator to verify the information contained within the NPI application. The NPI is obtained through the National Plan and Provider Enumeration System (NPPES).

The use of the NPI is covered under Section 1173 of the Social Security Act, which authorized the adoption of a standard, unique healthcare identifier for all healthcare providers who conduct transactions electronically. The NPI and its adoption was for the purpose of improving the efficiency and effectiveness of standard healthcare transactions, including the Medicare and Medicaid programs and private healthcare programs. It streamlines identification of providers and reduces the administrative burden on healthcare providers who would otherwise carry different identifiers for each health plan.

There are two types of NPI numbers: Type 1 and Type 2. Type 1 includes individuals such as dentists, physicians, surgeons, and therapists. A professionally licensed provider is eligible for only one NPI. Type 2 NPIs are assigned to organizations that may include acute care facilities, healthcare systems, hospitals, physician groups, assisted living facilities, and healthcare providers who are incorporated. The assignment of an NPI is not required for a provider to practice. A healthcare provider who is not covered by HIPAA, has opted out of Medicare/Medicaid, and accepts absolutely no third-party payments does not need an NPI.

The NPI does not replace the provider's taxpayer identification number, DEA state license, or social security number, because these identifiers are used for other purposes. Once enumerated, a provider's NPI will never change. The NPI remains with the professionally licensed provider regardless of a job or location change.

There is no charge to obtain an NPI. It takes five to ten days from initiation of application to receipt of NPI.

According to CMS, an NPI does not:

- Change or replace your current Medicare enrollment or certification progress
- Enroll you in a health plan
- Ensure you are licensed or credentialed
- Guarantee payments by a health plan
- Require you to conduct HIPAA transactions

Besides demographic information, the NPI contains a taxonomy code that identifies specialties or provider type. The taxonomy code for an NPI is self-selected and there is no verification process by the NPPES. (Taxonomy is explained in the following section.)

The NPI is quite different from other insurance provider numbers in that the individual professional may only obtain one NPI regardless of the number of specialties, licenses, or business practices they may possess. The application for the NPI also requires the submission of social security number or Individual Taxpayer Identification Number (ITIN). The social security number and ITIN are never reported to the public.

When applying for an NPI, one provides basic information, including:

- The purpose of the application, including:
  ~ Initial application
  ~ Change of information
  ~ Deactivation
  ~ Reactivation

The application must report the provider's entity type, either that of an individual who renders or furnishes healthcare to patients, or an organization that renders healthcare or furnishes healthcare supplies to patients. This includes hospitals, home health agencies, ambulance companies, group practices, HMOs, etc.

When an individual applies, they must provide their legal name and other names that they might be personally associated with so there is no confusion of who the NPI was assigned to. Organizations/groups, which includes physician groups and hospitals, must provide their organization or group's name, their legal name used to file tax returns with the Internal Revenue Service (IRS), or the Employer Identification Number (EIN), also called the Tax Identification Number (TIN), assigned by the IRS, and any other name that the group might be associated with.

The NPI reflects the professional's or entity's mailing address, a business practice location address, a provider taxonomy code (provider type/specialty), and license number information.

Some individually licensed providers are required to submit their state license number associated with their profession. These include physicians/osteopaths, nurse practitioners, chiropractors, licensed nurses, pharmacists, et cetera.

What Is Taxonomy?

A taxonomy code is a unique 10-character alphanumeric number. It has three different levels: provider type, classification, and area of specialization, which allows an individual, like a physician or physical therapist; a group, like a physician's group; or an institution provider, like a home health agency or hospital to identify their specialty category or categories in a HIPAA-compliant transaction.

Taxonomy codes are not assigned. Taxonomy codes are self-selected by the provider from the Health Care Provider Taxonomy Code Set maintained by the National Uniform Claim Committee.

Even though the taxonomy code is self-selected, the choosing of a taxonomy code does not mean you meet the requirements of the taxonomy code.

Why Are Taxonomy Codes Important?

- Taxonomy codes are required to complete the National Provider Identification application.
- Taxonomy codes are a required component on claims for commercial healthcare plans as well as all public plans, including Medicare, Medicaid, and TRICARE, et cetera, to identify the specialty/qualifications of the provider.

As noted before, the taxonomy codes are self-selected by the provider. The codes are organized based on education and training and used to define a specialty rather than specific services that are rendered. Taxonomy codes do not replace any credentialing or validation process. Many of the codes specify certifying boards as a source. The selection of such a code does not indicate that the provider selecting the code meets the requirements as specified in the code. Although one can self-select more than one taxonomy code, the individual or group must select one taxonomy code as primary. For instance, if someone was a licensed physician and a licensed pharmacist, they could identify themselves by two taxonomy specialty codes but must designate one as primary.

Once one selects a taxonomy code, one can complete the NPI application. Penalties for falsifying information on the NPI application form is governed by 18 U.S.C. 1001, which "Authorizes criminal penalties against an individual who in any manner within the jurisdiction of any department or agency of the United States knowingly or willfully falsifies, conceals or covers up by any trick, scheme or device a material factor or makes false statement, fictitious or fraudulent statements or representation, or makes any false writing or document knowing the same to contain any false, fictitious, or fraudulent statements or entry. Individual offenders are subject to fines of up to $250,000 and imprisonment for four years. Offenders that are organizations are subject to fines of up to $500,000. Doubling the gross gains derived from the offender if it is greater than that specified in the sentencing statute allows for fines up to twice the gross gain derived from the offender in 18 U.S.C. 3571(d)."

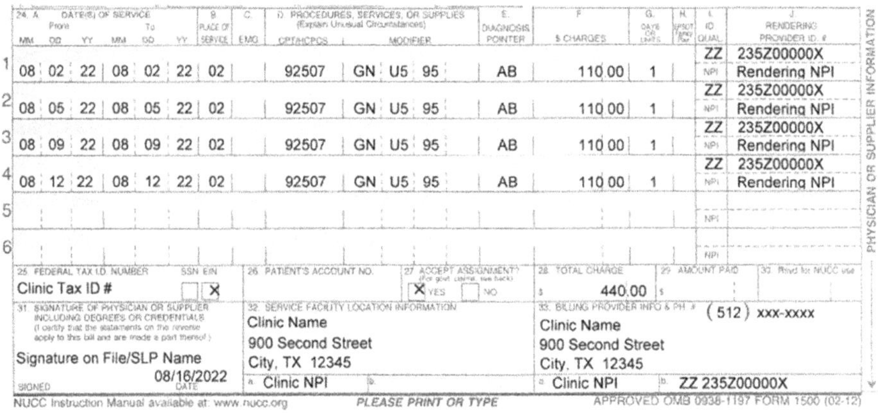

	24. A. DATE(S) OF SERVICE From MM	DD	YY	To MM	DD	YY	B. PLACE OF SERVICE	C. EMG	D. PROCEDURES, SERVICES, OR SUPPLIES (Explain Unusual Circumstances) CPT/HCPCS	MODIFIER			E. DIAGNOSIS POINTER	F. $ CHARGES	G. DAYS OR UNITS	H. EPSDT Family Plan	I. ID QUAL.	J. RENDERING PROVIDER ID. #
1	08	02	22	08	02	22	02		92507	GN	U5	95	AB	110 00	1		ZZ NPI	235Z00000X Rendering NPI
2	08	05	22	08	05	22	02		92507	GN	U5	95	AB	110 00	1		ZZ NPI	235Z00000X Rendering NPI
3	08	09	22	08	09	22	02		92507	GN	U5	95	AB	110 00	1		ZZ NPI	235Z00000X Rendering NPI
4	08	12	22	08	12	22	02		92507	GN	U5	95	AB	110 00	1		ZZ NPI	235Z00000X Rendering NPI
5																	NPI	
6																	NPI	

PHYSICIAN OR SUPPLIER INFORMATION

25. FEDERAL TAX I.D. NUMBER SSN EIN: Clinic Tax ID # [ ] SSN [X] EIN

26. PATIENT'S ACCOUNT NO.

27. ACCEPT ASSIGNMENT? (For govt. claims, see back) [X] YES [ ] NO

28. TOTAL CHARGE $ 440.00

29. AMOUNT PAID $

30. Rsvd for NUCC use

31. SIGNATURE OF PHYSICIAN OR SUPPLIER INCLUDING DEGREES OR CREDENTIALS (I certify that the statements on the reverse apply to this bill and are made a part thereof.)
Signature on File/SLP Name
SIGNED DATE 08/16/2022

32. SERVICE FACILITY LOCATION INFORMATION
Clinic Name
900 Second Street
City, TX 12345
a. Clinic NPI b.

33. BILLING PROVIDER INFO & PH # (512) xxx-xxxx
Clinic Name
900 Second Street
City, TX 12345
a. Clinic NPI b. ZZ 235Z00000X

NUCC Instruction Manual available at: www.nucc.org PLEASE PRINT OR TYPE APPROVED OMB 0938-1197 FORM 1500 (02-12)

Image 2. Sample Components of HCFA 1500 Claim Form

What Is the National Correct Coding Initiative (NCCI)?

The NCCI is a compilation of processing edits. Edits are employed to act as safeguards for specific CPT code pairs for automated claims. In 1996, CMS developed the "edits to promote national correct coding methodologies and to control improper coding that leads to inappropriate payments of Medicare Part B claims."

Coding policies were developed based upon coding conventions defined in the AMA CPT manual.

The NCCI program includes two types of edits:

- Procedure to Procedure (PTP) edits
- Medically Unlikely Edits (MUEs)

PTP edits ensure that payment is not made for codes that generally should not have been performed on the same date of service for the same beneficiary. MUE edits ensure that payment is not made for "an inappropriate number/quantity of the same service, on the same day to the same beneficiary."[10]

The Affordable Care Act of 2010 required all state Medicaid programs to incorporate all compatible Medicare NCCI edits to claims processing. All five Medicare NCCI methodologies were determined to be compatible.

Some states have voluntarily required their Medicaid MCOs to incorporate the NCCI edits. Texas is one of those states. Many commercial carriers have also incorporated compatible Medicare edits.

CMS requires that NCCI edits be applied to Medicare claims before applying any other specific edits during processing.

With All These Controls, How Do You Scam the System?

How did one individual, "Dr. Dave" (a pseudonym), bill for $2.3 million in medical services as a physician when in actuality he was providing private personal training services, either provided by himself personally or by individuals who worked for him, none of whom were physicians?

"Dr. Dave," a highly educated individual who held a PhD in kinesiology, was previously convicted of two felonies. The first instance when he falsified invoices for a nonprofit organization where his son was provided treatment. "Dr. Dave" indicated that his child received therapy at the facility but in fact the child had not, thus creating false bills that he then presented to a county agency for cash reimbursement.

"Dr. Dave" pleaded guilty in Tarrant County District Court to felony theft in November 2008. He was sentenced to 18 months in jail and was released on bond. While released on bond, he was arrested for "causing bodily harm." "Dr. Dave" pled guilty to that and again was convicted of a felony. With the addition to the bail violation, he served about two years in jail.

Due to "Dr. Dave's" background, he could provide personal training services and other related services. Individuals would pay cash for these services, but if they were recognized as "therapeutic healthcare services," health insurance would pay for them. Insurance would pay twice as much as an individual willing to pay in cash for the same service.

So how did Dr. Dave bill Aetna, Cigna, and UnitedHealthcare for millions of dollars for bogus medical services? He used an NPI containing the taxonomy code of a licensed physician; Dr. Dave is not and was never a licensed physician. He coded personal training services using CPT codes for therapeutic services and billed these services to insurance companies using information obtained voluntarily from his clients. He billed the claims as an out-of-network provider, avoiding the vetting/credentialing process of the insurance companies for in-network providers.

So did the sophisticated coding system recognize that Dr. Dave was providing medically unnecessary services and was not qualified to have an NPI with the taxonomy of a physician? No. Over the course of four years, Dr. Dave submitted claims for $4 million with one commercial insurance company and received $2.5 million in reimbursement.

As the scheme progressed, Dr. Dave was flush with cash and bought some high-priced electronics, including iPads, for his two children. His ex-wife became suspicious as Dr. Dave had been without funds for some time, recently having served his two-year jail sentence. Unfortunately for Dr. Dave, he used the same account for his children's iPads that he used for filing his "health care claims." The ex-wife and her father, who were knowledgeable in this area, recognized the fraud and reported it to the insurance companies, who initially did not move against Dr. Dave for fraud. Only later did the they press charges against Dr. Dave for fraudulently filing claims as a licensed physician.[11]

- How are data points derived from standardized coding and billing processes used in investigating overutilization?

Claims submissions contain critical data points and identifiers allowing for tracking of services for possible identification of over- and/or underutilization. Healthcare organization and health plans use data points for the tracking of services and the possible identification of over and underutilization of services. The Texas Health and Human Services agency, the sole Medicaid agency, in a letter dated June 2, 2014 to the Associate Regional Administrator of CMS, Division of Medicaid and Children's Health, Region Six, published in the *Austin American Statesman*, December 2014 indicated that HHSC tracks services by beneficiary and regions and specific services provided and then compares this data to other regions of state and uses the same standard data identifiers. The stark difference in utilization of service by region was likened to a pandemic.

"HHSC-OIG began the therapy initiative with an assessment of utilization rates for therapy services in the state. That preliminary review is full of staggering comparisons, each one equally or more damning that the one before.

"Yet while speech therapy expenditures in the Valley counties are four times greater than in the highest non–Valley counties, the Medicaid population is less than a third as large.

"The unbalance comparisons between the highest utilizing counties of therapy services and the rest of the state go on virtually for as long as the analyst cares to make comparisons. Indeed, with rare exception, even the rank order of counties for utilization of different therapy types remains unchanged. These facts indicate the only two explanations for the extraordinarily high and consistent utilization rates in the Valley region were overbilling through an established practice and pattern, or an epidemiological even of such magnitude that its lack of identification would roughly equate to overlooking the disappearance of the dinosaurs."[12]

- Can data points derived from standardized coding and billing processes identify shifting trends in healthcare?

The Texas OIG published "Texas Medicaid Speech Therapy, Informational Report on Payment Trends and Service Delivery, February 28, 2017" (page 15), which tracked the provision of speech therapy services to answer a question posed by Texas Medicaid MCOs relative to increasing cost associated with the provision of therapy services. The OIG tracked utilization of a specific code, CPT 92507, as it represents 75 percent of all speech therapy codes reimbursed by Texas Medicaid. Using this method, the OIG was able to pinpoint service provision by provider type.

The information obtained by tracking by provider type and location leads us to the curious case of CPT 92507. In the next three chapters we will examine this specific code as a major case in point, from which we will be able to see not only how the sophisticated systems in place are allowed to not work, but also how the systems can be made to work and achieve the objectives related to providing optimal care while also keeping costs under control. For years, author Famiglietti has utilized the CPT 92507 code and has also dealt with a variety of challenges in trying to straighten out rate-setting discrepancies related to provider type and place of service. The author's experiences over the years inform Chapters 7–9 from the perspective of an "insider."

CHAPTER 7

The Curious Case of CPT Code 92507

In this chapter and the following two we discuss a specific healthcare code and describe in detail various matters related to this code, such as diagnosis, billing, and payment disparities. This will shine a light on healthcare cost issues that are difficult to observe from a distance or from a macro analysis.

Healthcare costs are usually studied from a macro level, examining large-scale patterns of expenditures. The American Medical Association (AMA), in its publication, *Policy Research Perspectives: National Health Expenditures, 2019; Steady Spending Growth Despite Increases in Personal Health Care Expenditures in Advance of the Pandemic*, indicated that the United States spent $3.8 trillion on healthcare in 2019. The AMA report breaks down spending in multiple categories:

Hospital care
Physician services
Clinical services
Prescription drugs
Nursing care facilities
Home health care

Other personal healthcare costs
Government administration
Net cost of health insurance
Government public health activities
Investment spending

Using the same investigative protocols of epidemiology, one can explore the cost of healthcare using a micro-level empirical analysis of specific individual healthcare codes rather than a macro approach.

A micro-level analysis of a reported overutilization of therapy services in the Texas Medicaid program demonstrates the effectiveness of this approach in identifying cost drivers.

Medicaid is a state and federal cooperative program. It is a publicly funded healthcare plan and is therefore relatively transparent, allowing for several levels of inquiry. The Texas Medicaid program was selected for this empirical analysis as Texas has the third largest Medicaid expenditure

Chapter 7. The Curious Case of CPT Code 92507

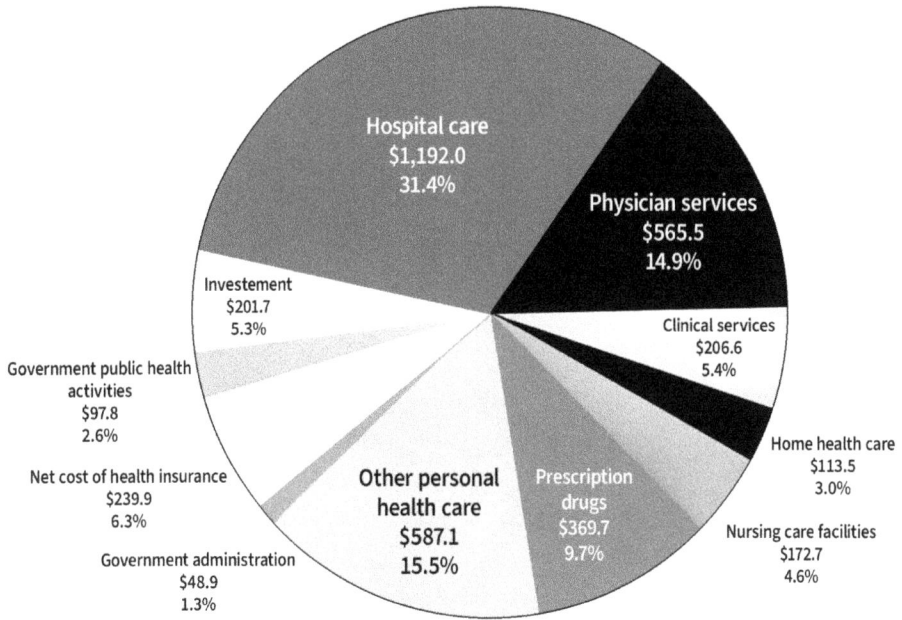

Chart 5. U.S. Spending on Healthcare in 2019

and has not expanded coverage, allowing for microanalysis over an uninterrupted period of time.

The Texas Medicaid program, in a 2016 correspondence with the Centers for Medicare and Medicaid Services (CMS), reported overpayments in excess of $300 million for a specific speech therapy service, CPT 92507.

This estimate was derived from analyses of claims information by mapping data from standard transaction codes and comparing the rate paid for the specific code to the benchmark rate of Medicare services.

What Is Data Mapping?

John Snow is not only regarded as the father of epidemiology, but is also viewed as a pioneer in the field of disease mapping. Using data collected regarding the number of deaths from cholera and location of the deaths, John Snow was able to create a geographic map. Plotting the deaths on a map revealed clustering in specific locations. A pump at the intersection of Broad and Cambridge Streets in the Golden Square district of London was identified as the possible source of cholera infection. John Snow's data and map were presented to the Cholera Inquiry Committee of St. James parish in 1855.[1]

Map 2. The Location of the Broad Street Pump on Dr. John Snow's Map of the 1854 London Cholera Epidemic

The plotting of relevant data led to identification of a possible source of infection based upon clustering data points. The identification of the source led to the decommissioning of the pump in the interest of public health and safety, and added to the knowledge of how cholera spread. Close and systematic examination allows for the development of theories of what happened, the way an event happened, and the impact of an event.

Policies leading to overutilization and increased healthcare costs can be identified using Snow's approach, a micro-level analysis which is illustrated in the curious case of CPT 92507.

Tracking of CPT 92507 revealed non-compliance:

- With required rate-setting methodologies
- With mandated transactional standards
- With AMA copyrights
- With mandated prior authorization requirements
- With mandated provider qualifications

Similar to John Snow, we can examine the significant increases in costs of providing therapy to children by plotting data points. By juxtaposing additional data points collected from claims for outpatient therapy

Chapter 7. The Curious Case of CPT Code 92507

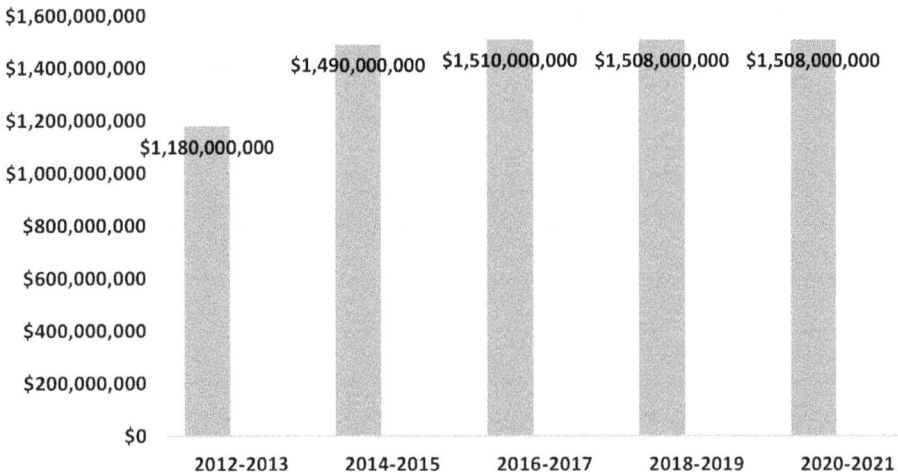

Chart 6. HHSC Consolidated Budget by Fiscal Years, Combined Amounts

services, one can, like Snow, use data clusters to seek additional understanding of the source of healthcare costs.

For our investigation, we have chosen a healthcare cost concern identified by Texas Medicaid.

To begin our investigation, we first have to determine how much a provider was paid for a therapy service and how the rate for the service was established.

Recall that the Medicaid program is a joint venture of the state and federal government, funded by both.

To obtain federal Medicaid matching funds, the federal government delineates very specifically what healthcare services it will cover, which professionals it recognizes as qualified to provide these services, and requires the establishment of "medical necessity" for the services to be partially paid by the federal government. It leaves to the state the administration of the program, including setting the rates for individual services. Each state must establish a "sole" agency for administration of the state's program. For Texas, the "sole" Medicaid agency is the Texas Health and Human Services Commission (HHSC).

The definition of "medical necessity" as established by the state must be based upon guidance from professionals and governmental agencies.

In 2016, the Texas HHSC submitted a report to CMS regarding proposed reductions in the state's rate paid for therapy services.[2] HHSC proposed reducing rates due to rapid and uncontrollable acceleration in cost of therapy services to children. The report concludes that "analysis performed in 2015 indicated that for state fiscal year (SFY) 2016, payments made under existing Texas Medicaid acute therapy rates would exceed the payments that would have been made had Texas Medicaid used the Medicare Fee Schedule rate for reimbursement by $315 million." HHSC indicated the examination of rates was prompted by legislative directive.[3] According to *Texas Medicaid and CHIP Guide 13th Edition*, 43 percent of Texas children are currently covered by Medicaid and CHIP (less than 1.02 percent are covered under CHIP). Children account for 76 percent of individuals covered under Texas Medicaid.

Texas HHSC, as the "sole" administrator of the Texas Medicaid program, is in control of who receives the service, under what conditions, and how much will be paid for the service. At the request of the legislature, HHSC reviewed rates paid for therapy services for children. Over the years, the pricing for therapy had gotten so confused that the state felt the need to self-report to the federal government that it had overpaid and intended to make corrections in the fee schedule to address the issue. The federal government requires that all policies the sole agency uses in developing rates to pay for services be consistent with federal and state legislative mandates.

How Did Texas Medicaid Determine, in One Year, a Potential Overpayment of $315 Million for Therapy Services?

Texas HHSC, through its data collection obtained from analysis of paid claims, determined that 54 percent of all monies funding therapy were for speech therapy services. Speech therapy comprises 1 to 3 percent of total Medicaid payments. Ninety-five percent of speech therapy services provided were coded as CPT 92507.[4]

CPT Code 92507 is defined as *treatment of speech, language, voice, communication, and/or auditory processing disorders, individual*. CPT codes reflect outpatient procedures.[5]

What Can Be Purchased for $315 Million (or $630 Million Per Two-Year Texas Budget Cycle)?

In 2021, building a hospital costs anywhere from about $60,000,000 to $187,500,000. The national average cost is $112,500,000 for a new 300,000 square-foot hospital that includes administrative areas, emergency and

Chapter 7. The Curious Case of CPT Code 92507

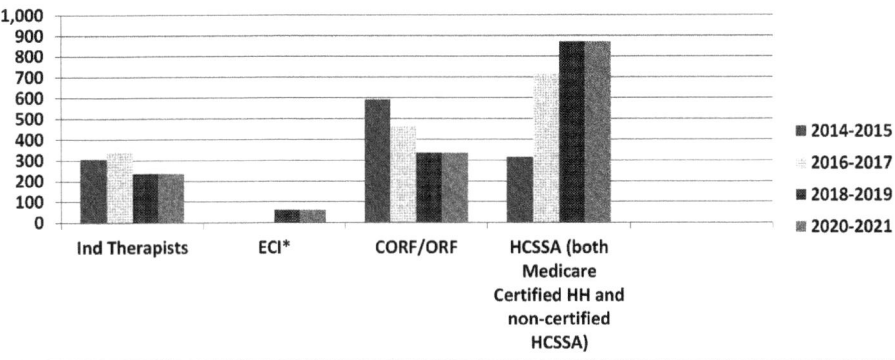

*ECI was separated from Independent Therapist Totals beginning in 2018

**Texas Medicaid policies refer to HHA which is defined as a Medicare-certified Home Health Agency, but reimburses non-certified, at-home, therapy-only providers at the same rate as HHA.

Chart 7. Texas Health and Human Services Commission Consolidated Budget by Fiscal Years. Levels of spending reflect only therapy services (children 0–21). All Texas Health and Human Services Commission information was obtained using Freedom of Information Act.

operating rooms, and enough space for 120 beds.[6] At the low end, the cost can be as low as $52,2a00,000 for a 150,000 square-foot micro hospital with 60 beds, an emergency department, outpatient surgical facilities, and limited administrative areas. So the overpayments for the one procedure code for a two-year cycle could have paid for as many as ten micro hospitals and at least three bigger ones.

How Were the Overpayments Identified and Quantified? What Was the Systemic Weakness That Allowed the Overpayments? What Other Systemic Overpayments Are Likely and How Can They Be Determined?

In its 2016 report, Texas HHSC stated that Texas Medicaid rates adopted by HHSC must comply with the statutory requirements of Section 1902(a)(30)(A) of the Social Security Act and 42 Code of Federal Regulations (CFR) 447.203-204. State Medicaid payment rates are to be developed by:

- Comparison to Medicare rates
- Comparison to other states' Medicaid rates
- Comparison to Texas commercial insurance rates

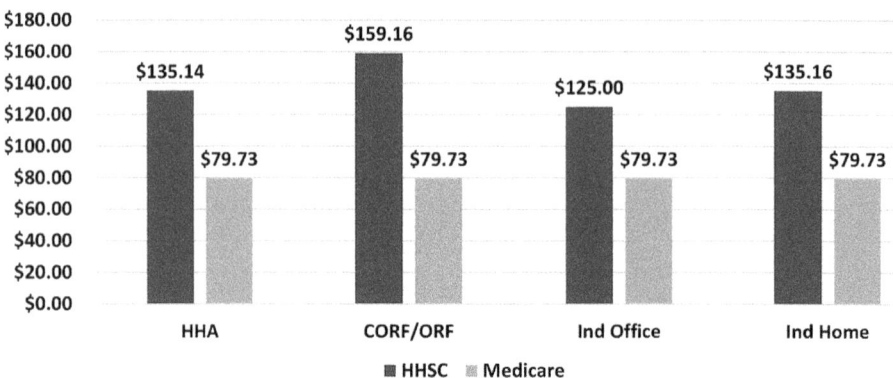

Chart 8. Comparison of Maximum Payment from Texas Medicaid vs Maximum Payment from Medicare (2016)

The report compares each provider type providing procedures/services defined by the code, CPT 92507, to children.

The Medicare rate for the outpatient therapy services defined by CPT 92507 is site neutral. "Site neutral" is the concept of paying the same amount for the same outpatient service, regardless of place the service was provided (POS). Medicare pays by procedure, one encounter per patient per day for all provider types. The Medicare rate reflects the maximum allowable for all provider types.

The Social Security Act requires that payment for Medicaid healthcare services are "consistent with efficiency, economy, *and* quality of care."[7]

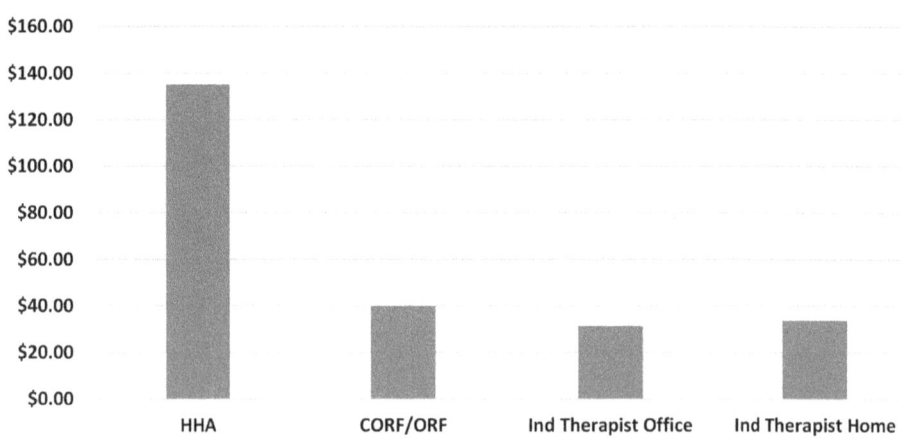

Chart 9. 15-Minute Units Maximum Texas Medicaid Payment, CPT 92507

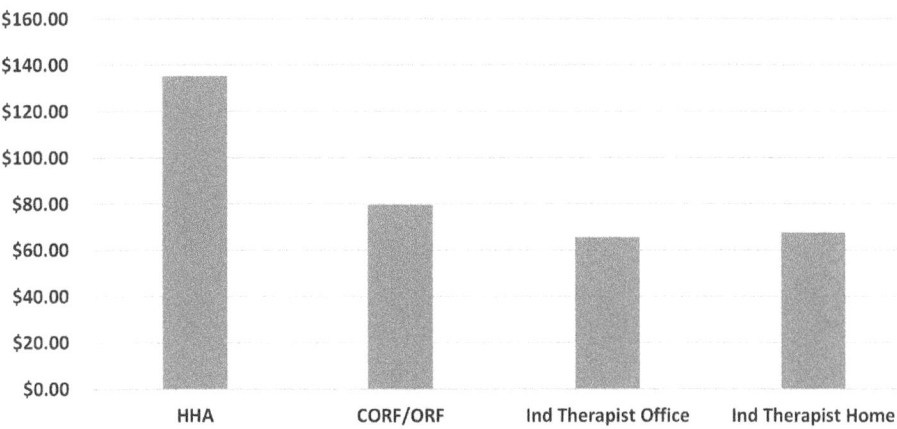

Chart 10. 30-Minute Session Maximum Texas Medicaid Payment, CPT 92507

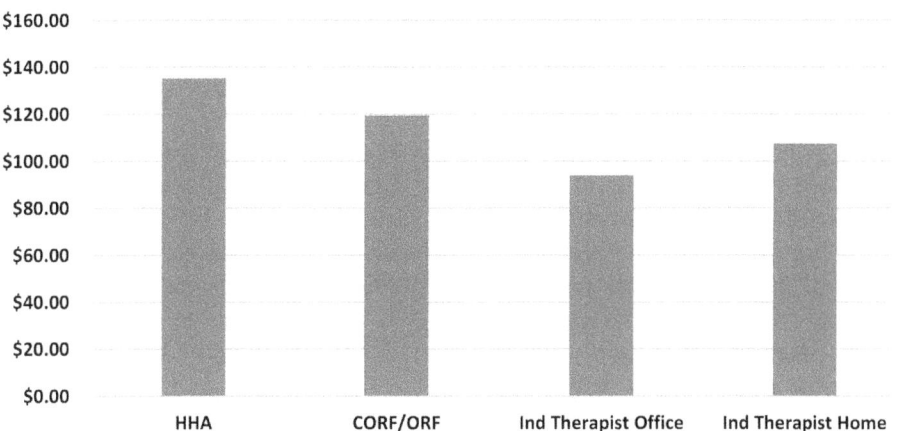

Chart 11. 45-Minute Session Maximum Texas Medicaid Payment, CPT 92507

Texas Medicaid established a fee schedule that paid two provider types in 15-minute units (up to four units per date of encounter at different rates) and one provider type at an untimed rate, creating a three-tiered system.

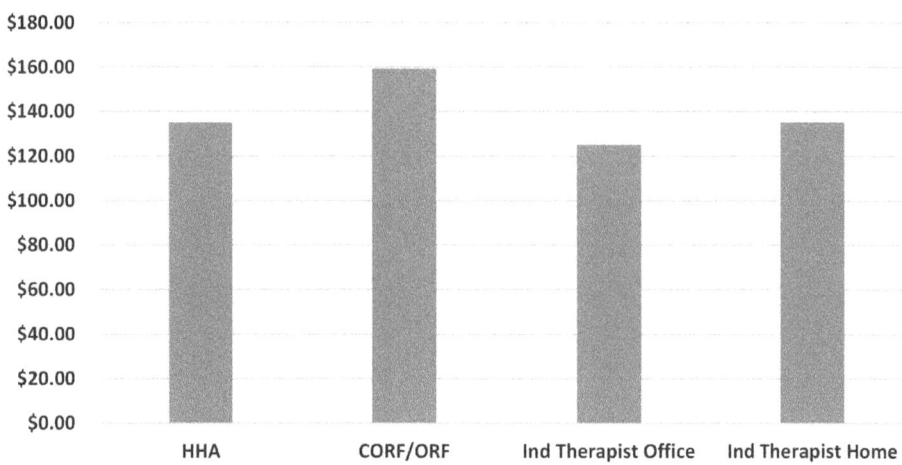

Chart 12. 60-Minute Session Maximum Texas Medicaid Payment, CPT 92507

How Did HHSC Determine the Impact of the Rate Structure on the Cost to the Medicaid Program?

HHSC analyzed data and compared rates to the Medicare rate for the same CPT code. Data collected is prescribed by the federal government, as are the guidelines for comparison. In 2010, the administrative simplification provision of the Health Insurance Portability and Accountability Act (HIPAA) required all healthcare providers, health plans, clearinghouses and other entities covered by HIPAA to comply with use of standard transactions, code sets and identifiers. Under HIPAA, the U.S. Department of Health and Human Services (HHS) adopted code sets including the Current Procedural Terminology (CPT) codes for outpatient services and identifiers for providers and health plans. The standardization of data contained on a claim was to allow for accurate and useful data collection for research and audit.

Federal regulations require that states "ensure that payments are consistent with efficiency, economy, and quality care and are sufficient to enlist enough providers so that the care and services are available under the plan to at least the extent such case and services are available to the public in the geographic area." According to 42 CFR 447.203 (b) (1) (iv), CMS therefore requires fees developed to undergo a Medicaid to Medicare comparison, and requires that rates not exceed the "reasonable estimate of the upper provider limit."[8]

CMS accepts a reasonable estimate of the upper provider limit using a comparison of Medicaid payments to equivalent Medicare payments or Medicaid costs using Medicare principles.

- To demonstrate Medicaid payments to Medicare payments, states must compare CPT codes based on Medicare "non-facility" fee schedules.
- To demonstrate Medicaid fees as a percentage of Medicare, states must use the Medicare non-facility fee schedule.
- To demonstrate the rates for nonequivalent services or services not covered under Medicare, the state chooses a Medicare CPT code that is reasonably similar to the Medicaid service code, provider type, and place of service.
- To demonstrate upper limits, one must compare Medicaid payments to Medicare payments.

State Medicaid programs must provide all mandatory services, which include all medically necessary healthcare services for children. The federal requirement for coverage of therapy services provided to children was delineated in a landmark lawsuit, *Alberto N. v. Traylor*. In a partial settlement with the federal government, Texas Medicaid agreed to certain provisions, and these were required to be included as components of the *Texas Medicaid Provider Procedures Manual*. The settlement also requires that MCOs adhere to these provisions. In Section C of this agreement,

- "The parties agree that no limitation exists for the provision of medically necessary physical therapy services, occupational therapy services, and services for an individual with speech, hearing, and language disorder, for which federal financial participation is available. The Agency shall approve medically necessary physical therapy, occupational therapy, and services for individuals with speech, hearing, and language disorders, except for where federal participation is not available."
- "The Agency shall provide medically necessary physical therapy, occupational therapy, and services for individuals with speech, hearing and language disorders if there is or will be progress made towards a goal and supported by documents from the prescribing physician and the treating therapist. Therapy goals include improving function, maintaining function, or slowing the deterioration of function."
- "The agency will revise the *Medicaid Provider's Procedures Manual* to conform with the policies described in Paragraph 31 and 32 of this Agreement. The *Manual* provision will also include

a description of the documentation that must be submitted by the prescribing physician and treating therapist when seeking authorization for therapy services. The Agency will provide the Plaintiff's counsel with a copy of these revisions for review and comment prior to publication in the *Medicaid Provider Procedure Manual*. Any corrections or clarification will need to be made in the subsequent *Texas Medicaid Bulletins*."[9]

Section C is specific, delineating that the documentation from the prescribing physician and the treating therapist is required for preauthorization of all therapy services.

In adhering to the requirements of the lawsuit agreement, the *Texas Medicaid Provider Procedures Manual, Volume 2*, was adjusted and includes Section 6.2.1.1: "Documentation to establish medical necessity for therapy services must include evaluation, treatment plan, and/or plan of care signed and dated by the treating therapist."

Despite the investigation that was initiated at the request of the legislature, the issue of overutilization of therapy services has been an ongoing concern since 2010, most notably in a letter written by HHSC dated June 2, 2014, to the Associate Regional Administrator of CMS Division of Medicaid and Children's Health, Region 6, published in the *Austin American-Statesman* December 2014.

What Is the Medicare Rate?

A fee-for-service schedule refers to the rate that "providers" are paid for certain specified services. Fees vary by procedure, by specialty, and by place of service (POS). The most highly recognized fee-for-service schedule is that developed by CMS. The Medicare rate can be considered a benchmark rate given its importance in rate setting for Medicare, Medicaid, commercial insurance carriers, and other governmental healthcare programs.

Before 1992, the federal government reimbursed Medicare-covered services based on the payment of charges. In 1992, CMS developed the Resource-Based Relative Value Scale (RBRVS). Howard University is credited with creating the RBRVS system and published its creation in the *Journal of the American Medical Association* on September 29, 1988. The system was based upon an interdisciplinary team of researchers, which included input from statisticians, physicians, economists, and "Medicare measurement specialists." The Healthcare Financing Administration, now known as CMS, adopted the system, and it was signed into law by the

Ombudsman Budget Reconciliation Act of 1989. Medicare has used the RBRVS system since that time.

RBRVS is reviewed annually. It places a value on each CPT code for physician and non-physician practitioner's bill (request reimbursement) for services. A Specialty Society Relative Value Scale Update Committee (RUC) meets three times a year to set new values and to review and reevaluate existing values at least once every five years. The RUC is made up of 29 members and is appointed by national medical societies. Committee seats are also held by an appointee of the chair of the AMA, an AMA representative, a representative of CPT Editorial Panel, a representative of the American Osteopathic Association, a representative of the Healthcare Advisors Committee, and a representative from the Practice Expense Review Board Committee.

An RBRVS value is assigned for each CPT code. Values are based on three factors with different weights. The average relative weights are 52 percent for physician work, 44 percent for practice expense, and 4 percent for malpractice expense. Payments under the RBRVS system also reflect a geographical adjustment of cost.

The formula uses a conversion factor (CF) that converts the relative units to actual dollar amounts. The multipliers (or the CF) are updated on an annual basis according to a formula specified by a congressional statute. The statutory formula establishes budget neutrality (42 CFR 412.352).

Budget neutrality prohibits CMS from changing the overall budget for Medicare expenses by more than a prescribed percentage. The conversion factor ensures that the total Medicare payments comply with the allowed budgeted Medicare funding.

The RBRVS formula also addresses the issue of facility/non-facility-provided services. This designation identifies a type of service provider. Facilities include hospital outpatient and inpatient departments, or hospital outpatient clinic settings, while non-facility services are generally provided in freestanding physician or non-physician practitioner's offices and other freestanding outpatient settings. The fee-for-service program is referred to as the Medicare Physician's Fee Schedule (MPFS). The fee schedule includes non-physician practitioners like physical therapists, speech-language pathologists, nurse practitioners, respiratory therapists, etc.

The RBVRS or the fixed fee schedule established by CMS is recognized as the most updated and accurate fee schedule for providers. It is used by publicly funded health plans, including Medicare, Medicaid, and TRICARE. Commercial insurances often use the fee-for-service schedule established by CMS as a basis for their reimbursement in the private sector.

The State Medicaid Director's Letter (SMDL) 13–003 requires that states annually submit upper payment demonstrations. CMS requests cost data by using a standard template. The template helps the state determine if the aggregate fee-for-service for a particular specialty exceeds what Medicare would have paid based upon the fee-for-service schedule established by RBVRS. CMS also requires a code-by-code comparison, which Texas HHSC performed in its report to CMS in 2016.[10]

Our concentration here is on how the CMS Medicare fee-for-service schedule was used to determine overpayment.

HHSC appealed to CMS to reduce rates for therapy services including CPT 92507 due to perceived overpayment when compared to the Medicare rate. HHSC cited rapid increases in use and cost when compared to Medicaid enrollment for the period examined as evidence of overpayment.

In the 2016 correspondence, HHSC reviewed the statutory and regulatory requirements governing rate setting by the Texas Medicaid program. Rate determination for Medicaid state plan programs is governed by Section 1902(a) of the Social Security Act (the Act), which states that a state plan for medical assistance must "provide such methods and procedures relating to the utilization of, and the payment for, care and services available under the plan (including but not limited to utilization review plans as provided for in section 1903[i][4]) as may be necessary to safeguard against unnecessary utilization of such care and services and to assure that payments are consistent with efficiency, economy, and quality of care and are sufficient to enlist enough providers to that care and services are available under the plan at least to the extent that such care and services are available to the general population in the geographic area." 41 U.S.C. 1396(a)(30)(A).

The report reviewed the current HHSC fee-for-service rates in 2016 for the primary providers of the speech therapy code CPT 92507. HHSC identified CPT 92507 as driving the "aggregate access."

Primary provider types of CPT 92507:

- Home health agencies (HHA)
- Comprehensive outpatient rehabilitation facility (CORF)/ Outpatient rehabilitation facility (ORF)
- Independent speech therapy providers

The three provider types were paid different rates based on:

- Units of service
- Place of service
- Provider type

All providers must report modifier GN on all filed claims, indicating CPT

Chapter 7. The Curious Case of CPT Code 92507   89

92507 is provided under an outpatient speech-language pathology plan of care per *Texas Medicaid Provider Procedures Manual* (*TMPPM*), Section 6.3.5.

Although a portion of the *TMPPM* often refers to an AT+ modifier for speech therapy services, according to the claims filing section of the same manual, the AT modifier is only appropriate to delineate "the necessity of an acute condition for occupational therapy (OT), physical therapy (PT), osteopathic manipulation (OMT), or chiropractic services."[11]

The report notes the difficulty comparing rates with the benchmark Medicare rate, other state Medicaid rates, and commercial rates. Texas Medicaid reimbursed CORF/ORF and independent speech therapy providers for CPT 92507 for up to four 15-minute units per day, which is inconsistent with mandated transactional standards for CPT code set, inconsistent with the mandated modifiers, and inconsistent with the definition of the CPT code.

Does the Medicare Program Have the Same Providers as the Texas Medicaid Program?

CMS indicates that speech therapy, as defined by CPT 92507, can be provided to Medicare-covered adults and a limited number of children with specific health conditions in these settings, consistent with coverage guidelines of the Texas Medicaid program:

- Offices of privately practicing therapists
- Many medical offices
- Outpatient hospital departments
- Critical access hospital (CAH) outpatient departments
- Rehabilitation agencies (sometimes called "other rehabilitation facilities" [ORFs])
- Comprehensive outpatient rehabilitation facilities (CORFs)
- Skilled nursing facilities (SNFs) (when Medicare Part A [Hospital Insurance] doesn't apply)
- At home, from certain therapy providers, including privately practicing therapists and certain home health agencies (if the beneficiary is not under a Home Health Plan of Care). Medicare covers the same POS locations as Texas Medicaid.

Adhering to national transactional standards mandated by HIPAA and CMS, Medicare considers:

- CPT 92507 is an untimed outpatient procedure code
- CPT 92507 encounters are not to exceed one time/day/beneficiary.

The Texas Medicaid program reimbursed inconsistently with the regulatory mandates.

Do the National Transactional Regulatory Requirements Apply to Commercial Carriers?

Commercial plans adhere to the national transactional standards in the same manner as Medicare.

Blue Cross Blue Shield claims filing guidelines:

Proper Speech Therapy Billing
Current Procedural Terminology (CPT) codes 92507 and 92508 are defined as speech/hearing therapy codes. Codes 92507 and 92508 are not considered time-based codes and should be reported only one time per session; in other words, the codes are reported without regard to the length of time spent with the patient performing the service.

Because the code descriptor does not indicate the time as a component for determining the use of the codes, you need not report increments of time (e.g., each 15 minutes). Only one unit should be reported for code 92507 and 92508 per date of service. Blue Cross and Blue Shield of Texas (BCBSTX) adheres to CPT guidelines for the proper usage of these CPT codes.

Current Procedural Terminology (CPT), copyright 2008 by the American Medical Association (AMA). CPT is a registered trademark of the AMA.[12]

The FFS established by HHSC and in use in 2016 resulted in a three-tiered rate system paying three different rates for the same service provided by a professional with the same qualifications under the same coverage guidelines and under the same established requirements for medical necessity, while Medicare and commercial carriers all adhered to mandated requirements and AMA copyright.

In the 2016 report, HHSC indicated that it had attempted to control spending by reducing the disparate rates by percentages, but the percentage reductions were also disparate. HHSC stated the percentage reductions "had little effect on utilization."[13] Percentage reductions ranged from 1.5 percent to 7 percent depending upon provider type.

HHSC had planned to initiate additional rate reductions in 2015, but their initiation was blocked by the filing of a lawsuit by non–Medicare certified licensed, at-home therapy-only and community support service agencies (HCSSAs), which provide at-home therapy services in the home or "other" setting. The HCSSAs were subsequently joined by relatives of children with disabilities who received therapy from the licensed-only, at-home providers.

In response to the filing of the lawsuit, the lower state court temporarily blocked state officials from implementing the therapy reductions.

The case was heard in the Texas Third Court of Appeals in April 2016. The court ruled that the HCSSAs' lawsuit was invalid "per lack of jurisdiction" and therefore overruled the lower court's decision and removed the temporary order blocking implementation of the rate cuts. The Appeals Court ruled only on whether or not providers were entitled to sue the state over rates. It did not address any other questions, including access to care or the legitimacy of the rates.

HHSC's proposed rate reductions continued the three-tiered system but with additional inequitable rates of reductions that were not based on access to care or any other metric.

There appears to be no justification given for continuation of the three-tiered system nor for the unequal percentage of reductions, even after the legislative-mandated investigation was completed.

Qualifications

There are no heightened educational or certification requirements for speech-language pathologists that work for HHAs and CORFs/ORFs. All Texas speech-language pathologists must meet the same requirements of state licensure. Providers of speech therapy in Texas, including those participating in the Texas Medicaid program, must possess the education and experience required for a Certificate of Clinical Competence in Speech-Language Pathology granted by the American Speech-Language-Hearing Association or meet the educational requirements and be in the process of accumulating the supervised experience required for certification and be licensed by the state if the state has such licensure requirements. The requirements are the same for all SLP providers: a master's degree and 36 weeks of full-time supervised professional experience (Texas Occupational Code, Chapter 401).

Equal or Greater Costs

Speech-language pathologists in private practice can enroll in Medicare and bill directly for their services. A 2009 CMS transmittal addressed speech therapy reimbursement for independent therapists, HHAs, and CORFs/ORFs. The transmittal explains that when providing speech therapy covered by Medicare Part B, independent speech therapists, HHAs providing outpatient speech therapy, and CORFs/ORFs are all to be reimbursed under the Medicare Physician Fee Schedule (MPFS) and reimbursed at the same levels, except for one reimbursement code for which

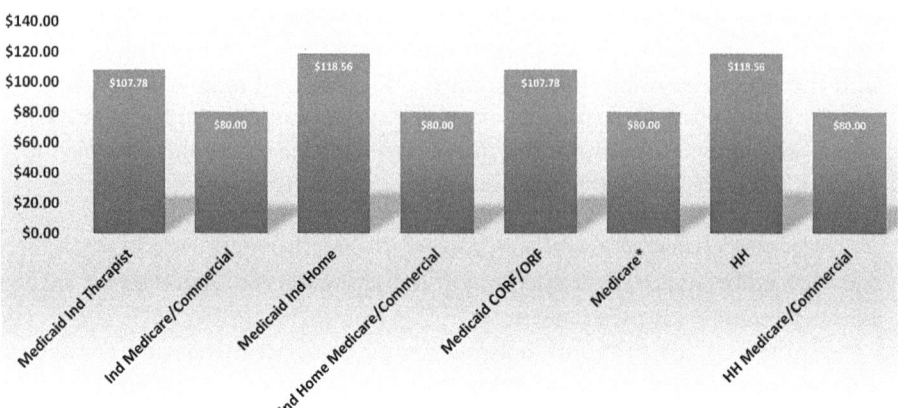

Chart 13. HHSC FFS Rates vs Medicare/Commercial Rate, CPT 92507, 2019 Texas Medicaid

independent therapists are reimbursed at a higher level. According to the CMS transmittal:

> The **non-facility rate** (that is paid when the provider performs the services in its own facility) accommodates overhead and indirect expenses the provider incurs by operating its own facility. **Thus it is somewhat higher than the facility rate**.[14]

Medicare is mandated as the benchmark and/or linchpin rate for the Medicaid program. In the case of CPT 92507, the benchmark/linchpin rate is site neutral. Texas HHSC was able to determine a projected overpayment by comparing its rates to the Medicare benchmark/linchpin rate for the specific code, CPT 92507.

While HHSC identified overpayment, it overlooked the lack of compliance with universally mandated regulatory requirements.

Indeed, the case of CPT 92507 and the recognized overutilization exceeding $300 million is a curiosity as the agency could not compare data collected to the established benchmark, the Medicare rate, as its HHSC fee schedule violated required AMA definitions of the CPT code for two provider types and disregarded the site neutral concept of the Medicare rate.

Despite acknowledging this, HHSC's previous attempts to alter the fee schedule failed to curb the rapid increase of cost to the Medicaid program.

The curious case of CPT 92507 becomes curiouser and curiouser.

Chapter 8

Curiouser and Curiouser

In this chapter we continue our review of how one state overpaid by over $600 million for one procedure code in one two-year period, and what can be learned from it. To convey the significance of the situation, we will need to discuss some dry regulations that govern Medicaid. All of the regulatory frameworks will need to be considered as we continue our inquiry into where the healthcare money goes and what can be done to tame healthcare costs in the complex twenty-first-century systems that have developed.

The Social Security Act requires that payment for Medicaid healthcare services are "consistent with efficiency, economy, *and* quality of care,"[1] effective for claims filed on or after October 1, 2010, must incorporate compatible methodologies of the National Correct Coding Initiative administered by the Secretary (or any successor initiative to promote correct coding and to control improper coding leading to inappropriate payment) and such other methodologies of that Initiative (or such other national correct coding methodologies) as the Secretary identifies" (Sec. 1903. [42 U.S.C. 1396b]).

As noted earlier, and it bears repeating, that in 2010, the Administrative Simplification provision of the Health Insurance Portability and Accountability Act (HIPAA) required all healthcare providers, health plans, clearinghouses and other entities covered by HIPAA to comply with use of standard transactions, code sets and identifiers. Under HIPAA, the U.S. Department of Health and Human Services (HHS) adopted codes sets including the Current Procedural Terminology (CPT) codes for outpatient services and identifiers for providers and health plans.

1. Does lack of compliance with required rate-setting methodologies impact healthcare spending?

Please refer to chart on page 81, HHSC Consolidated Budget, Fiscal Years, Chapter 7.

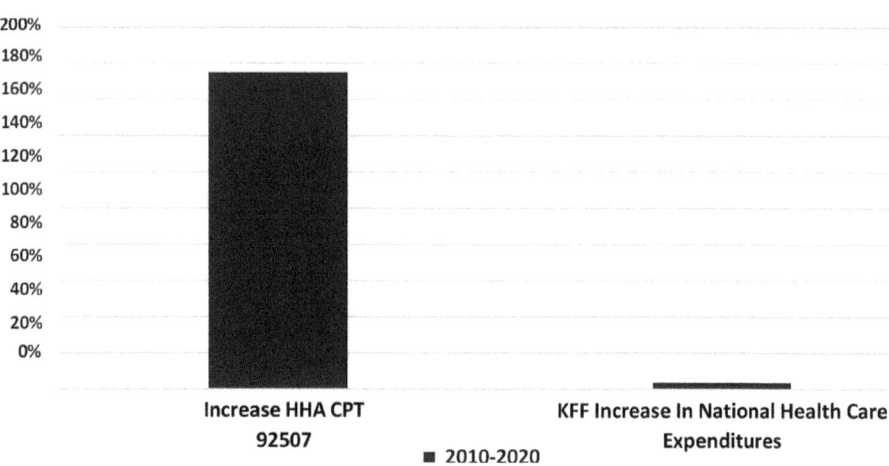

Chart 14. Percentage Increase in Therapy Provided by a HHA Compared to Increase in Total National Health Expenditures Based Upon Data from KFF, 2010–2020

2. What was the cataclysmic change that increased the number of children needing therapy services provided by a home health agency?

Does Lack of Compliance with Required Rate-Setting Methodologies Impact Healthcare Spending?

In 2014, the Texas HHSC had initiated a review of utilization for therapy services due to rising costs. By using data points collected from claims, HHSC found that of the "top 10 counties utilizing speech therapy in Texas, half are in the Rio Grande Valley. Five non–Valley counties have a population of 7,667,178 or roughly 29 percent of the state's total population. The five Valley counties account for 1,601,238 people or about 6 percent of the state's population in 2013."[2] Twelve percent of the Medicaid population resided in the Valley counties identified. In its analysis, HHSC compared the utilization of therapy services by Valley counties to utilization by non–Valley counties with consideration of the percentage of the population that were enrolled in Texas Medicaid. The data revealed that the use of speech therapy in the five identified Valley counties were four times greater than the use in non–Valley counties. HHSC indicated that the Texas Medicaid program spends $25.64 per eligible recipient on speech therapy services

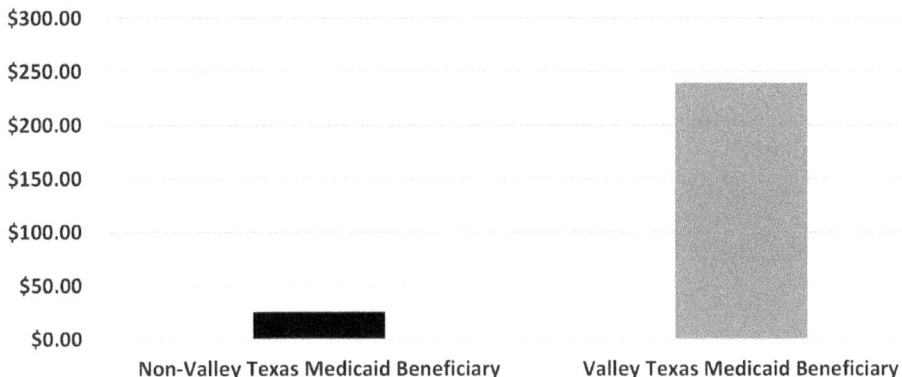

Chart 15. Comparison of Medicaid Spending for Texas Medicaid Beneficiaries Based On Location

in non–Valley counties, while it spends $239.40 per eligible recipient in the Valley counties. In the highest utilizing counties, Texas Medicaid spent $308.48 per eligible Medicaid recipient on speech therapy services while the non–Valley counties spent an average of $23.47 per eligible recipient.

The Texas HHSC pondered if this unbalanced utilization in the Valley region was secondary to overbilling through an established practice or pattern or "an epidemiological even of such magnitude that its lack of identification would roughly equate to overlooking the disappearance of the dinosaurs."[3]

HHSC went on to suggest that policy gaps might account for some of the issues related to overutilization, including lack of ability to track the rendering provider for the services provided by CORFs/ORFs and HHAs and the high use of assistants.

In the 2014 letter to CMS, HHSC identified CORFs/ORFs as a type of provider but did not delineate other types of providers permitted to bill for outpatient speech therapy services (HHAs and independent therapists), nor did they make reference to reimbursement rates for all of the tracked therapy services.

The report did highlight a reduction in total reimbursement for therapy services from 2013 to 2014, suggesting that changes in HHSC policy regarding transportation services may have accounted for the reduction, as many CORFs/ORFs relied on Medicaid-reimbursed transportation services to bring the eligible beneficiaries to their facilities. Texas Medicaid prohibits CORFs/ORFs from receiving reimbursement for any service *not* delivered at the CORF/ORF location facilities and prohibits transportation to clients by the CORF/ORF.[4] (See chart on page 81.)

The HHSC publication in 2016 did review moratoriums placed on Medicare-certified HHAs in Texas during the report period and expressed "concerns that the overly generous Medicaid reimbursement may have made this industry (HHA) a profitable target for fraud, waste, and abuse."[5]

According to the Peterson-KFF Health System Tracker, as of December 23, 2020, growth in healthcare spending grew by 3.7 percent for the period 2010–2019.

What Was the Cataclysmic Change That Increased the Number of Children Needing Therapy Services Provided by a Home Health Agency?

During the period of review, Home and Community Support Services Agencies (HCSSAs) were licensed by the Texas Department of Aging Disability Services (DADS). Types of HCSSAs include (1) licensed-only HCSSA providers (non–Medicare-certified HCSSAs) and (2) licensed and certified Home Health Agencies (Medicare HHAs), which are Medicare-certified.

According to federal and Texas regulations governing Medicaid, licensed-only non–Medicare-certified HCSSAs, or at-home therapy providers, who do not hold Medicare certification are *not* "Home Health Agencies," nor do they provide "Home Health Services."

"Home Health Services" means services provided in the patient's place of residence, as part of a plan of care approved by the patient's physician every 60 days. "Home Health Agency" means a public or private agency or organization, or part of any agency or organization, that meets requirements for participation in Medicare, including the capitalization requirements under 42 CFR 489.28 of this chapter (42 CFR 440.70(d)).

Home health agencies' ability to be recognized providers is regulated by Texas Administrative Code (TAC) Chapter 354.1033.

    a. Home Health Agencies. To participate in the Texas Medical Assistance (Medicaid) Program, a home health agency must:

    1. Be certified for participation as a home health agency in the Medicare program;

    2. Agree to operate and furnish services in compliance with all federal, state, and local laws and regulations. This includes holding a valid state license as a Home and Community Support

Chapter 8. Curiouser and Curiouser

Services Agency (HCSSA) with the category of service of licensed and certified home health services.

The Texas definition of Home Health is regulated by Texas Administrative Code (TAC) Chapter 354.1031:

> b. Definition. The following words and terms when used in this subchapter, shall have the following meanings, unless the context clearly indicates otherwise.
>
> 1. Home health services—Covered services, equipment, appliances and supplies which are provided to qualified Medicaid recipients at their place of residence by home health agency staff, providers of durable medical equipment, or expendable medical supplies under federal regulations 42 CFR 440.70 and TAC Chapter 354.1037 of this title (relating to Written Plan of Care) and TAC Chapter 354.1039 of this title (relating to Home Health Benefits and Limitations).
>
> 2. Home health agency—A public or private agency or organization, licensed by the state to provide home health services and qualified to participate as a Medicare home health agency under 42 CFR, Part 484, 42 CFR 484.1–484.52 (Conditions for Participation of Home Health Agencies).

This is consistent with requirements for the provision of therapy services in the *Texas Medicaid Provider Procedures Manual, Vol. 2—Children's Services*.[6]

2.1.2 Enrollment

Comprehensive Care Program (the name for the children's program under Texas Medicaid) providers must meet Medicaid and HHSC participation standards to enroll in the program. All CCP providers must be enrolled in Texas Medicaid to be reimbursed for services.[7]

According to the Chief Counsel of HHSC in a letter to stakeholders, dated July 19, 2012, "CCP enrollment does not mean that CCP providers are regulated."[8]

From the *Texas Medicaid Provider Procedures Manual*:

> "Home health services (e.g., intermittent skilled nursing, physical therapy, occupational therapy and hoe health aide) are provided under Texas Medicaid as Title XIX services. To enroll, a provider must be a licensed HCSSA that is also Medicare certified. These facilities will have the Licensed and Certified Home Health (LCHH) category listed on the DADS

issued license. Home health providers may render traditional Title XIX Medicaid home health services, telemonitoring services, and CCP services.

"Licensed Home Health–CCP. Licensed Home and Community Support Services Agencies (HCSSA) that are not Medicare certified, but have the licensed home health category on their DADS issued license may provide only Private Duty Nursing, CCP therapy to children (0–20), telemonitoring services, or Personal Care Services (PCS) under Texas Medicaid Comprehensive Care Program. HCSSAs that also wish to provide Title XIX, Medicaid home health services must also be Medicare certified.

"Speech Therapist (SLP). HHSC allows enrollment of independently practicing licensed speech-language pathologists under the THSteps-CCP. Texas Medicaid enrolls and reimburses speech-language pathologists for CCP services only."

"Physical Therapist (PT-CCP). The Medicare enrollment requirement is waived for therapists providing services only to THSteps-eligible clients who are 20 years of age and younger and who are not receiving Medicare benefits. Physical therapy services may also be provided by a licensed HCSSA. CCP physical therapy may be provided by either a licensed and certified home health provider or licensed HCSSA, and physical therapy through Medicaid home health services may be provided by a licensed and certified HCSSA."

"Occupational Therapist (OT-CCP). HHSC allows Medicaid enrollment of independently practicing licensed occupational therapists in CCP. Licensed HCSSAs are also able to provide occupational therapy in CCP."

Beginning in 2005, every healthcare provider in the United States had to register for a National Provider Identifier (NPI) number. Final NPI rules were published by Centers for Medicare and Medicaid (CMS) on January 23, 2004, codified at 45 CFR Part 162. The NPI system is administered by CMS.

Taxonomy codes are published by a third party publisher—West Publishing Company: http://www.wpc-edi.com/reference/

Home Health Agency Taxonomy Code

251E00000X—"A public agency or private organization, or a subdivision of such an agency or organization, that is primarily engaged in providing skilled nursing services and other therapeutic services, such as physical therapy, speech-language pathology services, or occupational therapy, medical social services, and home health aide services. It has policies established by a professional group associated with the agency or organization (including at least one physician and one registered nurse) to govern the services and provide for supervision of such services by a physician or a registered nurse; maintains clinical records on all patients; is

Chapter 8. Curiouser and Curiouser

licensed in accordance with State or local law or is approved by the State or local licensing agency as meeting the licensing standards, where applicable; and meets other conditions found by the Secretary of Health and Human Services to be necessary for health and safety. Source: CFR 42 Chapter IV Part 484."

42 CFR 484

42 CFR 484.1(b) "This part also sets forth additional requirements that are considered necessary to ensure the health and safety of patients."

42 CFR 484.18(b) "The total plan of care is reviewed by the attending physician and HHA personnel as often as the severity of the patients condition requires, but at least once every 60 days."

42 CFR 484.32 Allows for the use of licensed assistants for physical and occupational therapy, but not speech therapy assistants.

Upon enrollment with Texas Medicaid, both Licensed Only Non-Medicare Certified HCSSAs, or at-home therapy providers, and Medicare HHAs were issued a Texas Provider Identifier (TPI) number. Each TPI was assigned a corresponding provider type and number, such as Home Health Agency (44), CCP Provider (50); or Early Childhood Intervention Provider (11).

Texas Medicaid Reimbursement Rates were based upon provider type established by TPI assigned at enrollment which contained links to the provider's NPI.

TAC Chapter 355.8021 sets forth HHA reimbursement methodology. HHSC sets rates based on per-visit amount for speech therapy.

TAC Chapter 355.8441 governs reimbursement of the Early and Periodic Screening, Diagnosis, and Treatment (EPSDT) Services (in Texas, CCP services).

For CCP speech therapy, HHAs were paid per visit and CCP providers, including individually enrolled therapy providers and CORF/ORF, were paid in 15-minute units.

Step-by-step Summary of LICENSED ONLY NON-MEDICARE CERTIFIED HCSSA, at-home therapy services agency, state licensing process and enrollment in the Texas Medicaid program:

1. Non-Medicare-certified HCSSA, at-home therapy provider, registered for NPI number and selected taxonomy code *before* being licensed.

2. Non-Medicare-certified HCSSA, at-home therapy provider, submitted application to Texas Medicaid, using NPI and taxonomy code for Medicare-certified Home Health Agency.

3. Non-Medicare-certified HCSSA, at-home therapy provider,

could obtain license from DADS as licensed-only HCSSA, at-home therapy provider.

4. Texas Medicaid issued Texas Provider Identifier (TPI) that is associated with Provider Type 44 (Home Health Agency).

5. Non-Medicare-certified HCSSA, at-home therapy provider, were enrolled as a CCP provider, but were reimbursed on a different fee schedule than other CCP providers including Independently enrolled therapists and Independently enrolled ECI therapists and physician's offices rendering speech therapy services.

6. This results in non–Medicare-certified HCSSA, at-home therapy provider enrolled as a CCP provider, being paid an encounter instead of per 15 minutes of care.

A Medicare-certified HHA and Medicaid HHA must adhere to Conditions of Participation (CoPs) for ALL patients, even non–Medicare patients. MEDICAID recipients who require home health services *do not* have to meet the homebound status of Medicare recipients. Part of the mission of Medicaid is to ensure enrollees can continue to reside in a community setting.

From *Medicaid State Operations Manual*, Appendix B: "all Conditions of Participation apply to a Medicare certified HHA as an entity and to all individual or patients under the HHA's care. (See Section 1861[m], 1861[o][3] and 1891[a][1]) of the Social Security Act."

Summary of Authority from 79 FR 61165:

"Under the authority of sections 1861(o) and 1891 of the Act, the Secretary has established in regulations the requirements that an HHA must meet to participate in the Medicare program. These requirements are set forth in regulations at 42 CFR part 484, Home Health Services. Current regulations at 42 CFR 440.70(d) specify that HHAs participating in the Medicaid program must also meet the Medicare Conditions of Participation (CoPs). Section 1861(o)(6) of the Act requires that a HHA must meet the CoPs specified in section 1891(a) of the Act, and other CoPs as the Secretary finds necessary in the interest of the health and safety of patients. Section 1891(a) of the Act establishes specific requirements for HHAs in several areas, including patient rights, home health aide training and competency, and compliance with applicable federal, state, and local laws. The CoPs for HHAs protect all individuals under the HHA's care, unless a requirement is specifically limited to Medicare beneficiaries. Section 1861(o) of the Social Security Act (the Act) describes a HHS for purposes of participation in the Medicare program in broadly descriptive terms. All the requirements are stated generally as applicable to the HHA's overall activity, and not specifically to the Medicare patient. This provision, which was reaffirmed by Congress in the OBRA 1987 amendments to section 1891(a) of the Act, has been in the law since the inception of the Medicare program, and CMS' interpretation of it has remained the same."

79 FR 61165 explains why Medicare CoPs apply to all patients under care of Medicare-certified HHA:

"As the single largest payer for healthcare services in the United States, the federal government assumes a critical responsibility for the delivery and quality of care furnished under its programs. Historically, we have adopted a quality assurance approach that has been directed toward identifying health care providers that furnish poor quality care or fail to meet minimum federal standards. Facilities not meeting requirements would either correct the inappropriate practice(s) or would be terminated from participation in the Medicare or Medicaid programs."

Medicaid-only HHAs (providing services only to Medicaid-enrolled beneficiaries) must meet the requirements of Medicare Conditions of Participation (CoP). Medicaid does not require those individuals requiring the need for home health services to be homebound and does not require home health services to be provided exclusively in the home. However, other CoP must be met.

Licensed-only HCSSAs, at-home therapy providers, did not meet HHA CoP as licensed, Medicare-certified HCSSAs. Requirements not met by non–Medicare-certified HCSSAs, at-home therapy providers:

- Used licensed speech therapy assistants, which are not permitted under the Medicare CoPs. Medicare CoPs does not allow the use of speech therapy assistants even if licensed by the state.
- Obtained physician approval of therapy plan every 180 days instead of every 60 days. Medicare CoPs requires physician certification of plan of care to be approved every 60 days (Texas Medicaid CCP authorization periods are 180 days).
- Provided services to those without medical need for home health. Medicare CoPs do not permit providing therapy to patients that do not have medical need for home health services.
- Did not have personnel to meet Texas state HCSSA licensing requirements that all licensed-only HCSSAs **AND** Medicare-certified HCSSAs provide an in-home health assessment prior to initiating services.

According to the Texas A&M report commissioned by the Texas HHSC to investigate overutilization of therapy services, only 2 percent of home health therapy services reviewed were provided by a Medicare-certified HHA.[9]

HHSC publications in 2014 and 2016, and that of TX OIG in 2017, point out the high use of assistants for the provision of CPT 92507 reimbursed by Texas Medicaid.

HHA and CORF/ORF must be Medicare-certified to enroll in Texas Medicaid. The Medicare Conditions of Participation (CoP), applicable to both, prohibit the reimbursement of funds for speech therapy services delivered by a speech-language pathology assistant, even if licensed by the state. Texas Medicaid reimburses both provider types for CPT 92507 services delivered by a speech-language pathology assistant.

Until 2017, all speech therapy services delivered by a licensed speech-language pathologist or speech-language pathology assistant were paid at the same rate as a fully licensed therapist.[10]

Supply Creates Its Own Demand: A Twist on Say's Law

In the rational world of economics, dealing with supply and demand, Say's Law of Markets states that people's ability to purchase something depends on their ability to produce and thereby generate income. This dictum was shortened to "supply creates its own demand" and was taught down through the years in economics classes in the English-speaking world.

In the world of healthcare, the dictum has taken on a non-rational, some would say absurd, connotation. In the case of CPT 92507, the supply of governmental money, with disparate rates of reimbursement, created a demand for services from specific provider types for habilitative and rehabilitative services.

Excerpts from Advance Magazine, *a Trade Publication for Rehabilitation Therapists (2011)*

"Monday afternoon arrives, and the waiting room is full of pre-school children anxiously waiting for their speech and occupational therapy sessions. The front office staff has a long line of family members trying to check in. The children keep playing with the elevator button, water fountain, or anything else they find to pass the time."

"You have just walked into a pediatric rehabilitation facility in South Texas. It has contracted with my firm to convert from a rehabilitation program doing business under individual professional licenses with

Medicare/Medicaid, to a Medicare Part A certified outpatient rehabilitation facility (OPT/ORF) as classified by the federal government."

"Most of these facilities start out operating under therapists' individual professional licenses. Subsequently, they are encouraged to transition their operations to a licensed Medicare/Medicaid CORF or OPT, due to greater reimbursements from Texas Medicaid."

Excerpts from Advance Magazine on Decreasing No-Show Rates

"Achieving a targeting patient census is another major obstacle. In working with more than 60 rehabilitation programs in seven years, we have found that those offering transportation services averaged patient no-show rates of between 12 and 20 percent of their monthly scheduled visits. Those not offering transportation services averaged patient no-show rates between 25 percent and 30 percent. Unfortunately, with the present high cost of fuel, many rehabs must weigh these transportation-related costs against the added revenue resulting from a decrease in patient no-shows."

"Two other strategies have proven to decrease patient no-show rates. One strategy is to institute a patient attendance incentive program."

"The second strategy is cooperating with your local Medicaid/Medicare transportation provider to meet the transportation needs of the facility."

"Most Medicaid programs are required to offer transportation to their beneficiaries. Depending on the amount of Medicare/Medicaid business provided, these facilities will cooperate with your program if the facility assists in providing the paperwork necessary for approval by the payer."

"Use your professional staff appropriately by hiring PTAs, OTAs and speech-language pathology assistants to perform treatments under the supervision of a master's level therapist. This allows the provider to be available for new patient appointments and timely re-evaluations."

This last recommendation from above is confusing, to put it mildly, as Medicare certification has Conditions of Participation (CoP), which outline permissible personnel. Medicare will not reimburse any services provided by speech-language assistants, even if they are licensed in the state, and does not recognize assistants as qualified personnel under the CoP. Policy gaps create a situation under which CORF/ORFs are required to enroll under their Medicare certification, but do not have to maintain

CoP in the Texas Medicaid program. The situation is ripe for the birth of a moral dilemma—pass up an oversight sanctioned by the government, or violate program CoP to increase profit.

Consultants also provided services to assist SLP practices in opening a non–Medicare-certified, licensed at-home therapy-only HCSSA. This would allow for billing on an untimed basis rather than in 15-minute units. Additionally, SLPs who work for HCSSAs and CORFs/ORFs are not required to individually enroll in Texas Medicaid or Texas Medicaid MCOs, a process that could take up to six months in 2016 for a therapist enrolled based on their individual license.[11]

Enrollment as an at-home therapy-only HCSSA:

- Enrollment as a facility provider allows the facility to hire licensed therapists and bill for their services under the facility NPI. Independently enrolled therapists must be individually vetted by Texas Medicaid and Healthcare Partnership (TMHP) and enroll separately in each MCO before providing services to Medicaid beneficiaries. While some independently enrolled providers can enroll as a group, each licensed provider must be individually vetted, a process that can take up to six months. This created a scenario in which independently enrolled therapists were paid for months by their employer but could not treat Medicaid beneficiaries.
- Before December 2017, HHA billed in daily encounters. All other provider types billed in 15-minute units. For a 30-minute encounter, HHA was paid $70.00 more per encounter than any other provider type.
- While enrollment as a facility provider was advantageous for both CORF/ORFs and HCSSAs, it also created a significant issue for tracking and use of integrity measures, as claims could not be tracked by the rendering provider, the professional providing the service, but rather the entity. This precludes monitoring for excessive numbers of patients seen in a 24-hour period.

The 2002 publication of the *AMA Journal of Ethics* suggests that artificial intelligence–based systems can be used to identify waste, fraud, and abuse. The required fields in the information to be carried on electronic claims is reviewed in the coding and billing chapter of this book. CMS currently uses the fraud prevention system, which is a form of data analytics and "big data" to monitor and analyze claims and payments. With the use of this data collection, the Office of Inspector General should be able to compare:

- Patient volume for similar professional claims to identify abnormally high reimbursement submissions;
- Unnatural practice growth patterns;
- Unusually high numbers of procedures based on specialty and practice size which may highlight excessive numbers of patients seen by an individual within a 24-hour window;
- and other patient visit anomalies.

Let's go back to the curious case of 92507. The data analytics as proposed by the above *AMA* article would require the use and NPI of the individual professional rendering the service.

Three provider types provide CPT 92507 to the Texas Medicaid program:

- Home health agencies, including Medicare-certified home health agencies and at-home service providers, often referred to as licensed at-home, therapy-only agencies;
- Comprehensive outpatient rehabilitation facilities/outpatient rehabilitation facilities (CORF/ORF);
- Individually enrolled speech-language pathologists and/or physicians.

The following represents a chart of growth in utilization of services over several years (see chart on page 81).

A non–Medicare HCSSA could provide CPT 92507 for any duration of time and receive the same rate as an independent SLP who provided direct services for 60 minutes in their office.

If site-neutral payments were implemented throughout healthcare, the decrease in expenditures could total as much as $672 billion over a decade.[12]

Provider Type	Length of Treatment	Rate Paid to Fully Licensed Therapist	Rate Paid (Provided by SLP-Assistant)
HHA	30 minutes	$135.14	$135.14
Independent Office	30 minutes	$62.00	$62.00
Independent Home	30 minutes	$68.08	$68.08
CORF	30 minutes	$79.58	No assistants allowed in CORF/ORF per Medicare CoP

Table 5. ***2016 Texas Health and Human Services Commission (30 Minutes of Direct Contact) Fee for Service Rates, CPT 92507***. *All information taken from Texas Health and Human Services Commission via Freedom of Information Act.*

In 2016, there was no rate differential for assistants, so a fully licensed Medicaid-enrolled SLP, who might also be vetted by Medicare, would be reimbursed 67 percent less than a SLP-Assistant employed by a CORF/ORF. This was clearly an opportunity to increase revenue for the same service by the same qualified professional under the same coverage guidelines. (Medicare does not recognize SLP-Assistants in CORF/ORF as eligible personnel.)

An assistant employed by an HHA could be reimbursed the Medicaid HHA rate for a 20-minute session at the daily encounter rate, approximately 50 percent more than a fully licensed SLP individually enrolled in Texas Medicaid, resulting in an even greater opportunity for revenue increases for the same service.

Restructuring clinical staffing to include extended use of medical assistants to perform some patient care related to function can be constituted as unlicensed practice.[13]

Effective July 1, 2017, HHSC equalized the rates between provider types and applied NCCI edits to CPT 92507 following an investigation initiated by CMS, secondary to provider complaints that HHSC forced independents to bill CPT 92507 in 15-minute units rather than as an untimed code, in violation of the AMA copyright. All Medicaid providers are required to accept the restrictions established by the AMA for the use of copyrighted CPT codes. Appropriate use of CPT codes is also mandated as part of the national transactional standards.

Providers required to bill in 15-minute units also violated mandated HIPAA policy. According to U.S. Department of Health and Human Services, HIPAA "gives the Secretary the authority to impose monetary

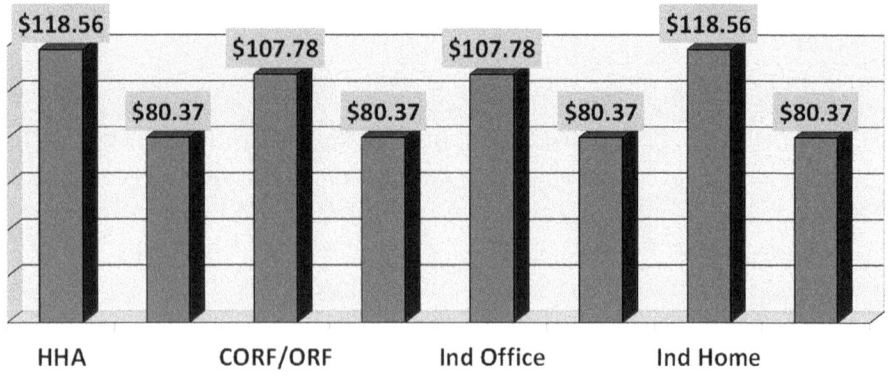

Chart 16. HHSC Adopted Rates 2019 for CPT 92507 vs Medicare Rate

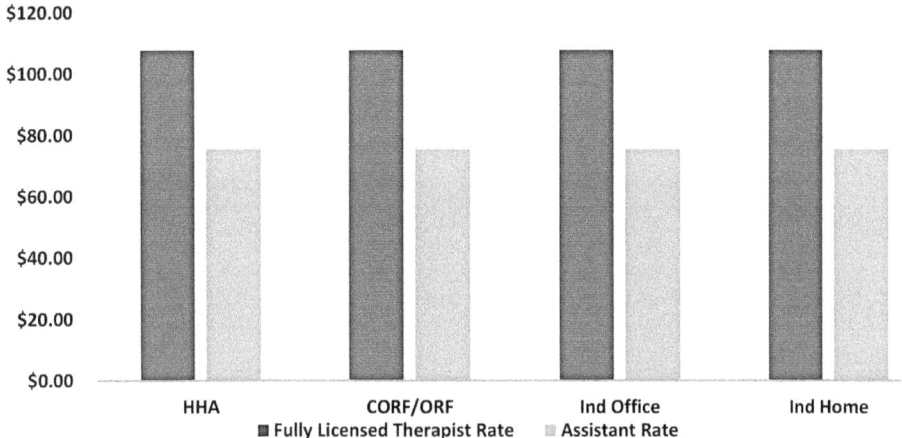

Chart 17. HHSC Rates (Adopted 12/01/2017) CPT 92507

penalties for failure to comply with a standard. The Secretary is required by statute to impose penalties of not more than $100 per violation on any person or entity who fails to comply with a standard except with the total amount imposed on any one person in each calendar year may not exceed $25,000 for violations of one requirement. Enforcement procedures will be published in future regulation."

To paraphrase, "If the standard adopted stipulates that HCPCS codes will be used to describe procedures, then the health plan must abide by the instructions for the use of HCPCS codes."

CPT codes are the standard for outpatient procedures, and state Medicaid programs are defined as health plans and are therefore covered entities under HIPAA.

The equalized rates adopted by HHSC were implemented effective September 1, 2017.

By that same date, a large Medicaid MCO in Texas reinstated the three-tiered disparate rates, rekindling the incentive for different provider types to obtain greater reimbursement from Texas Medicaid.

In September 2019, HHSC reinstated a portion of the tiered rates by increasing reimbursement based upon place of service (POS), rather than provider type Medicare and most commercial insurance plans consider outpatient services, like CPT 92507, delivered in the home as "at-home" services, not home health services under a home health plan of care, and, pays no rate differential for POS Home for outpatient codes. Texas HHSC states the increase payment for POS Home was secondary to a legislative directive that would be inconsistent with federal and state guidelines.

Individual Therapist Group
Therapy Fee Schedule

Effective September 1, 2017

PROC	M1	RATE	YMDEFF	YMDEND	AGE	Notes 1
92507		31.25	20130901	20170831	21 - 999	
92507		125.00	20170901	99991231	21 - 999	
92507		31.25	20130901	20170831	0 - 20	
92507		125.00	20170901	99991231	0 - 20	

Home Health
Therapy Fee Schedule

Effective September 1, 2017

PROC	M1	RATE	YMDEFF	YMDEND	AGE	Notes
92507		115.46	20130901	99991231	21 - 999	
92507		135.14	20130901	99991231	0 - 20	

Comprehensive Outpatient Rehabilitation Facility
Therapy Fee Schedule

Effective September 1, 2017

PROC	M1	RATE	YMDEFF	YMDEND	AGE	Notes
92507		39.78	20130901	20170831	0 - 999	
92507		159.12	20170901	99991231	0 - 999	

Image 3. MaxROI Rates for Speech Therapy

Medicare does not reimburse for SLP services (such as CPT 92507) if provided by a licensed SLP-Assistant, even if licensed by the state.

The change in rates for therapy services delivered in POS Home were paid at 10 percent greater rate for HHA and independently enrolled therapists and Early Childhood Intervention ECI) for CPT 92507 effective September 2019. With the increase in Assistants' rates and increase in POS rates, the SLP-Assistants were paid more than a fully licensed SLP enrolled in Medicare.

The use of a micro-level analysis suggests the increase in utilization of speech therapy services is likely related to:

- policy gaps that incentivize the provision of services by specific provider types

Chapter 8. Curiouser and Curiouser

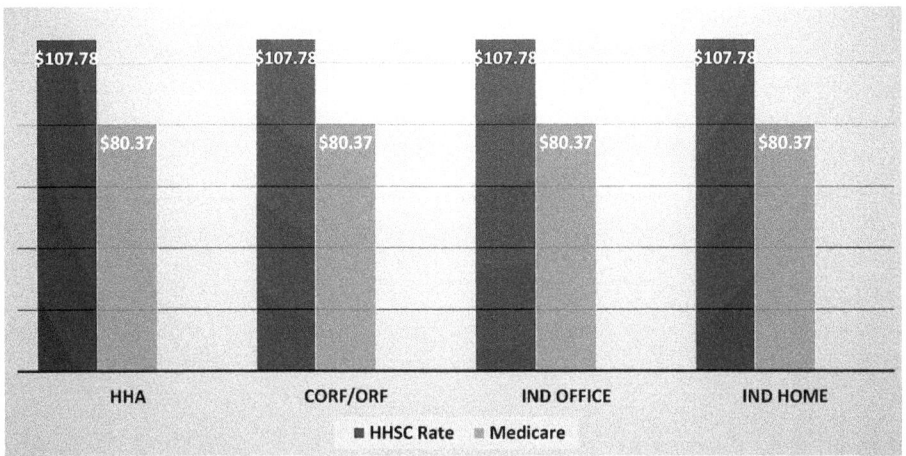

Chart 18. Texas HHSC Rate for Fully Licensed SLPs

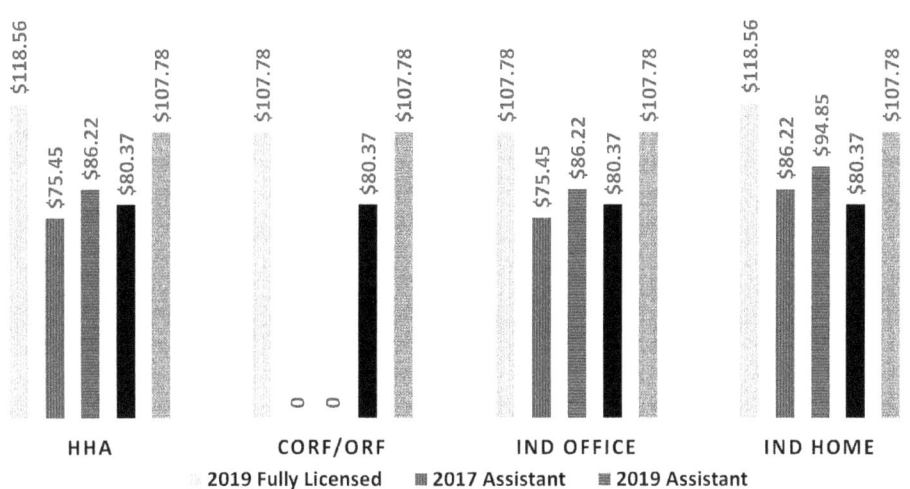

Chart 19. HHSC Rates for Fully Licensed SLPs vs SLP-Assistants for Years 2017 and 2019

- lapses in oversight and corrective action once overutilization is identified
- poor implementation of integrity measures and coding prohibitions

The investigation into the acceleration in speech therapy utilization that grossly exceeded growth in enrollment lacked a more sophisticated investigation—a micro-level analysis of data, that led to the location of the well.

This reflects only one healthcare discipline, only one healthcare code, and only one healthcare plan.

What are the implications to the total cost of healthcare if this scenario repeats itself in multiple healthcare disciplines, for multiple procedures, and for all health plans?

9

Managed Care Organizations

Down the Rabbit Hole

In this chapter we will continue examining how existing evaluation tools can evaluate healthcare costs and trends. The federal government funds the largest share of healthcare services, including Medicaid. The United States Census Bureau indicated that 17.8 percent of the U.S. population was covered by Medicaid in 2019. Texas, ranked second in population, is among the few states that has not expanded its Medicaid program under the Affordable Care Act, but it ranks third in Medicaid spending. According to the Kaiser Family Foundation (KFF) in 2019, Texas spent 22 percent of its "state general funds" on Medicaid while the state with the largest population, California, spent 16 percent.[1]

Data contained in *Texas Medicaid and CHIP Guide 13th Edition* indicates that 4.3 million Texans were receiving services through Texas Medicaid, which accounted for 15 percent of the Texas population.[2] Of those 4.3 million Texans served, 4.1 million or 94 percent of Texans were served by Medicaid MCOs. Spending by service provided: 52 percent of the Medicaid monies was spent on acute care services, which include therapy services; 34 percent was spent on long-term services and supports; 14 percent on prescriptive drugs; and five percent on behavioral health.

This book has concentrated on children's services funded by Texas Medicaid and a specific code, CPT 92507. The majority of cost of providing CPT 92507 is funded by the Children's Comprehensive Care Program (CCP), the Texas name for the Early and Periodic Screening, Diagnostic, and Treatment (EPSDT) benefit for children under the age of 21 who are enrolled in the Texas Medicaid program.

EPSDT was introduced in 1967 as part of Social Security Act addendums. Children under 21, enrolled in Medicaid based upon their eligibility, are entitled to access covered Medicaid services that are medically necessary, generally without limitations.

We will review a Texas MCO plan and determine how the issues concerning CPT 92507 were addressed.

Can You Track the Effectiveness of Medicaid MCOs in Curbing Costs by Tracking a Single Healthcare Service, CPT 92507?

In 2016, Texas's sole Medicaid agency, HHSC, reported to CMS its concerns regarding overpayment for therapy services. It cited the high utilization of CPT 92507 as "a driver" of the "aggregate access" in therapy cost. In its report, HHSC detailed its three-tiered rate structure based upon provider type.[3]

HHSC also made reference to a lawsuit filed to block proposed rate reductions that were to go into effect in 2015.[4]

Following the conclusion of the lawsuit, the rate reductions were imposed effective December 15, 2016. HHSC readjusted rates for therapy effective July 1, 2017, in response to a CMS investigation prompted by complaints of therapists who were concerned that the HHSC rate structure continued to require SLPs to bill untimed CPT codes in times units in violation of AMA copyright and NCCI edits.[5]

This book highlights the impact of circumventing legislative and administrative agency requirements and policy and the ramifications on healthcare cost and quality. To that end, we chronicle a Medicaid MCO with a specific provider, an exclusive provider. We will refer to the Medicaid MCO as MAXROI, ROI standing for Return on Investment. The larger the census of the Medicaid MCO, the greater the impact on the healthcare cost.

It is unclear if any other Medicaid MCO engaged in any other arrangements. This arrangement was initiated 01/30/2018 and continued for over 3.5 years. The arrangement was finally terminated 11/1/2021.

Following the adoption of the readjusted rates, MaxROI reinstated a tiered rate determined by provider types and place of service; however, they adjusted the rates to reflect CPT 92507 as an untimed code. All therapy rates for MaxROI exceeded the HHSC fee-for-service schedule. For one provider type, the rate for CPT 92507 exceeded the Medicare rate by 98 percent.

The amount the rate exceeds the HHSC fee structure is more startling if one realizes that MCO-capitated rates are based upon the commissioner's rate (the HHSC rate).

9. Managed Care Organizations   113

From a Pure Mathematical Perspective, How Can MCOs Reduce the Cost of Healthcare Services to the Taxpayer If a Contracted MCO Is Reimbursing at a Rate Greater Than What the State Would Have Paid Directly to the Provider?

Adjustment to reflect CPT 92507 as untimed code allowed direct comparison of rates paid by the MaxROI to each of the three provider types. This comparison could not have occurred prior to HHSC's eliminating the time requirement for CPT 92507 in accordance with legally mandated requirements.

Provider	CPT Code 92507 Medicare	CPT Code 92507 MaxROI	CPT Code 92507 HHSC
Independent Therapist/Physician Office	$80.37	$125.00	$107.78
Independent Therapist Home	$80.37	$135.14	$107.78
HHA 0–20	$80.37	$135.14	$107.78
CORF/ORF	$80.37	$159.12	$107.78

Table 6. *Texas Medicaid Managed Care Organization Rate for CPT 92507 by Provider Type Compared with Texas Health and Human Services Commission Fee-for-Service and Medicare Rates*. MaxROI Fee Schedule Effective July 1, 2017 (individual, 0–20 years of age, CPT 92507 billed at outpatient services [GN modifier], untimed code vs. Medicare Rate). All information taken from Texas Health and Human Services Commission via Freedom of Information Act.

Do MCOs Reduce the Cost of Service While Increasing Quality of Care?

Following the lawsuit and the rate reductions, MaxROI not only raised the fee-for-service rates of providers, but also initiated a dramatic alteration of the current service delivery model by collaborating with one of the plaintiffs of the lawsuit,[6] an at-home therapy-only service agency owned by a private equity company. This essentially monopolized the provision of therapy services, including CPT 92507, by establishing an

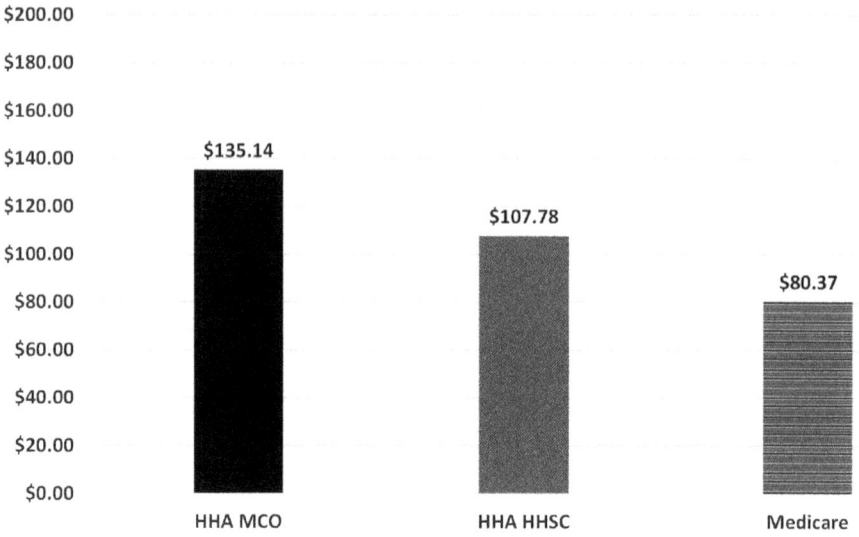

Chart 20. CPT Code 92507, MCO Rates for Provider Type HHA

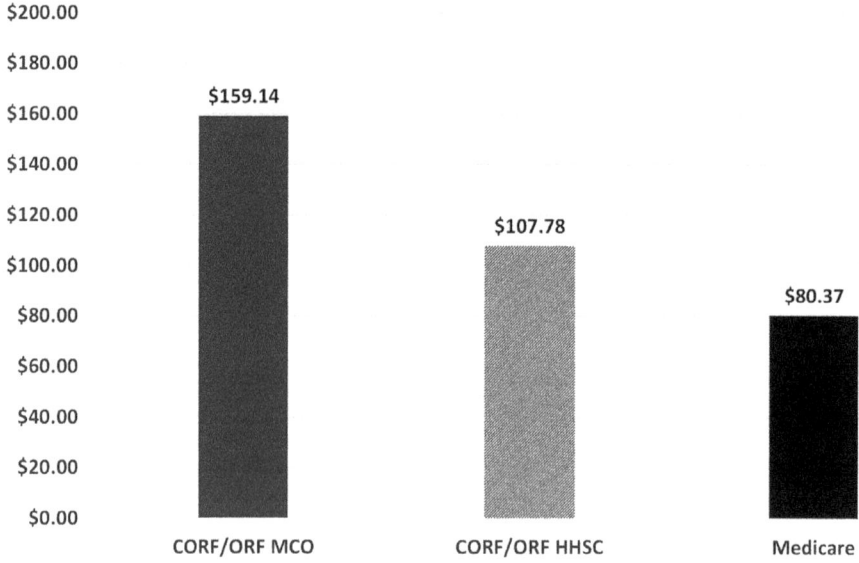

Chart 21. CPT Code 92507, MCO Rates for Provider Type CORF/ORF

exclusive provider in a Medicaid service region. Private equity-owned, at-home, therapy-only services agencies ranked highest in payment from Medicaid MCOs and ranked third for payment for the traditional Medicaid fee-for-service program for CPT 92507.[7] The altered service delivery model arrangement stayed in effect until November 1, 2021.

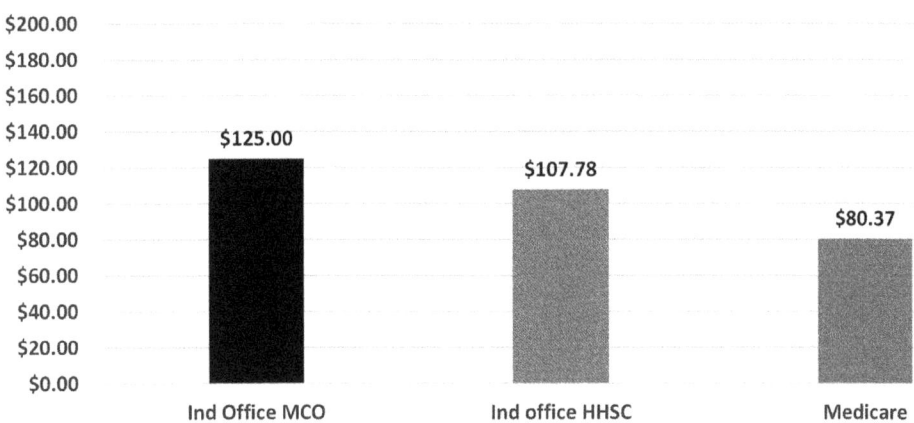

Chart 22. CPT Code 92507, MCO Rates for Provider Type Independent (Place of Service—Office)

Chart 23. CPT Code 92507, MCO Rates for Provide Type Independent (Place of Service—Home)

Effective March 1, 2015, MaxROI notified beneficiaries ("members," in the parlance of MCOs) of its plan that therapy evaluations/reevaluations must be obtained from an exclusive provider, an at-home therapy-only service agency. This requirement would apply to the STAR, STAR Health, STAR+PLUS and CHIP members assigned to the 39 counties in the Travis and Central Service Delivery Areas. While the Uniform Managed Care Contract, which Texas requires for all Medicaid MCOs, permits the use of preferred providers as a way to encourage quality-based alternative payment models, such programs must be designed to improve health outcomes for members, improve members' experience of care and lower healthcare cost trends, and must allow members to opt out. It is unclear how this model could accomplish any of these goals.[8]

Before MaxROI established an alternative exclusive provider for the provision of therapy services, it made a presentation to the Texas legislature. The MaxROI detailed the basis of reasoning on the structure of the "alternative plan," purporting that if a therapist evaluated a member, the therapist was incentivized to recommend treatment.

While at first glance, this might seem a reasonable statement, a closer look would reveal its absurdity: If an oncologist evaluated a patient, would they be incentivized to treat the patient for cancer, or would they also provide treatment for a cancer that was diagnosed through the evaluation process? Also recall the federal government, in its settlement in the *Alberto N. v. Traylor* case, mandated that the treating therapist establish the plan of care based upon completion of an evaluation. This is also a mandate of the Medicaid program.

All children in Texas Medicaid who are seen for therapy evaluation and treatment must first be screened by their primary care physician, who determines whether there is a high suspicion or concern needing assessment by a physical therapist (PT), occupational therapist (OT), or speech-language pathologist (SLP) before making a referral for evaluation.

MaxROI's concern is a ludicrous assertion. If the proposed tenet was supportable, then one could reasonably assume an oncologist, endocrinologist, or other specialist who evaluated an individual on the referral of the primary care provider (PCP) would also be incentivized to initiate treatment and testing and charge for follow-up visits.

An investigation of the utilization of speech therapy reimbursed by MCOs, published on October 2, 2017, by the Texas OIG, Report No. INS-16-00Z, tested this assertion and concluded that "all treatment records contained sufficient evidence for documenting medical necessity based upon a review by a subject matter expert."

This would suggest that recommendations for therapy were based on documented need rather than a source of potential income.

In recent years, Texas Medicaid dealt with what many considered excessive therapy costs. The Texas legislature intervened to control costs, and, in response, a group of HCSSAs, including the later designated exclusive provider (which identified itself as a pediatric home health agency), led a lawsuit against the state.

Background

Medicaid pays for acute care services[9] and long-term services and supports (LTSS).[10] Medicaid clients are served through a traditional fee-for-service (FFS) model or a managed care model. Under the FFS model, healthcare providers are paid through the Texas Medicaid and Healthcare Partnership (TMHP) for each acute care service they provide, such as an office visit, test, or procedure. HHSC pays LTSS FFS claims directly to providers through the Claims Management System.[11] Under the managed care model, the Texas HHSC contracts with MCOs, also known as health plans, and pays a monthly per-person amount called a capitation payment[12] to MCOs. Speech therapy is universally recognized as an outpatient service, unless provided under a Home Health Plan of Care.

Under the managed care model, the MCO contracts with Medicaid providers for the delivery of healthcare services to Medicaid enrollees.[13] The MCO contracts directly with doctors and other healthcare providers to create provider networks their members can use. MCOs are required to provide all covered medically necessary services to their members, including speech therapy, and must have an adequate network of providers. The managed care model was based on the theory that by coordinating Medicaid program healthcare services through an MCO, states would reduce Medicaid program costs and improve care outcomes. MaxROI's decision to direct all Medicaid business to a particular HCSSA deviates from this theory. Instead, it created an elaborate scheme that bypassed regulations that ensure children and the disabled receive the same services as the general public under the same standards of care. It directed acute care, outpatient services to a LTSS provider. It also eliminated more conveniently qualified providers for at-home care, increasing the burden on its members.

I. Medical Necessity

HHSC has tried to curb the use of in-home therapy services that are for the convenience of the provider who bypasses the cost of a brick-and-mortar facility. It changed Texas Medicaid policy in 2017 to require that all "medically necessary criteria for therapy services provided in the home must be based on need."

MaxROI appeared to recognize the need to have medical necessity criteria for therapy in the home consistent with OIG reporting and new policy and created a "Provider Attestation Statement for At-home Therapy" prior to 2017. When this form was announced, MaxROI was attempting to limit the amount of at-home therapy consistent with HHSC policy regarding medical necessity.

II. Inability to Offset Costs Through Other Payors

MaxROI's plan causes waste by forfeiting third-party liability payments from commercial insurance providers. This is because the exclusive provider, licensed only by Department of Aging and Disability for Travis County (i.e., not a Medicare-certified HCSSA), is not a healthcare entity recognized by commercial insurance carriers for outpatient services. In contrast, when therapy services are provided by therapists in outpatient settings enrolled in commercial health plans, payments by commercial carriers offset some of the costs. The program changes in referral and authorization carry significant cost for an area of Texas that has demonstrated more than adequate control over overutilization.

III. The Service Delivery Area Already Has Low Utilization

By allowing this agreement with the exclusive provider, MaxROI implemented a pilot study to curb costs by using a non-standard healthcare protocol. MaxROI had and continued to reimburse private practice providers 15 percent below the HHSC fee-for-service rate. Until 2017, MaxROI had paid individually enrolled therapists at the lower rate. The area targeted by MaxROI had the lowest utilization of all MCO regions and

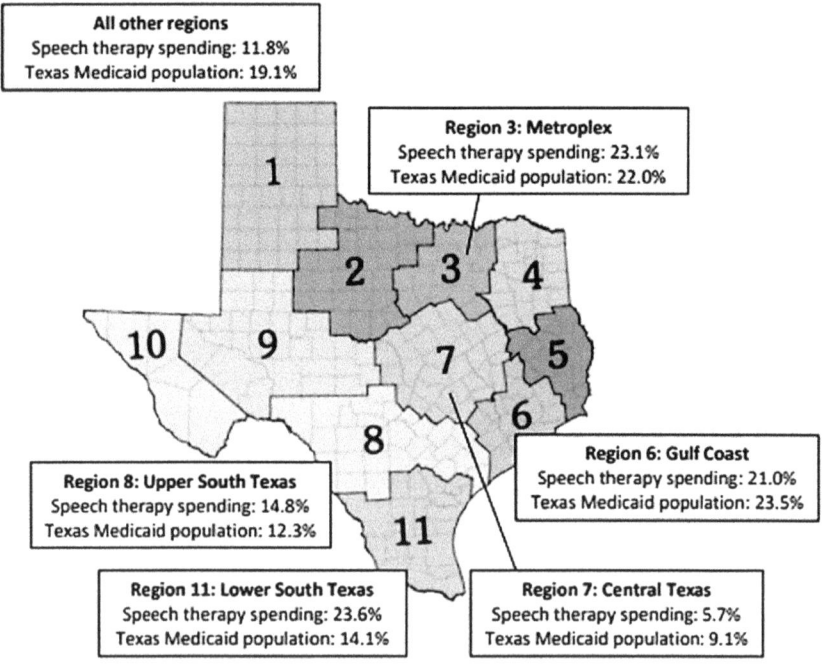

Map 3. Service Delivery Areas for Texas Medicaid Managed-Care Organization

accounted for only 5.7 percent of speech therapy payments (in the Central Texas region).

The data reported by HHSC showed that regions with the largest Medicaid populations were generally where most of the speech therapy payments were made. However, Region 11 (Lower South Texas) had a notably larger proportion of speech therapy spending relative to its Medicaid enrollment, while payments in the targeted Region 7 (Central Texas) were lower than would be expected based on its Medicaid population.

1. The Exclusive Provider Plan Violates All Recognized and Accepted Standards of Healthcare

According to the American Speech-Language-Hearing Association (ASHA), the American Physical Therapy Association (APTA), and the American Occupational Therapy Association (AOTA), MaxROI mandates are inconsistent with recognized standards of care.

Texas Health and Human Services secures federal financial participation for the Texas Medicaid program through the State Plan. HHSC has clarified that Medicaid MCOs must follow all federal and state laws and HHSC rules.

MaxROI's plan designates a "dedicated," (exclusive) provider of a type not recognized as an acute care outpatient service provider in Texas Medicaid. Medicare-certified home health agencies (HHAs), therapists in private practice, comprehensive outpatient rehabilitation facilities (CORF), outpatient rehabilitation facilities (ORF), hospitals and physicians' offices may provide therapy to Texas's Medicaid beneficiaries under age 21. Medicare-certified HHAs (with the exception of speech therapy services), hospitals, physicians' offices, and therapists in private practice (with the exception of SLP employed by a hospital or physician) may provide services to adults.

The exclusive provider was an at-home, therapy-only agency in Travis County. The exclusive provider could enroll in Texas Medicaid to provide OT and PT services to children eligible for CCP services. HHAs can only provide therapy services under a Home Health Plan of Care to categorically needy individuals.

The Provider Participation Requirements to be recognized by Texas Medicaid as an HHA are outlined in TAC 354.1033(a).

The Medicaid Government Waiver Program Technical Guidelines outline the use of Home and Community-Based Services in the Early Periodic Screening Diagnostic and Treatment Program:[14]

> "If an extended state plan coverage is proposed in order to provide a service in an amount greater than permitted under the state plan, the coverage may only

apply to adults (individuals aged 21 and older). When children are served in a waiver, the services that are included in the waiver must take in account the Early and Periodic Screening Diagnostic and Treatment benefits requirements. Federal requirements concerning EPSDT mandate that Medicaid eligible children receive all medically necessary services coverage under 1905 (a), Other Act, regardless of whether such services are specifically included in the state plan. The waiver may not provide for the coverage of service that could be furnished to children under EPSDT. If a waiver targets children exclusively, it may not provide the coverage of any service that can be offered through the state plan."

The use of Home and Community-Based Services is restricted to rehabilitative services, occupational therapy (OT), and physical therapy (PT). Speech thrapy (ST) can only be provided in assisted living arrangements.

The Texas State Plan is consistent with Social Security Act 1861 and does not identify Home and Community-Based Services as outpatient speech therapy providers.[15]

For clarification, MaxROI entered into an exclusive provider agreement and implemented a plan to deliver the covered benefits of occupational therapy (OT), physical thcrapy (PT), and speech therapy (ST), all initial evaluations and initial plan of care creation, reevaluations and subsequent plan of care creation, and a "preferred provider" for treatment. While the beneficiaries could have opted out of the exclusive provider for treatment, they could not opt out of using the exclusive provider for initial evaluation and initial POC creation and the reevaluations and POC creation. The MaxROI program dictated that the treating therapist must *not* be the same professional who completed the evaluation and POC creation or subsequent reevaluation and subsequent POC creation. The MaxROI program also dictated that the treating therapist must follow the initial POC established by the evaluating or subsequent reevaluating therapist employed by the exclusive provider.

MaxROI mandated this plan for those with Medicaid as primary as well as for those with commercial or other publicly funded health plan coverage as primary and Medicaid as secondary.

It should be noted that another aspect of the exclusive provider agreement was the burden of prior authorization of any providers who were not the exclusive provider. The exclusive provider did not have to go through the normal channels of approval for therapy services. If a patient opted out of treatment with the exclusive provider, the provider that had been elected simply obtained the physician's signature on the evaluation report (that they did not author) and then the exclusive provider set up the authorization with MaxROI. This process circumvented any communication between the doctor and the therapist providing services to the patient and the related provisions of the Alberto N. Settlement Agreement.

9. Managed Care Organizations

Preferred providers are generally contracted by the health plans to deliver services to the plan's members at a discounted rate. For example, selecting a preferred provider may not require a copayment or may limit the amount a patient might be charged for a service.

Medicaid providers cannot bill the patient for any service, so the use of an exclusive provider provides no benefit to the beneficiaries. In fact, in some cases it created a hardship as the designated exclusive provider did not have adequate locations or bilingual therapists.

The scheme was shortsighted, as the selected exclusive provider did not have adequate resources to address the number of individual health plan members. To circumvent this, the exclusive provider attempted to contract directly with providers already enrolled and providing services to MaxROI members through a contractual relationship with MaxROI.

The scheme was to alter recommendations for frequency of treatment and POCs if completed by a "subcontractor" to reduce the number of therapy visits authorized.

In summary, the HHSC requires MCOs to follow state and federal laws, HHSC rules, and the provisions of the *Texas Medicaid Provider Procedures Manual* (*TMPPM*).

Providers enrolled with HHSC and contracted with Medicaid MCOs must comply with all requirements of the provider manual (*TMPPM*) and must sign the HHSC provider agreement:[16]

"By signing an HHSC Medicaid Provider Agreement (through the enrollment process) and submitting Medicaid claims, each enrolled provider agrees to abide by the policies and procedures of Medicaid, published regulations, and the information and instructions in manuals, bulletins, and other instructional material furnished to the provider."

    1. Agreement and documents constituting Agreement. The current *Texas Medicaid Provider Procedures Manual* ("Provider Manual") may be accessed via the internet at www.tmhp.com. Provider has a duty to become educated and knowledgeable with the contents and procedures contained in the Provider Manual. Provider agrees to comply with all of the requirements of the Provider Manual, as well as all state and federal laws governing or regulating Medicaid.[17]

    2. Nondiscrimination. Provider must not exclude or deny aid, care, service, or other benefits available under Medicaid or in any other way discriminate against a person because of that person's race, color, national origin, gender, age, disability, political or religious affiliation or belief. *Provider must provide services to Medicaid clients in the same manner, by the same methods, and at the same level and quality as provided to the general public.* Provider agrees to grant Medicaid recipients all discounts and promotional offers provided to the general public.

Section 5 of *TMPPM* (March 2023) indicates that documentation to establish medical necessity for therapy service must include evaluation, treatment plan and/or plan of care signed and dated by the treating therapist.[18]

By signing and dating the documents submitted, the treating therapist declares authorship. Authorship attributes the original creation of particular information to a specific individual acting at a particular time.

In signing the document and submitting for authorization, the treating therapist attests to its validity, accuracy and completeness. To attest to documents completed and developed by another individual compromises patient care, care coordination and quality, as well as creating potential for fraud and abuse.

MaxROI's plan to require separation of clinical data from evaluation and POC creation and reevaluation and POC creation from treatment makes the treatment process for MaxROI beneficiaries different from every other Texas Medicaid beneficiary, those exempted from participation in the MaxROI plan, and the general public. This plan creates a two-tiered system that precludes some MaxROI beneficiaries from receiving the benefit of having integrated care based upon the essential relationship of evaluation, plan of care creation and therapeutic treatment, nor do these beneficiaries receive the benefit of having a therapist acting independently on their behalf that can adapt the POC as needed.

> Principles of Ethics I
> M. Individuals who hold the Certificate of Clinical Competence shall use independent and evidence-based clinical judgment, keeping paramount the best interests of those being serviced.
>
> Principles of Ethics IV
> B. Individuals shall exercise independent professional judgment in recommending and providing professional services when an administrative mandate, referral source, or prescription prevents keeping the welfare of persons served paramount.[19]
>
> Principle of Ethics IV
> Individuals shall not provide professional service without exercising independent professional judgment, regardless of referral source or prescription.[20]

Merriam Webster defines "best practice" as "a procedure or protocol that has been shown by research and experience to produce optimal results and that is established or proposed as a standard suitable for widespread adoption."

In 2011, the Institute of Medicine (IOM) defined clinical practice guidelines as "statements that include recommendations intended to optimize patient care that are informed by a systematic review of evidence and an assessment of the benefits and harms of alternative care options." Trustworthy guidelines should be based on a systematic evidence review, developed by a panel of multidisciplinary experts, and should provide a clear explanation of the logical relationships between alternative care options and health outcomes and ratings of both the quality of evidence and the strength of the recommendations.

The IOM further states that expert panels are created to conduct systematic evidence reviews to enable clinical practice guidelines development. An expert panel is a committee of unpaid experts. Members are chosen mainly for their scientific and clinical expertise. Excluded are individuals with clear financial conflicts and those whose professional or intellectual bias would diminish the credibility of the review.

MaxROI's rationale for implementing this program in no way establishes nor meets the requirements of best clinical practices. Best clinical practices include the conscientious, explicit and judicious integration of the available, evidence-based approach from systematic research and should not reflect decision-making practices based upon anecdotal reporting.

MaxROI's plan also makes the evaluations and POCs subject to review and modification by someone who did not conduct the evaluation or create the POC. The licensed therapist is mandated to agree to allow the review, modification (falsification) and approval of plans of care and clinical evaluation documentation by a third party. This violates 16 TAC 111.155(b)(13), the provision of the Code of Ethics that prohibits the falsification of records.

MaxROI acknowledges that the plan is based on anecdotal reporting: "Exclusive Provider has had success with this model, moving patients to meet plan of care goals faster."

The Texas Office of Inspector General (OIG) references the American Speech-Language-Hearing Association (ASHA) publication, *Preferred Practice Patterns for the Profession of Speech-Language Pathology*, and Texas Administrative Code 353.2 (65) as criteria for establishing medical necessity and best practices. Texas Administrative Code (TAC) 353.2 (65) defines medical necessity as (iii) consistent with healthcare practice guidelines and standards that are endorsed by professionally recognized healthcare organizations and governmental agencies; and (vi) not experimental or investigative.[21]

Best practices include recommendations from governmental agencies including CMS, which requires the treating therapist to establish the plan of care. The POC prescribes the type, amount, frequency, and duration of therapy services to be furnished. Changes in the POC are the individual responsibility of the therapist providing the therapy services

The MaxROI plan currently requires any dissatisfaction with the POC to be appealed through exclusive provider, addressed through a second opinion.

Appealing to the exclusive provider makes an unbiased appeal unlikely. Furthermore, the member is subjected to multiple evaluations, one of which may have been tainted by validation issues, as the standardized tests used by speech-language pathologists can be invalidated by testing and retesting within narrow time frames and is inconsistent with Texas Medicaid, Medicare and third-party appeals processes.

Principles of Documentation in Healthcare Settings

Documentation plays a critical role in communicating to third-party payers the need for evaluation and treatment services (medical necessity) and why those services require the skill of the speech-language pathologist (SLP). Documentation requirements vary by practice setting and by payer. Medicare outpatient therapy documentation guidelines serve as the standard for many other insurance plans.[22]

Evaluation involves creating the POC and is in and of itself a critical part of the therapeutic process. For good reason, the CMS directs Medicare, like other public and private health plans, to require that, unless a physician or physician extender creates the POC, the therapist who established the POC must also provide the treatment thereunder. Physician extenders can be nurse practitioners or physician assistants.

Internal training materials used by CMS to determine when payment is appropriate for outpatient therapy state that a POC must meet the following requirements:

- Services must relate directly and specifically to a written treatment plan;
- Must be established by the therapist who will provide the services (PT, OT, SLP), physician/NPP; and
- Must be signed, dated and have the professional's identification (e.g., MD, PT, OT).[23]

Section C of the *Alberto N. v. Traylor* Partial Settlement Agreement referred to required components:

- The parties agree that no limitations exist for the provision of medically necessary physical therapy, occupational therapy, and services for individuals with speech, hearing, and language disorders, for which federal financial participation is available. The Agency shall approve medically necessary physical therapy, occupational therapy, and services for individuals with speech, hearing, and language disorders, except where federal financial participation is not available.
- The Agency shall provide medically necessary physical therapy, occupational therapy, and services for individuals with speech,

hearing, and language disorders if there is or will be progress made towards a goal, as supported by documentation from the prescribing physician and the treating therapist. Therapy goals include improving function, maintaining function, or slowing the deterioration of function.
- The Agency will revise the *Medicaid Provider Procedures Manual* to conform with the policies described in paragraphs 31 and 32 of this Agreement. The *Manual* revisions will also include a description of the documentation that must be submitted by the prescribing physician and treating therapist, when seeking authorization for therapy services. The Agency will provide Plaintiffs' counsel with a copy of these revisions for review and comment prior to publication in the *Medicaid Provider Procedures Manual*. Any corrections or clarifications will be made in subsequent *Texas Medicaid Bulletins*.[24]

Section C is very specific that medically necessary physical therapy, occupational therapy, and services for individuals with speech, hearing and language disorders are based upon supporting documentation from the prescribing physician and the treating therapist. It also clearly states that the agency, HHSC, was directed to revise the *TMPPM* to include a description of the documentation that must be submitted by the prescribing physician and the treating therapist when seeking authorization for therapy services.

In conclusion, Speech-Language Pathologists are autonomous professionals licensed by the state of Texas who are the primary care providers of speech-language pathology services. SLPs are enrolled and participate in Texas Medicaid based upon their license to practice in the state of Texas.

Separating evaluation from treatment is in direct conflict with the Texas OIG requirement for medically necessary speech therapy services which requires compliance with all final court decrees, the Texas Medicaid program, governmental agencies including CMS, and recognized professional organizations. In addition, services to members should not be experimental or investigational in nature.

MaxROI has excluded certain beneficiaries from the pilot program, creating separate clinical guidelines based on health status requiring that two separate and unequal clinical protocols be imposed on MaxROI beneficiaries.

The MaxROI plan results in disparate levels and quality of care and interferes with contractual agreements between other parties.

MaxROI's plan also makes the evaluations subject to review and modification by someone that did not conduct the evaluation/create the

POC. This has the potential to further diminish the quality of care provided. And to the extent it results in alteration of medical records (e.g., by the "reviewer" modifying the evaluation and treatment plan), it requires violation of Texas laws that prohibit such alterations.

The curious case of CPT 92507 continues to baffle all who inquire into it, and does little or nothing to support the adoption of an MCO service delivery model. The purpose and concept of MCOs is to reduce cost and increase quality of care.

So now we have completed our analysis of CPT 92507. We discussed Dr. Snow from the Victorian Age and how his insights into epidemiology could be used to analyze and help contain costs. In the next chapters we return to studying healthcare costs from a macro point of view, starting with the importance of accurate estimates and how they relate to regulations and the legal framework governing healthcare costs.

Chapter 10

Regulations and Estimates

In this chapter we return to a macro or "big-picture" outlook and discuss appropriations for healthcare costs, estimates related to healthcare costs, and some of the political nuances that affect healthcare finance at a state and national level.

An Insured Arrangement

In 1999 George W. Bush was the governor of Texas, with intentions of running for the U.S. presidency. One of his claims was that he was a good businessman and a fiscal conservative. He ran on a record of having been a good custodian of the Texas state budget.

Part of the Texas state budget process entailed using actuarial projections to estimate the cost of Medicaid for the biennial budget; this was critical, since Medicaid expenditures used from a fifth to a quarter of the Texas state budget. In 1999 the estimates of population and utilization of Medicaid were calculated in the usual way, but at some point, reductions to estimates were made so that over the next two years Medicaid had a shortfall of approximately $600 million. Some people thought pressure had been applied to make the Texas budget show a surplus. In any case, it turned out that the original actuarial projections were quite accurate.

At the time Texas administered the Medicaid program through an EDS subsidiary called National Heritage Insurance Corporation (NHIC), which has already been discussed in Chapter 4.

The eligible Medicaid population was put into risk categories and estimates of utilization were made to determine premiums to be paid by the state to NHIC. At the time, this was referred to as "an insured arrangement." A fund was set up where the premium payments were deposited, and from which NHIC would pay eligible claims from Medicaid providers. NHIC was compensated for their work via a different fund. At the end of each year, there would also occur a sharing of any "profits" from the insured arrangement, in the event that the state and NHIC had successfully economized on claims.

In the two years between the 1999 and 2001 legislative sessions, a kind of eerie foreboding lingered over the Texas Medicaid program. Administrators and stakeholders knew there would be a big shortfall, and then there would be finger pointing about whose fault it was.

During the same time period, the state was experimenting with managed care models. These were based on capitated rates, whereby providers would be paid based on the number of patients who received covered services. Gradually, subtle changes in the healthcare dialogue contributed to the push toward managed care. For example, the standard fee-for-service payments were referred to as "acute care" while the capitated rates were "managed care." (Of course, "managed" sounded better.) Managed care represented a departure from standard Medicaid, which required wide coverage of qualified populations, usually on a fee-for-service basis. State Medicaid programs invested substantial time in obtaining waivers from the federal Medicaid rules, usually with the goal of saving money.

When the 2001 legislative session and budget preparations got rolling in Texas, the Medicaid shortfalls were front and center during the discussions. The legislature in general was reticent about the known underfunding related to the actuarial projections. Instead, there was a great emphasis on so-called rampant fraud in the Medicaid program. To be sure, some fraud did occur, but it was not the reason for the shortfall.

But the opportunity was taken to "shake up Medicaid" and divide the administrative contracts among various corporate contractors. A trend toward corporatizing began and continues to this day.

By 2018, 94 percent of Texas Medicaid beneficiaries were enrolled in comprehensive Medicaid managed care plans, a higher proportion than in any other state.[1]

Spiraling Costs Under Managed Care

As noted in Chapter 2, Texas Medicaid costs have increased greatly in the past two decades. A substantial part of the increase can be attributed to increased administrative costs for managed care. According to Jack Charles Shoenholtz, MD, in his book *The Managed Health Care Industry: A Market Failure*, the change to healthcare managed by MCOs "portended a shift from the non-profit, 3% administrative costs center of government health care programs to a for profit one ranging from 15 to 40%, permitting cost to soar out of proportion to population growth and secular inflation trends."[2]

Chapter 10. Regulations and Estimates

Why Do Managed Care Organizations Cost More?

MCOs basically add layers of overhead onto healthcare costs. The corporate structures also make the costs harder to track. Recent federal and state audits of MCOs have disclosed common areas of overpayments in the MCO framework. It is important to note that in managed care, much faith is put in actuarial assumptions. When actual practices do not comport with actuarial assumptions of treatment and flows of transactions, the result can be uncontrolled higher costs that become built into the system.

A 2018 Texas State Auditor's Office (SAO) report revealed that the state's single Medicaid agency, the Health and Human Services Commission (HSSC), allowed MaxROI, the subject of the audit, to include "$29,574,454 of bonus and incentive payments paid to employees of affiliate companies" as part of their rates charged to the Medicaid program. MaxROI also "included affiliate profits in its financial statistical reports" that are used to establish rates charged to the Medicaid program.

The audit's scope only samples the costs that go into the rate setting, not the entire cost pools, an analysis of which would identify more questionable costs. The incentive payments are administrative bonuses on top of administrative costs. The underlying medical costs were not addressed by that particular finding.

MaxROI, the subject of the audit, responded that they were "disappointed that the auditor chose to omit the fundamental contextual issues related to this issue." MaxROI stated further that "the staffing agreement between (company) and (affiliate) provides a level of simplicity for the holding company system in which company is a wholly owned subsidiary."[3]

As to the questioned costs noted in the report, MaxROI said, "the ambiguity in the cost principal language should be resolved consistent with the usual contract construction principles, which would properly consider the course of performance of the parties to the agreement. This well understood contractual interpretation principle is expressed in numerous sources."[4]

If this sounds to the reader pretty much like MaxROI was saying the costs are whatever they say they are, it is also what it sounds like to me (MS) based on years of auditing contracts. Yet this example is not just the tip of the iceberg for this particular contract; it is more remarkable since MaxROI's contract is subject to much more scrutiny than other MCO contracts. Overcharges and questionable costs are likely more prevalent in contracts that undergo less scrutiny.

In addition to overpaying MCOs for administrative costs, federal audits have identified that the medical costs themselves are often overpaid. A July 2018 GAO report (GAO 18–528)[5] stated that Medicaid managed care suffered from

> 1. incorrect fee-for-service payments from MCOs, where the MCOs paid providers for improper claims, such as claims for services not provided; and
>
> 2. inaccurate state payments to MCOs resulting from using data that were not accurate or including costs that should be excluded in setting payment rates.

Such overcharges are, from the standpoint of the MCOs, a gift that keeps on giving. They are added to the rate calculations and estimates for future periods, to the extent they are not identified and corrected.

The result of the proliferation of MCO costs has been rapid increases in Medicaid managed care spending over the last two decades. "Total managed care spending, including the federal and state share, in federal fiscal year 2020 across all 50 States and 6 territories was $359.6 billion, up from $313.5 billion in federal fiscal year 2019." This represented a 14.7 percent increase in one year, when the inflation rate was 1.23 percent.

According to the *Harvard Business Review*, "Poor costing systems have disastrous consequences. It is a well-known management axiom that what is not measured cannot be managed or improved. Since providers misunderstand their costs, they are unable to link cost to process improvements or outcomes, preventing them from making systemic and sustainable cost reductions."[6]

The study of improper cost accounting for medical services adds, "Poor cost measurement has also led to huge cross-subsidies across services. Providers are generously reimbursed for some services and incur losses on others. These cross-subsidies introduce major distortions in the supply and efficiency of care. The inability to properly measure cost and compare cost with outcomes is at the root of the incentive problem in health care and has severely retarded the shift to more effective reimbursement approaches."

We will examine some of the controversies surrounding cost-shifting in Chapter 12. According to the *HBR* article, "Existing costing systems, which measure the costs of individual departments, services, or support activities, often encourage the shifting of costs from one type of service or provider to another, or to the payor or consumer."

Healthcare costs and projections are by necessity evaluated using estimates. One major estimate that must be made is the rate of inflation. Before the pandemic in 2020, inflation rates were one or two percent per year. In 2022, inflation rose to 8.4 percent.

In 2019 and 2020, according to CMS, "the FY 2020 Medicare fee for service (FFS) estimated improper payment rate is 6.27 percent, representing $25.74 billion in improper payments. This compares to the FY 2019 estimated improper payment rate of 7.25 percent, representing $28.91 billion in improper payments."[7]

In Medicare prior to the pandemic, improved oversight created progress in reductions of overpayments: "For FY 2020, the Part C improper payment estimate is 6.78 percent, representing $16.27 billion in improper payments. This represents a decrease from the FY 2019 rate of 7.87 percent, representing $16.73 billion in improper payments, and was driven primarily by Medicare Advantage organizations submitting a greater number of medical records that validated the diagnoses for which they were paid."[8]

For Medicaid and CHIP, the challenge of correcting overpayments is more difficult.

The FY 2020 national Medicaid improper payment rate estimate was 21.36 percent, representing $86.49 billion in improper payments. The FY 2020 national CHIP improper payment rate estimate was 27 percent, representing $4.78 billion in improper payments. There are several factors that led to these improper payment rates.

- One area driving the FY 2020 Medicaid and CHIP improper payment estimate is the continued reintegration of the Payment Error Rate Management (PERM) eligibility component, which was revamped to incorporate the Affordable Care Act requirements in the PERM eligibility reviews. CMS will complete the review of the remaining 17 states and the District of Columbia under the new eligibility requirements over the next year and establish a baseline in FY 2021 once all states are measured under the new requirements.

Based on the measurement of the first two cycles of states, the major drivers of the increased Medicaid and CHIP eligibility improper payments are a result of the following:

- Eligibility errors are mostly due to insufficient documentation to affirmatively verify eligibility determinations or noncompliance with eligibility redetermination requirements. The majority of the insufficient documentation errors represent both situations where:
  ~ The required verification of eligibility data, such as income, was not done at all; and
  ~ There is indication the eligibility verification was initiated but there was no documentation to validate that the verification process was completed, and non-compliance with eligibility redetermination requirements.

The CHIP improper payment rate was also driven by claims where the beneficiary was incorrectly determined to be eligible for CHIP, but upon review was determined eligible for Medicaid, mostly related to beneficiary income calculations, household composition, and third party liability coverage:

- Noncompliance with requirements for provider revalidation of enrollment and rescreening.
- Continued noncompliance with provider enrollment, screening, and National Provider Identifier requirements.[9]

As can be seen, proper payments are dependent on consistent testing and evaluations of claims and payments.

11

Regulation Failures

Third-Party Recovery and Site-Neutral Requirements

In previous chapters we discussed the importance of estimates in computing expected costs and budgeting for them. This pertains to both private insurance plans and government-funded plans. We discussed the so-called "pay and chase" philosophy that came to be accepted in Medicaid, that is, the payors would err on the side of paying a claim, then "chase" it to recoup it if it was later deemed erroneous. In this chapter we will discuss two significant examples of how non-enforcement of rules can cost the healthcare system and the taxpayer.

Medicaid is a voluntary healthcare plan jointly funded by the individual states and the federal government. All 50 states and the District of Columbia have chosen to participate. The federal government funds a portion of the cost (up to 60 percent). The Medicaid program allows great variety in eligibility requirements, covered benefits and payment policies, which vary by state. However, some benefits are mandatory—the state must provide these services to receive federal matching funds. The provision of Early Periodic Screening, Diagnosis, and Treatment (EPSDT) of all medically necessary healthcare services to children is mandatory and is required of all state participants.

Whether the service is optional or mandatory, states are statutorily required to ensure that provider payment rates are consistent with efficiency, economy, and quality of care. We assess whether or not the federal requirement is effective at the state administrative level by examining third party liability and site-neutral payments.

Site-Neutral Payments

In March 2021, a publication of the Healthcare Finance Management Association stated, "If site-neutral payments were implemented throughout healthcare, the decrease in expenditures could total as much as 672 billion dollars over a decade."[1]

Site-neutral payments pay the same rate for the same services, regardless of setting. Most references are to physician-provided evaluation and management services for healthcare conditions. The rates for freestanding physician offices are reimbursed on the Medicare Physician Fee Schedule, while rates for the same service provided in a hospital outpatient facility are paid at a different rate, generally much higher.

Our illustrations of disparity in payment rates for the same service are seen in the curious case of CPT 92507. In this case, rates for two of the approved providers were billed in 15-minute units, a maximum of four units per day. The third was paid a flat rate per encounter regardless of time.

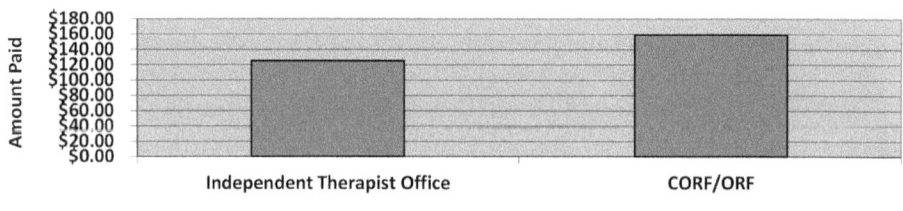

Chart 24. HHSC Fee for Service, CPT 92507 Billed with GN Modifier, Comparison Year 2014

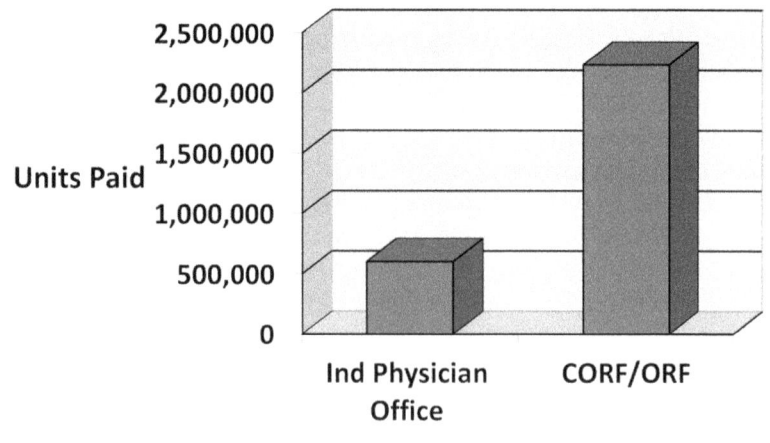

Chart 25. TX HHSC Units Paid by Provider Type, Same Licensed Professionals, Same Coverage Guidelines and Limitations, Comparison Year 2014

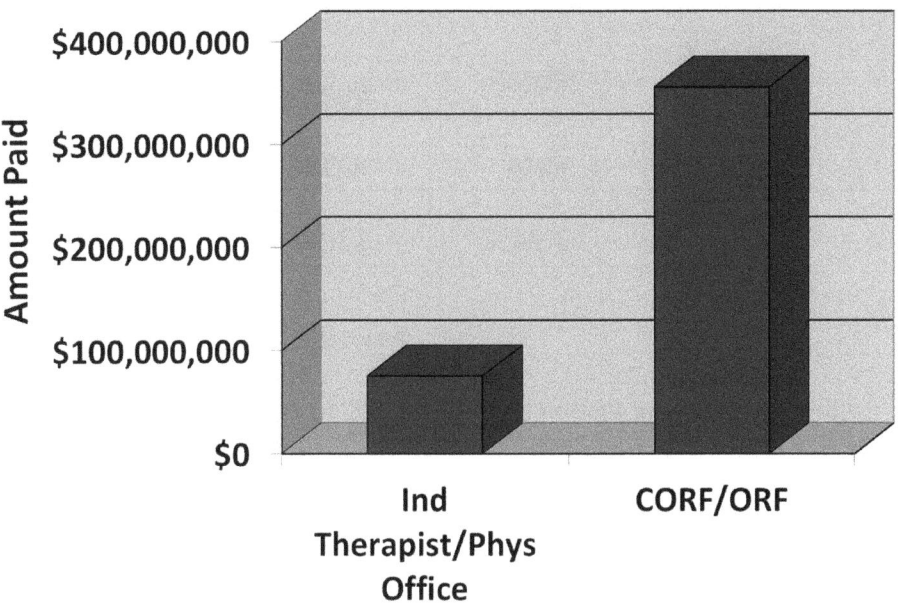

Chart 26. Texas HHSC Utilization Summary for 2014 (15-minute unit rate x number of encounters = amount paid by Texas Medicaid for each provider type for CPT 92507)

Money saved using site-neutral payments based upon the lowest rate for the same service by the same qualified professional under the same coverage guidelines (2014 HHSC Utilization Summary). Multiply rate by encounter units:

$355,616,811 (CORF/ORF)
$75,205,500 (Independent Therapist/Physician Office)
Savings would have been $280,411,311

HHA rates were not used in illustrating site neutrality savings because HHA were paid a daily encounter rate rather than in 15-minute units.

Our comparison is the Texas Medicaid program for various reasons, in general due to its essential transparency, and in particular due to its lack of expansion. Although most likely unintended, the consequences of disparate rates can be seen in the growth of therapy services provided in the home from 2013 to 2021. The growth was further aided by disparities in credentialing and enrollment requirements.

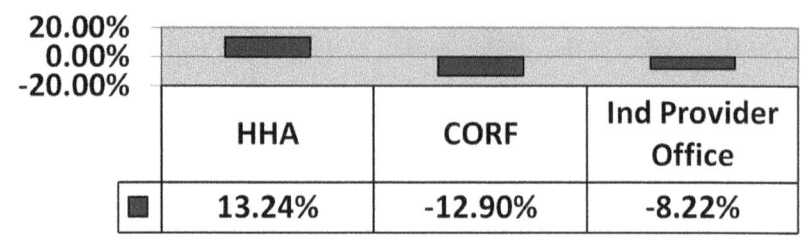

Chart 27. Change in Utilization of CPT 92507 by Provider Type 2014–2016 Based Upon HHSC Utilization Summaries

The Bipartisan Budget Act of 2015 altered the way that off-campus providers, meaning providers who were not on the same campus as the hospital, were reimbursed for outpatient services rendered to Medicare patients. The law required that these services be paid according to the Medicare Physician Fee Schedule. Although the law became effective in 2015, it exempted existing off-campus provider-based departments from the requirement. Under the exemption, existing off-campus provider-based departments could continue to be paid as before under the Outpatient Prospective Payment System. The 21st Century Cures Act gave some providers the ability to claim an exemption for the site-neutral payment requirement if the department was "mid-build" at the time of the enactment of the Bipartisan Budget Act of 2015. CMS was to audit providers to determine which were eligible for the mid-build exemption and could continue to be exempted from being reimbursed consistent with the Medicare Physician Fee Schedule.

The site-neutral payment cuts were in part developed to control the reported dramatic increases in the amount of hospital outpatient costs billed to the Medicare program.

There is some controversy about whether all outpatient services provided in physician offices are equivalent to those in hospital outpatient clinics. That discussion is beyond the scope of this book.

In its Outpatient Prospective Payment System Rule of 2019, CMS required a reduction of payment rate for evaluation and management services rendered by off-campus, provider-based departments. This rule was opposed by the American Hospital Association and dozens of hospitals, who suggested that CMS had exceeded its authority when it finalized the cuts.

11. Regulation Failures

A federal judge initially supported the American Hospital Association's argument and ruled that CMS had overstepped its authority to expand the site-neutral pay policy. The U.S. Court of Appeals of the District of Columbia reversed the decision in July 2020, finding that CMS's reduction of the rate for off-campus, provider-based department evaluation and management services fell within its authority to control increases in the volume of outpatient services. The American Hospital Association then asked the Supreme Court to review the U.S. Court of Appeals's decision. The Supreme Court declined to hear the arguments. In response to the Supreme Court decision, the payment reduction stayed in place, and CMS will reprocess all claims, paying the lower rate.

The issue of site neutrality may be controversial. However, in the curious case of 92507, one can see the dramatic effect on the trends in delivery of outpatient services when a disparity in outpatient fee schedules exists.

Site neutrality is a concept that Medicare embraced for therapy services for many years. Medicare reimburses outpatient therapy services, billed with a GN modifier to indicate that speech therapy services are provided under an outpatient plan of care, provided by a home health agency, CORF/ORF, physician's office, or individually enrolled therapist, in all recognized places of services, at the same rate. Rates for outpatient therapy reimbursed by Medicare established the neutral rate based upon the individual in private practice, as this type of provider has been recognized as having greater direct expenses, and therefore Medicare would reimburse HHAs, CORF/ORF, institutional or facility providers at the same rate as the individual outpatient provider for outpatient therapy services.

Despite the validity of the site-neutral concept relative to therapy services, Texas HHSC established a three-tier system based upon provider type and place of service.

As you recall, Medicaid is the payor of last resort, and requires that one seek third-party liability to protect funds and offset the cost of Medicaid services to states.

As we remember from the curious case of 92507, the Early Periodic Screening Diagnosis and Treatment program (EPSDT), which was introduced as part of the Social Security Act Amendment of 1967, is a mandatory part of all Medicaid programs. Its extension to include other healthcare services in 1989 was also mandated, meaning that state Medicaid programs do not have the option of *not* providing healthcare services to children. While services to the adults vary dramatically by state, services to children are mandatorily required and must be equivalent to the services available to the general public.

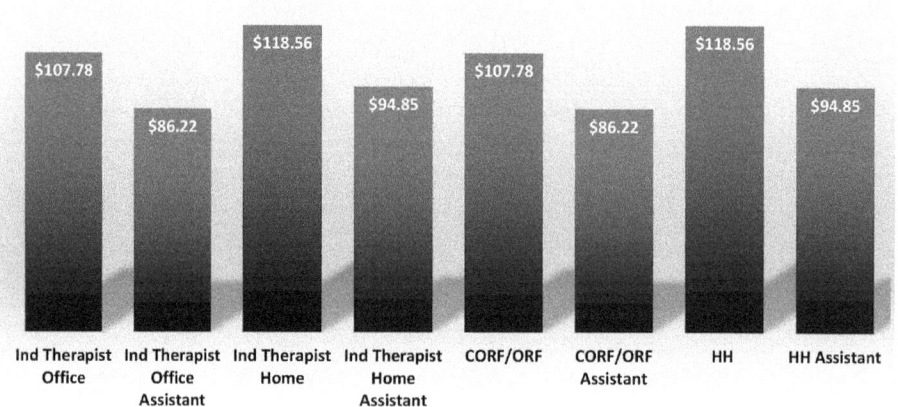

Chart 28. Texas HHSC Rates CPT 92507, 2019 FFS

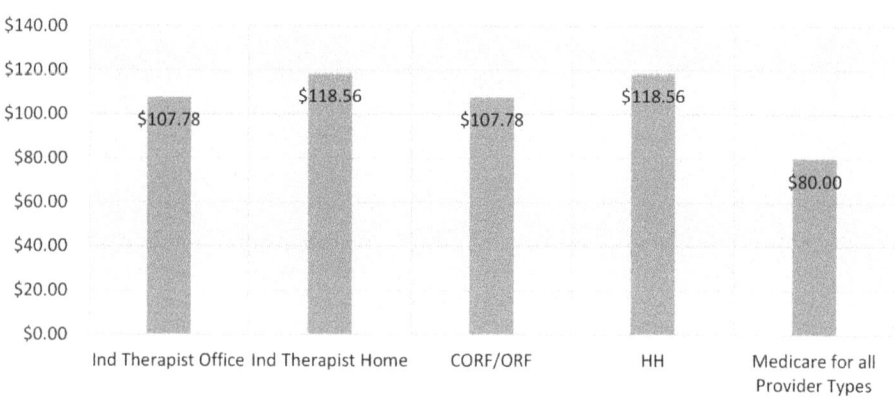

Chart 29. Medicare Rates for All Provider Types vs Texas Medicaid Office and Home POS Rates for CPT 92507, 2019

Hard limits (amounts of payments or number of visits), or caps on services, are not permissible in the EPSDT program. Soft limits may be employed, for the purpose of sustainability of the program (Utilization Code CMS 2014(a)). While there are no hard limits or caps allowed, and states are required to provide all medically necessary services, state programs can consider cost as part of the prior authorization process. Through the Home and Community-Based Service (HCBS) Waiver Program, children can receive services beyond those defined as medical assistance in the Social Security Act of 1905(a) to prevent institutionalization. Simply providing outpatient therapy services in the home for the convenience of the caregiver does not prevent institutionalization.

Reviewing the curious case of 92507, the concept of site neutrality was not considered, observed, or addressed. The state's ability to include cost effectiveness in its prior authorization process was not considered. Even if the fee schedules violated the site-neutrality concept and were not in compliance with the guidelines for rate-setting for fee for services, the state could have required that beneficiaries receive the services from the provider with the least maximum payment allowed. All therapy must be provided by a licensed therapist in the discipline for which the service is being provided, including occupational therapy, physical therapy, and speech therapy. Code 92507 is a speech therapy code. It must be delivered by a licensed speech-language pathologist who meets Medicaid provider eligibility requirements. Further, the services must be medically necessary, established by standard criteria of medical necessity based upon recommendations of governmental agencies and professional associations, and must be ordered by a physician and preauthorized by the Medicaid program or the Medicaid MCO. Texas HHSC set disparate rates but did not prescribe which beneficiaries could be served in the least expensive place of service or by the least expensive provider type.

Medicaid requires not only that it be the payor of last resort and that it cover all medically necessary services, but ensures that the individuals who are receiving healthcare services paid by Medicaid receive the same level and quality of services as those in the general population, which according to a study commissioned by Texas HHSC is an outpatient therapy private practice setting.

Third Party Liability

Medicaid is a state and federal cooperative program. As a public program, it is relatively transparent, therefore more easily assessed as to the integration between policy and payment.

Medicaid is generally considered by law to be the payor of last resort, which means that claims must be paid under other policies before Medicaid will pay for the care reflected in the claim. This responsibility, mandated by law, is referred to third party liability (TPL). The primary cost to the health service should be borne by a party other than Medicaid (42 CFR 447.10).

The U.S. Department of Health and Human Services (HHS), Office of the Inspector General (OIG), has reviewed the contribution of third party liabilities to the payment for Medicaid. Coordinating third party liability is important to the federal government for at least two reasons:

- It preserves Medicaid funds so that more services, or more beneficiaries, can be covered.
- It coordinates and shifts the cost from the federal government and the states to private insurance, if applicable, and from the states to the federal government if covered under more than one public plan.

The federal government pays approximately two-thirds of the cost of the Medicaid program, while states bear one-third of the cost. The Medicaid program has increased in scope and coverage. With additional increases in population and expansion of the Medicaid programs, Medicaid has become a high contributor to the cost of healthcare in the country.

By law, state Medicaid programs must pursue third-party payments. States are required to reject claims and instruct the provider to submit it to a potential primary payor if one has been identified (42 CFR 433.139). The provider must submit the claim to the primary carrier and then resubmit the claim to Medicaid along with the Explanation of Benefits from the primary coverage. Medicaid will pay the claim if the Medicaid allowable amount exceeds the amount of the primary payment. If the state Medicaid program is not aware of a particular beneficiary having coverage at the time a claim was paid, the state may pay the claim in full, then seek reimbursement from a primary insurance at a later date. This process is also often known as "pay and chase" (42 CFR 433.139). If a claim is rejected or applied to the deductible, or if there is any balance unpaid, Medicaid will reimburse for the claim only if the claim is "clean," the proper authorization has been obtained, and the Explanation of Benefits from the primary payor is submitted along with the claim to Medicaid.

With the advent of managed care, the states have several options for managing third party liabilities. States can exclude beneficiaries with third-party coverage from enrollment in Medicaid managed care plans. They may also enroll beneficiaries in the Medicaid managed care plan, and either retain the responsibility of pursuing third-party payments, or delegate the responsibility to the managed care program.

Due to the potential loss of income from not pursuing third party liabilities, federal legislation has attempted to increase the ability to coordinate benefits. The U.S. Department of Health and Human Services and the Office of the Inspector General has estimated the potential savings to state and federal Medicaid programs from third party liability to be $13.6 billion in 2011. So, the loss of the ability to obtain third-party assistance in the payment of coverage for healthcare service is significant.

11. Regulation Failures

There are public programs that have been statutorily designated as payors of last resort after Medicaid, including the Ryan White HIV/AIDS Program and the Title V Maternal and Child Health Block Grant Program. The Deficit Reduction Act of 2005 (DRA, P.L. 109–171) added a number of provisions to the legislative requirement of third party liability recovery and amended the Social Security Statute, Section 1902(a) (25), to require insurers, including self-insured plans, managed care plans, pharmacy benefit managers, or other parties that are by statute, contract, or agreement to be legally responsible for payment of claims for a healthcare item or service, to provide coverage information to a state upon request and must:

- accept the state's right of recovery;
- respond to claims and inquiries submitted by the state for up to three years after the date that service was provided; and
- agree not to deny a claim submitted by the state solely on the basis of the date of service (a reference to the fact that some insurers will not adjudicate a claim when the date of service falls outside the claims filing deadline).

The legislation has attempted to decrease some of the barriers to effective coordination of benefits, allowing states to conduct a variety of data matches to identify third-party resources, which includes the ability to conduct data matches with large insurers and data clearinghouses, and to determine if the third party is liable for healthcare services even if not identified by the beneficiary.

The state of Texas does require that all individuals who are beneficiaries in the Texas Medicaid program declare if there is a liable third-party insurer. There have been multiple legislative attempts to ensure protection of the Medicaid program from improper payment of claims that are the responsibility of a third party. These statutes include the prohibition against potential discrimination against individuals on the basis of their Medicaid eligibility.

As noted above, third party liability can be assessed to another public program. Generally, Medicare and other state and federal programs can be liable for third-party payments unless they are excluded, as noted above.

The U.S. Government Accountability Office, the GAO, published a report in response to congressional request entitled *Medicaid, Additional Federal Action Needed to Further Improve Third-Party Liability Efforts* (GAO-15-208). This report was published in January 2015.

The report emphasizes the number of individuals who also have third-party health insurance, including public healthcare programs such as Medicare, Veterans Administration, and TRICARE, as well as those that also have insurance through a commercial payor through an individual plan or an employer group plan, whether self-funded or fully insured.

The report also indicates that the states continue to leave a significant amount of funds "on the table" that could reduce costs to and protect the Medicaid program.

Barriers to obtaining third party liability to protect the Medicaid program include several issues related to coverage requirements of individual commercial carriers, which, like Medicaid, have their own procedural requirements for coverage. Commercial claims are often denied because:

- A referral from a participating or in-network primary care provider (PCP) was not obtained prior to the provision of the services.
- Services were not rendered by an in-network provider.
- Services were not provided in a participating place of service.
- Services were not prior authorized per insurance plans' requirements.

Our comparison to the Texas Medicaid program with commercial insurance illustrates how the Medicaid program has many of the same requirements as commercial carriers, including that a provider can be denied payment for services if:

- A referral from a participating or in-network primary care provider (in this case, the network is Texas Medicaid or a Texas Medicaid MCO) is not obtained prior to the provision of services.
- Services were not rendered by an in-network provider (payment to providers is contingent upon a provider's eligibility and enrollment in the Medicaid program and in each individual Medicaid MCO in which the beneficiary is a member).
- Services were not rendered in a participating place of service. Medicaid, like Medicare and commercial insurance, prohibits some services from being provided in a particular place of service, often requiring individuals to meet certain criteria to receive services in a particular place of service, i.e., hospital or through home health agencies.
- Prior authorization was not obtained from the Texas Medicaid program or the Texas MCO.

Provision for the delivery of occupational therapy (OT), physical therapy (PT), and speech-language pathology services (SLP) covered by the Texas Medicaid program are the same. Evaluations must precede the provision of therapy. State Medicaid programs and federal mandate must allow evaluations without prior authorization; however, an order from a Texas Medicaid-enrolled physician or specialist must be kept in the medical chart. Therapy, as recommended by the evaluation, must be preauthorized.

A significant number of low-income seniors and people with disabilities are dually covered by Medicare and Medicaid. For those who have this dual coverage, Medicare is the primary payor of medical healthcare needs, including physician visits, hospital stays, post-acute skilled care, and prescription drugs. The state Medicaid program covers certain benefits not covered by Medicare, including long-term services and support, and some cost of Medicare coverage including cost sharing, which includes deductibles and coinsurance.

Claims for Medicare coinsurance and deductibles are usually referred to as crossover claims. This is because the claim must first be submitted to Medicare, and then after processing, it is submitted to Medicaid. In fact, once filed with Medicare, the Medicare intermediary automatically submits the Medicare Explanation of Benefits to the state Medicaid program for payment of any additional amount due. State Medicaid programs are prohibited from reimbursing providers more than the maximum Medicare allowable amount. Any amount not covered by Medicare and Medicaid must be adjusted or "written off" by the provider. No balance billing to the beneficiary is ever permitted if the beneficiary is dually covered by Medicare and Medicaid, even for partial payment of claims.

The payment for these services for those beneficiaries with Medicare and Medicaid dual coverage is always limited to the maximum the Medicare program would have paid for those services.

If the beneficiary is dual-covered with a commercial carrier and Medicaid, Medicaid is the payor of last resort. The provider must file the commercial claim first. Many of the commercial plans are HMOs as well as PPOs. Each has different deductibles, coinsurance amounts, out-of-pocket maximum amounts and authorization requirements. HMOs require a referral from the PCP for both evaluation and treatment. Some PPOs will allow for evaluation and therapy with no prior approval for either, while others allow for evaluation with no preapproval, but require prior authorization or a predetermination prior to initiation of any therapy services. For most commercial insurance carriers that have such requirements, the plan will not pay if the referral or prior authorization is not obtained. These commercial carriers do not begin reimbursing providers for payment until the deductible is met for either the individual beneficiary or the family. The deductibles can range dramatically from as little as $200 to $6,000 or more per calendar year. Once the deductible is met, the individual might also be responsible for a coinsurance. For example, the allowable amount for a therapy session is $100. The beneficiary would pay the $100 to the provider until the deductible is met. Once the deductible is met, the beneficiary might have a 50 percent coinsurance, so the insurance company would then pay $50, and the individual receiving the service would be responsible for the other $50. If the beneficiary has dual coverage with commercial insurance and Medicaid, the deductible and coinsurance are paid by the Medicaid program.

In addition to the wide variety of deductibles and coinsurances, there may be different out-of-pocket maximums, meaning the insurance company will pay 100 percent of claims after the insured individual has reached a certain dollar amount.

Many of these plans have a different deductible amount for in-network and out-of-network benefits. For example, one might have a $500 deductible before the insurance company would directly pay an in-network provider. The same plan may have a $5,000 deductible before payment would be made to an out-of-network provider. The deductible is borne by the beneficiary. If dually covered, the cost is borne by the Medicaid program. The amount borne by Medicaid will differ dramatically if the provider is both in-network for the commercial carrier and also enrolled in Medicaid and/or the Medicaid MCO.

Provider Status	Deductible	Cost of 20 Sessions to the Medicaid Program	Total Paid by Texas Medicaid Program
In-network with commercial carrier and dual Medicaid enrollment	$500, then 50% coinsurance for remaining sessions	$500 deductible, then 50% coinsurance remaining 15 sessions	$500 + 15 visits × $50 coinsurance = $1,250.00
Out-of-network with commercial carrier and dual Medicaid enrollment	$5,000	Full charge for all sessions	20 × $100/session = $2,000.00

Table 7. *Third Party Liability Example*. Created by author (Famiglietti). Scenario: Beneficiary has $500 in-network deductible and 50 percent coinsurance; out-of-network deductible is $5,000 and 70 percent co-insurance; therapy allowable of $100 (deductible would be met after five sessions). The Texas Medicaid program saves nearly 40 percent in this scenario when the beneficiary uses an in-network, commercial provider who is also a Medicaid-enrolled provider.

Like Texas Medicaid, some commercial carriers not only require referral from the PCP, but also require preauthorization for therapy services. Some commercial carriers limit the number of coverable visits allowed. Medicaid cannot set hard limits for medically necessary children's therapy services.

Therefore, for maximum assurance of efficiency and economy of the Medicaid program, providers who serve dual-covered individuals need to be enrolled in both Medicaid and commercial insurance or Medicare and satisfy the referral requirements and preauthorization requirements before the insurer and Medicaid will reimburse for the healthcare services provided.

If the Medicaid provider receives Medicaid preauthorization but does not also obtain preauthorization through the commercial carrier (if required), the claim would be denied by the commercial carrier and Medicaid would be responsible for 100 percent of the Medicaid allowable for the claim. In the case of CPT 92507, Medicaid fee-for-service and at least one Texas Medicaid MCO reimburse therapy providers more than Medicare/commercial carriers.

The GAO's report, GAO-15-208, selected several states for review to determine inefficiency in addressing the coordination of benefits. Two states' Medicaid programs, Michigan and Minnesota, inform providers that Medicaid will not pay for denied claims "if rules of the third-party coverage were not followed," and further indicated that the state Medicaid program will not cover charges incurred when beneficiaries elect to receive services from a provider not enrolled in the third-party insurer's preferred provider network if dual-covered by Medicaid and a third-party carrier.

As we continue to discuss Texas Medicaid and therapy services for illustration, we remind the reader that the Texas Medicaid program identifies three primary types of providers: home health agencies, which includes non–Medicare-certified agencies and at-home, therapy-only agencies; comprehensive outpatient rehabilitation facilities (CORF), and/or outpatient rehabilitation facilities (ORF), and independently practicing therapy providers; and physicians enrolled under their individual professional credentials.

Commercial insurance does not recognize all of these therapy provider types to be coverable as eligible outpatient therapy providers. Commercial carriers generally do not enroll CORF/ORF, rather requiring that each individual licensed therapist be individually credentialed within the plan, rather than as an entity. Preauthorizations can be issued either to the group as a whole or in the individual provider's name. Texas Medicaid always preauthorizes services for independent therapists in an individual's name. Commercial insurances do not consider payment for home health services for individuals who do not meet the Medicare eligibility criteria for home health services and who are not seen under a Home Health Plan of Care.[2]

Claims submitted by two of the provider types for outpatient therapy would be procedurally denied after adjudication by commercial insurances and some public plans. Medicare does not recognize home health services provided by any other provider than Medicare-certified home health agencies. If an individual meets the criteria for CORF/ORF and the services are provided in accordance with the CORF/ORF Conditions of Participation, Medicare will pay the claims. Medicare pays for all outpatient therapy services provided by therapists in private practice based upon their professional credentials.

However, when commercial insurance is primary, the provider is required to file the claim first with the primary insured. Once denied or paid, the provider, not the intermediary, must submit the claim for reimbursement of deductibles and coinsurances. Unlike Medicare dual-qualified claims, if the commercial insurance pays less than the Medicaid program, then the provider will be paid the balance between the commercial insurance rate and the Medicaid reimbursement rate. In the case of CPT 92507, the Texas Medicaid program reimburses outpatient therapy services at a higher rate than Medicare and commercial insurance rates.

If Texas Medicaid and Texas MCO use providers who are not concurrently enrolled in Medicare and/or in-network therapy providers for commercial insurance carriers and Texas Medicaid, both commercial and Medicare/Medicaid will deny payment.

Although some might think it is restrictive that some states, including Michigan and Minnesota, require that dually covered Medicaid recipients go to an in-network commercial provider who is also enrolled in Medicaid, it is onerous to think it decreases access to care. It should be noted that the individual whose commercial insurance is primary would have been required to seek services from one of those providers or would be required to pay the differential between the network provider rate and

Commercial insurance/Medicare　　　　　　　　　　　　　　Texas Medicaid

Graphic 1. Comparison of Real-World Consequences of Inflated Payments by Texas Managed-Care Organizations

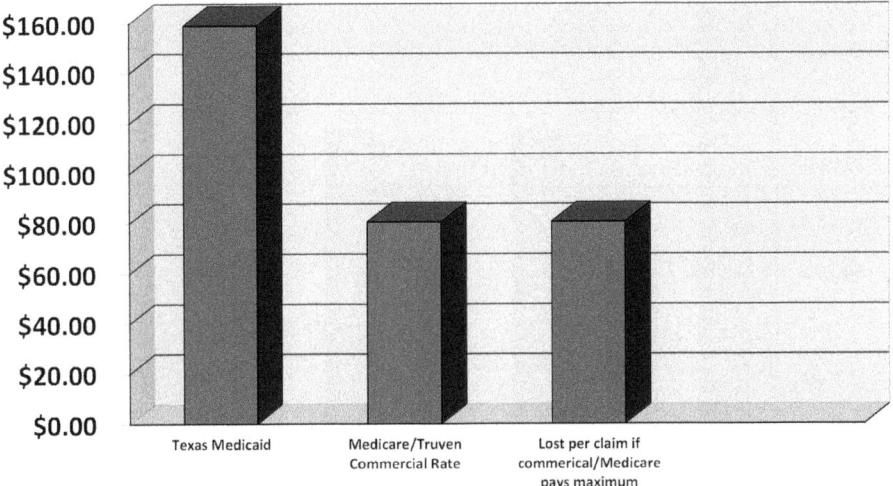

Chart 30. Loss of Third-Party Payment, CPT 92507, CORF/ORF

the non-network provider rate if the individual did not have additional Medicaid coverage.

When reviewing this possible access to care, remember, for outpatient therapies, beneficiaries covered by Medicare must go to a Medicare-enrolled provider in order for Medicare to pay for therapy. In fact, if one goes to a non–Medicare-enrolled provider, that therapy provider is required, by statute, to refer the patient to a Medicare-enrolled provider. Non-Medicare-enrolled therapy providers are statutorily prohibited from billing for therapy services that are covered by Medicare, as these services are a benefit of the Medicare program. This same prohibition does not apply to physicians. Physicians may opt out of the Medicare program.

In 2017, Texas HHSC created a rate differential for speech therapy services provided by a Speech-Language Pathology Assistant (SLP-Assistant). Medicare and most commercial carriers do not reimburse for services provided by SLP-Assistants and have no code modifiers to indicate services were provided by an assistant, thereby eliminating third-party reimbursement for all such claims.

We have reviewed the issue of the disparity of payment by provider types established by the Texas HHSC until September 2017, when it reorganized payments to be site neutral, consistent with Medicare. However, in September 2019, HHSC reinitiated disparate rates based upon place of service, inconsistent with the site neutrality established by Medicare for these outpatient therapy services. Additionally, the use of some provider

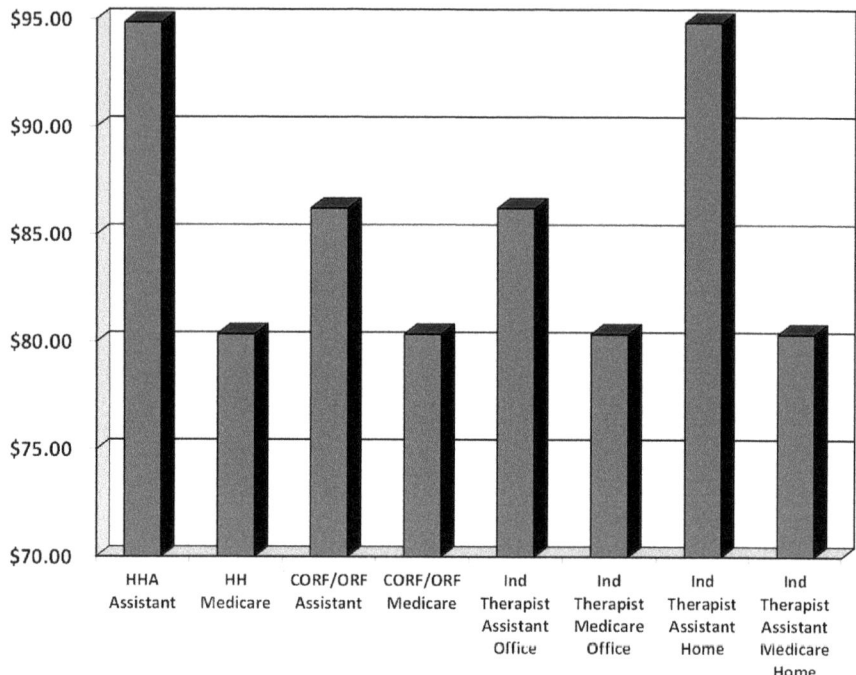

Chart 31. HHSC Adopted Rates Effective 09/01/2019 Comparing Licensed Assistant Rates to Medicare Rate for Fully Licensed SLP

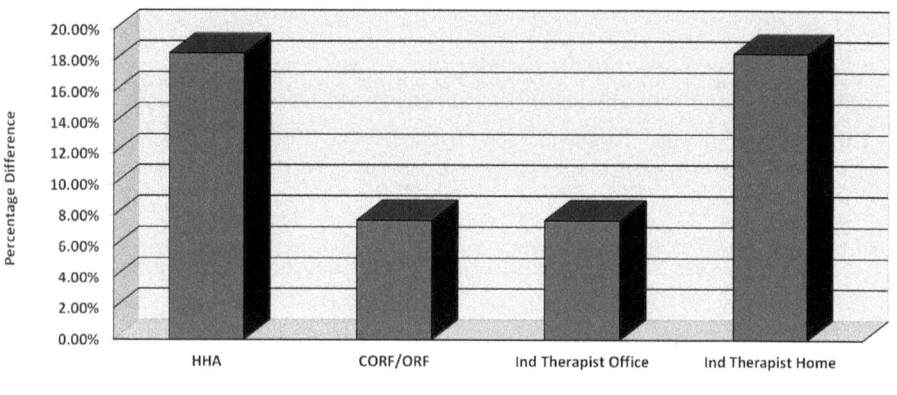

Chart 32. Percentage Difference Between Texas Medicaid Rate for SLP Assistants and Medicare Rate for Fully Licensed SLP, 09/01/2019

types and assistants precluded third-party payments that would offset the federal and state cost of the Texas Medicaid program.

In this chapter we have pointed out that there are established frameworks to prevent overcharging for healthcare services. Because of the complexity of the services and the many estimates and parties involved, enforcement of cost standards and payment recovery standards is required to rein in healthcare costs. The non-enforcement of two standards, site neutrality and third-party recovery, can add up to millions of dollars in healthcare costs to the taxpayer.

Chapter 12

Cost-Shifting and the Flip and Roll

In this chapter we will review the issue of allocation of healthcare costs, and how there are constant disputes about how to allocate them among population groups, diseases, and even time periods. Proper identification and allocation of healthcare costs is a major problem with controlling costs at the macro level. Some of the arguments in this arena have attained the status of conventional wisdom. Yet upon closer scrutiny, many of these arguments may also be part of political agendas.

A long-espoused complaint is that costs attributable to Medicare and other public-sector payors get shifted to the private sector, driving up the cost of private insurance. Xtelligent Healthcare Media states that "One factor that contributes to the high cost of health care for individuals and employers is a process called cost shifting. Cost shifting occurs when hospitals and other providers try to make up for lost revenue on public sector patients (Medicare and Medicaid) by charging private sector payors more than the expenses they incur. In order to control program costs, both the Federal and State governments pay hospitals and other providers less than the cost of care. According to one study, Medicare pays hospitals about 95% of the cost of the care delivered. The reimbursement for Medicaid is even lower.

"To make up for this shortfall, hospitals and other providers charge private sector payers more. A study by the actuarial firm Milliman estimates the cost shift adds $1,800 annually to the cost of health care per American family."[1]

This is the conventional wisdom espoused by the health insurance industry. Their views are echoed by some in the political realm. Tennessee state senator Dr. Mark Green's view, stated in October 2018, is that "The effect of cost shifting has devastated the health insurance industry. As the government pays less, physicians and hospitals raise the price for others, which leads to increased cost of care for those with health insurance. This

Chapter 12. Cost-Shifting and the Flip and Roll 151

increase is then in turn passed to their customers in increased cost. As the cost escalates, fewer people can purchase health insurance, leading to a need for insurance companies to increase prices further. Of course, with increased price, fewer people can afford the insurance. What followed was a vicious cycle which puts us where we are today."[2]

Some other voices in the healthcare field say that the problem of cost-shifting is overstated for political reasons. Under this view, cost-shifting as a problem is overstated by private insurance advocates, who see government insurance options as economically detrimental to private insurers.[3]

According to an editorial by Wendell Potter for the Center for Public Integrity, "Health insurance executives and lobbyists have for years told us that one of the main reasons they charge us so much for coverage is the cost-shifting that results from Uncle Sam's stinginess. The story goes like this: hospitals are paid so inadequately by government programs like Medicare and Medicaid that they have to charge private insurers more to keep their doors open."[4]

The editorial challenges the premise of cost-shifting. "Health care executives have talked about cost-shifting for so long it has become conventional wisdom. We've all come to believe it without challenging it. But what if it hasn't really been happening, at least not in recent years?"[5]

"Health economist Austin Frakt presented compelling evidence in a *New York Times* op-ed ... that, just because the government often pays a lower rate than many hospital executives would like, that doesn't mean they can simply force private insurance companies to pay more. In fact, as he pointed out, reduced government reimbursement rates often result in *lower*—not higher—private insurance reimbursement rates." This would go along with the basic economic theory of a greater supply having downward pressure on prices.

Frakt cited a study published in the May 2013 edition of *Health Affairs* that found "that a 10 percent reduction in Medicare payments was associated with an almost 8 percent *reduction* in private prices. In other words, not only did hospitals not charge private insurance companies more between 1995 and 2009 because of lower payments from the government, they actually charged them less." In the same article Frakt stated, "It seems that about the only time hospitals can get away with shifting more costs to private insurers is when there are not many other hospitals in the same geographical area competing with them."

The CFPI editorial indicates that some standard cost-shifting dialogue from corporate executives and their supporters are designed to maintain high insurance premiums. "Masters of spin that they are, insurance executives and lobbyists have led us all to believe that cost shifting is the inevitable result of government bureaucrats being too tightfisted. They can get away with it because so many Americans are willing to accept as truth just about any talking point that reinforces their deep-seated belief that the government is to blame for everything that ails us.

"So it's little wonder that we're willing to buy the insurance industry's suggestion that our premiums would be lower if it weren't for cost shifting.

"As long as we keep buying it, insurance company bureaucrats will keep jacking up our rates by more than they could otherwise get away with. And they'll keep grinning all the way to the bank as they do it."[6]

According to the *Journal of the American Medical Association* (*JAMA*), as well, cost-shifting is more of a political argument than one supported by accounting facts. "The cost-shifting theory persisted for a long time without being examined very rigorously. Data on private insurer payments to hospitals were not available at the transaction level, making such hypothesis testing difficult. The theory also held on because it was convenient. For hospitals, the cost shifting story could be used to argue against any reductions in public payment rates. For progressives, the idea that private patients were already paying for care for the uninsured through higher premiums offered an opportunity to argue that coverage expansions might not raise overall costs for taxpayers much at all. For conservatives, cost shifting implied that the needs of poor individuals were already being met and further reform was not needed. Economists differed because it is difficult to come up with a rational economic model of cost shifting, but their objections were drowned in a flood of anecdotes."[7]

According to *JAMA*, there is an important difference between fixed costs and variable costs that the cost-shifting dialogue was missing. "A series of studies by the Medicare Payment Advisory Commission and by academic economists found that hospitals did not cost shift. On the contrary, when public insurers reduced their payments, private insurance payment levels tended to decline as well. The pattern seen in the American Hospital Association's annual reports could be explained by the effect of private payments on the fixed cost of care. Most of the cost of running a hospital is fixed; equipment, buildings, and much of the staffing of the hospital must be paid for regardless of how many patients the hospital treats. Only a fraction of the cost of hospital care is variable, specific to a particular patient stay. Hospitals determine how much to spend on the costs of production based on the average payment levels they face. As private insurance payments increase, hospitals respond by spending more, often to attract ever-more valuable privately insured patients. If private insurer rates are higher than public insurer rates, private rates will exceed average total costs—the sum of fixed and variable costs—and public rates will fall below average total costs. But that is not cost shifting, it is just the law of averages."

The *JAMA* article posits that if cost-shifting were actually occurring at the level claimed by the insurance industry, there would have been more of a leveling out of the severity of COVID outcomes, as between wealthier patients with private insurance and those whose healthcare was paid by the public sector. The article concludes, "COVID-19 has washed away the last of the comforting cost shifting myth. It is simply not happening."[8]

The cost-shifting debate highlights an issue in healthcare finance that is very slippery indeed—the accounting. The *JAMA* article notes the high degree of fixed costs that go into healthcare. The accounting and auditing professions make frequent references to "Generally Accepted Accounting Principles," or GAAP. It is generally understood that the healthcare profession follows GAAP. However, this is usually discussed in the context of financial statement presentation. Accounting for costs is a less well-defined area. This will be discussed in a later chapter on hospital cost accounting, where the cost practices that become accepted practices seem to defy reason.

Macro-Accounting and Cost Identification

The costing/pricing for patient care is complicated by the need to allocate fixed costs among patients. The healthcare industry employs highly paid doctors, administrative staff, and clerical staff whose time and efforts must be compensated. As we will discuss more fully in the chapter on hospital costs, there is not necessarily a strong desire or political will to identify and account for costs.

Even with federal and state healthcare programs, where there are long established accounting principles, identification and allocation of costs can prove a challenge. And with both government and private healthcare, there is almost always an agenda among administrators to increase administrative costs.

With government programs, and especially with block grant programs having federal funds that require state matching funds, there are various accounting tricks in common use. One relates to how states draw down federal money in one year and then recycle it in the next year or biennium. If a program is 60 percent federal funds and 40 percent state funds, the state accountants can draw down all the federal funds the first year, then repay the feds from state funds just before the state funds lapse, i.e., "flip" the transaction, then "roll" the now unencumbered federal funds forward into the next federal year as something of a slush fund.

The "flip and roll" is especially common in block grants used for healthcare purposes. For basic Medicaid, the drawdowns are more easily traceable as to matching federal and state drawdowns. Block grants allow for more flexibility.

One problem created by the flip and roll is that the drawn-down money loses its identity as a federal healthcare expenditure. If $5 million is drawn down from a federal source in year one, then paid back (on the state ledgers to free up the account, but not refunded to the federal source) in year two by a state source, and then that same $5 million is used to cover administrative costs in year three, the validity of the accounting becomes very suspect indeed.

State and federal programs tend to be audited in a siloed environment. So, an individual transaction may be perfectly legitimate and well documented. Federal auditors should be aware of the tendency to utilize reversal entries, in order to re-utilize funds.

As federal funding grew rapidly in many areas of American life during the Roosevelt New Deal and later with LBJ's Great Society initiatives, accounting for the funds became challenging in several ways. The funds are sometimes distributed directly from federal agencies, sometimes from state agencies, and sometimes from counties, cities, or non-profit institutions. The federal government implemented an auditing and reporting system to deal with the new challenge. As we will see in a later chapter, the solutions for federal funds may provide future guidance for audits of healthcare costs.

With the flip and roll, funds lose identity and they are recycled. Another common problem with the proliferation of federal programs was the tendency to "double dip," i.e., charge more than one program for the same expenses. And during the 1970s, anecdotes became common wherein cities or other entities were using the same basket of receipts and charging the expenses to two or more programs. For example, a batch of salary, travel, and utility expenses would be charged to a health program, a transportation program, and maybe an education problem. Then when auditors from the transportation department came, they were shown a stack of receipts for expenses that were legitimate. Later the health and education auditors were shown the same stack of receipts, thus the charges for all three programs were documented. The problem obviously was that the federal government got charged three times for the same expenses. Toward the end of the 1970s, there was concern in government circles about getting government programs under control. Multiple audits by multiple jurisdictions were proving ineffective in preventing governmental entities and non-profits from keeping two sets of books.

What to do? In 1984 Congress passed the Single Audit Act. Many of the problems and solutions related to single audits and federal funds are analogous to issues of healthcare costs today. We will discuss these in a later chapter, in the context of proposing something akin to a "Single Audit Act" for healthcare costs. The Single Audit Act required that an entity receiving more than a certain amount of federal financial assistance must undergo a unified comprehensive audit, one that examines all of their funds within a single and consistent fiscal year.

The original threshold for a single audit was $25,000; today it is $750,000. The Single Audit Act was meant to prevent "double-dipping," keeping two sets of books, among other financial assurance objectives. Part of the original Single Audit Act reporting package was an "in relation to" opinion on the schedule of federal financial assistance, as compared with and in relation to the basic financial statements. This meant that the calculations of the amounts expended and reported to the individual finding agencies or computer were consistent with the way they were accounted for in the general-purpose financial statements.

This helped to promote consistent reporting of costs and prevent double-dipping. The reporting packages for Single Audits contained a standardized list of reports that had to be prepared and presented in a similar way for all entities receiving federal financial assistance.

Consistent reporting of costs was paramount to the administration of federal programs, and the Single Audit Act, along with various cost circulars, allowed for consistent calculation and recording of costs. Reported costs were compared against standards established for reasonableness. In a subsequent chapter on hospital costs, we will see how abandoning cost principles and reasonableness standards can lead to outrageous overcharges in healthcare.

Medicaid and Medicare payments were not included as subject to the Single Audit Act, as they are not grants but entitlement payments, and are not included in the Single Audit Act's definition of federal financial assistance. This had repercussions that we will discuss in a later chapter.

In this chapter we have pointed out how certain basic accounting practices, such as following cost principles, proper periodicity for funds, and reconciliations from period to period (known colloquially as "closing the books") are not routinely followed in healthcare accounting. The haze that this weak accounting adds to the general environment wherein healthcare costs are chronically out of control. We will discuss in the following chapter on hospital costs how standardizations that have been necessary in other industries could be applied in the field of healthcare.

CHAPTER 13

Scams with Teeth, Regulations without Teeth

In this chapter we address the cost of dental healthcare, the rise of dental support organizations (DSOs), and how fraud, waste, and abuse contribute to rising costs. We also address how government and corporate interaction create moral hazard, as attempts to profit while avoiding responsibility escalate. Some of the examples are several years old; however, the "gist" of how the healthcare system bears the cost for fraud, waste, and abuse can be seen in the examples, and the basic nature of the proclivity to commit fraud remains the same—where opportunity, motive, and rationalization of the financial behavior join up, there will always be a susceptibility to fraud.

Cost of Dental Healthcare

From the previous year, spending for dental services increased 4.2 percent in 2019 to $143.2 billion.[1] This represented 4 percent of total healthcare spending. Fraud, waste, and abuse have plagued the dentistry industry, with estimates of fraud between 5 percent and 10 percent.[2] Waste and abuse in the industry are driven by aggressive profit-maximizing behavior by DSOs.[3]

One of the most talked about and published Medicaid dental cases is that of a dentist in Dallas who had built a water park in his backyard. According to priceypads.com, the property connects two properties and includes bowling alleys, resort-style water park, and 18 bathrooms.

The actual allegations against the dentist were not necessarily that shocking. In some cases where he was supposed to be supervising procedures, it was proven that he was not on premises.

The case prosecution of the dental practice, All Smiles Dental Centers (ASDC), began in 2004, when federal and state investigators began

Chapter 13. Scams with Teeth, Regulations without Teeth 157

a probe into dental services that were allegedly not rendered but billed by ASDC to Medicaid. As one reporter noted, "the case was reassigned 3 times between the Texas Attorney General and the FBI ... and ended with a whimper seven years later in the Dallas County District Attorney's Office."[4]

The enigmatic aspect of the case against the dentist was that, while it might have seemed obvious that a provider was abusing a system meant to help poor people, it was difficult to say exactly where or if they crossed the line and committed an illegal act. In 2020, a court ruled that the dentist owed the state $16.5 million for improper billing, but the dentist in fact kept his license and the case may not be finally settled.

In 2010, Texas settled a lawsuit, originally filed in 1993 (*Frew v. Hawkins*), that alleged that Texas Medicaid Children's Program had failed to ensure access to preventive care and specialty healthcare, including dentistry. As part of the settlement, Texas was required to increase dental provider reimbursement by 50 percent.[5]

Texas Medicaid raised the rates paid for dental services as well as orthodontic services. Medicaid recipients under age 21 have no copayments or deductibles for dental services, which are often associated with private commercial plans.

Payment Structure 1	*Payment Structure 2*
DSO collects all revenue	Dentist collects all revenue
DSO pays dentists a base salary or a percent of payments received for dental services, whichever is higher. The DSO may also offer a productivity or profitability bonus.	Dentist pays DSO an agreed-upon amount, such as a percent of revenue or a fixed fee, for business support services provided by the DSO.

Table 8. **Examples of Dental Support Organizations and Dentist Payment Structures.** Source: Prepared by the IG Audit Division utilizing information from DSOs and the U.S. Senate Finance and Judiciary Committee.

The increased rate and patient base with publicly funded dental coverage created a tempting target for private equity funds through DSOs or corporate dentistry.

DSOs provide non-clinical services to dental practices including administrative, marketing, recruiting, bookkeeping, and financial services.

DSOs and physician practice management companies are largely owned by private equity companies. Most states' dental and medical practices must be owned by a licensed dentist or physician, not a non-dentist or non-physician entity. To circumvent laws prohibiting

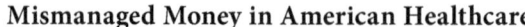

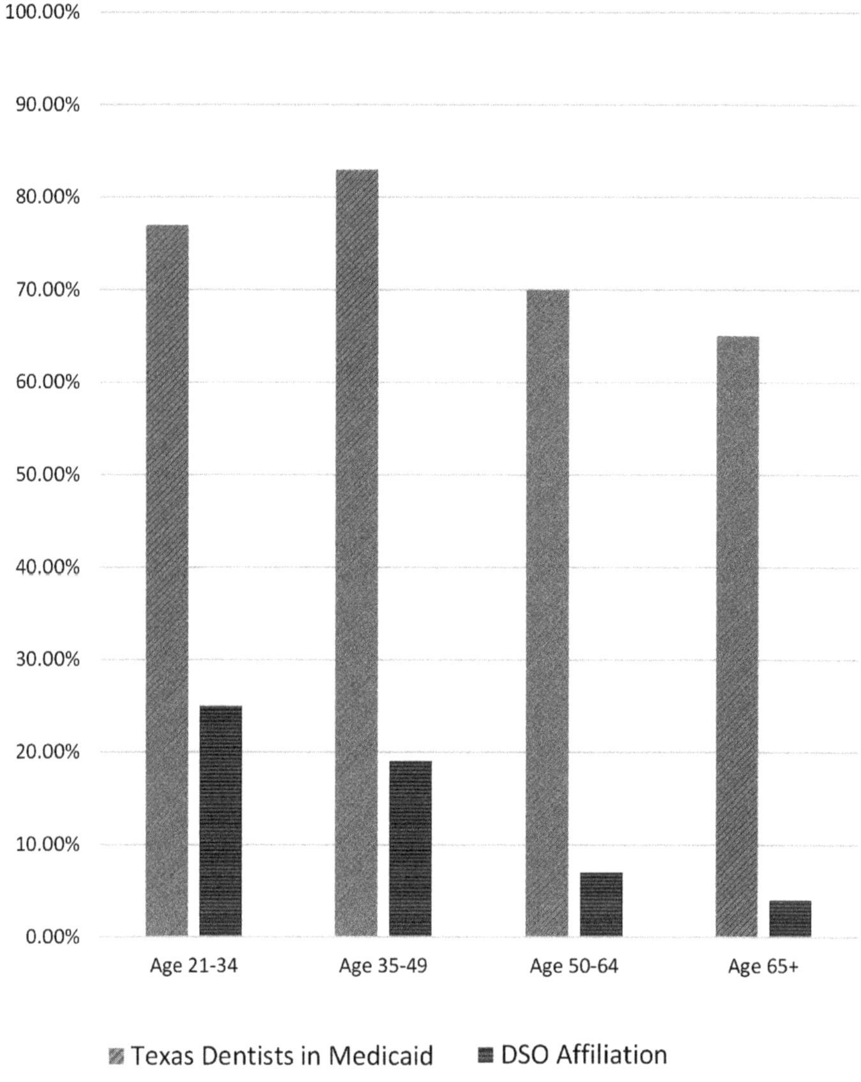

■ Texas Dentists in Medicaid   ■ DSO Affiliation

Chart 33. Texas Dentist Participation in Medicaid and DSO Affiliation, Fall 2015

ownership by non-professionals, the DSOs are created by investors to provide related services. The DSO hires the dentists. The payment structure between the dentist and the DSO often incentivizes overtreatment of patients, misleading advertising, and other practices in order to reach the target revenue of the DSO.

The rapid increase in Texas Medicaid care cost and the widely-published orthodontics scandal emboldened the Texas legislature to impose registration requirements on DSOs. The Texas State Board of Examiners was not granted authority over the DSOs, as the board can only regulate licensed dental professionals. The board did grant authority to maintain DSOs (Texas Senate Bill No 519, signed into law June 14, 2015).

According to the American Dental Association, 43 percent of dentists participated in Medicaid in 2019; of that number, 63 percent were enrolled in Medicaid and were affiliated with a DSO.[6]

All participating states must provide children's dental services—some states also provide adult dental care.

The All Smiles Dental Centers case did bring to light the dramatic increase in the number of DSOs and Medicaid MCOs.

Horror Stories, Corrective Actions and Opportunists

Part of the rise in dental healthcare fraud resulted from well-intentioned policies in response to medical disasters, where opportunists later took advantage of public generosity.

Tooth decay in children is an often overlooked problem. It is the most common chronic childhood disease—five times more common than asthma.[7] Poor dental health can lead to severe and sometimes tragic health outcomes.

One failure of the system that occurred in 2007 in Maryland captured nationwide attention. Alyce Driver had two sons, DeShawn and Deamonte, who both had routine dental issues in 2006 and 2007. Driver, even with the aid of an experienced attorney, could not navigate the complex web of the Maryland Medicaid managed care plan. Her son Deamonte would end up dying in 2007 from a toothache that would have cost just $80 to fix.[8]

In September 2006, Driver contacted Public Justice Center attorney Laurie Norris. Driver had met Norris, an attorney with the nonprofit Baltimore-based Public Justice Center, when Norris had been interviewing homeless families about their experiences with the public school system. Driver called Norris about how to find a dentist for her 10-year-old son DeShawn, who was suffering from pain and swelling in his mouth. Several of his teeth had become decayed and were infected.[9]

Even Norris, an experienced attorney, found the maze of the managed care system hard to navigate. DeShawn was in fact enrolled in a Medicaid managed care plan. His health coverage was provided through a Medicaid MCO. When Norris called the customer service telephone number to find a dentist, she was transferred to Dental Benefit Providers, a separate company that administered the plan's dental benefits.

Norris was told that DeShawn would first need to see a general dentist, who would then provide a referral to an oral surgeon. Dentists providing care would be contracted with Americhoice. Furthermore, only dentists who were under "Americhoice through the state" would provide care under DeShawn's Medicaid plan.

Norris contacted 26 of the dentists under the contract, and none of them accepted "Americhoice through the state." On October 5, 2006, DeShawn finally got to see a dentist, who cleaned his teeth and referred him to an oral surgeon for consultation in November. At the consultation, Alyce Driver learned that DeShawn needed to have six teeth extracted. She made a December appointment, then was told she needed to reschedule to January 16, 2007. But prior to the January appointment, Driver learned that her children's Medicaid coverage had lapsed due to some bureaucratic mishap—perhaps her paperwork had been mailed to the homeless shelter where the family no longer resided. Driver had to cancel the appointment.

The situation for Driver went from bad to worse. Her other son, 12-year-old Deamonte, developed an abscessed tooth, the extraction of which would have cost $80 if a timely appointment had been available. But Driver could not find a dentist to extract the tooth. As a result, bacteria from the tooth spread to Deamonte's brain. Despite two surgeries and six weeks of hospital care, Deamonte died. His operation, hospital care, and therapy totaled $250,000.[10]

The situation in Maryland had turned into such a bewildering maze in part because of a recurring pattern:

1. Government takes action to make healthcare more accessible.
2. Providers abuse and defraud the system.
3. Government cracks down on the abuse.
4. Some providers, incentivized to increase their income, create more intricate methods to increase revenue.

In 1970, Maryland gave dentists a rate increase to draw them in to the Medicaid program.[11] By 1972, state officials became alarmed by rapidly rising Medicaid costs. Rising dental fees came under special scrutiny. One dentist, Earlie Lee Trice, boasted in the *Washington Post* that "I've got the most Medicaid work of any dentist in Prince George's County—I've got four secretaries." He drew the attention of investigators, and eventually fraud charges were brought against him. In one instance he had billed for extracting 38 teeth from one patient's mouth, although an expert witness testified that humans rarely have more than 32 teeth. In 1976, the trial drew national headlines, such as "Medicaid also a Dentists' Goldmine."[12]

Chapter 13. Scams with Teeth, Regulations without Teeth

The political mood turned against Medicaid-funded dentistry. States are not allowed to reduce the number of children who are federally entitled to Medicaid, but they can reduce the reimbursement rates paid to dentists, which Maryland and other states did. Most individual dentists simply left the program because they said they lost money on Medicaid patients.

Managed care, by using business models to economize, was hailed as a potential solution. As Deamonte Driver's tragic situation demonstrated, however, it only created a bureaucratic maze. The state, thinking the managed care networks could solve the problem, considered the responsibility to have been transferred. The managed care network, operating with several companies like a shell game, mainly provided obstacles to obtaining care. Each of the parties involved made what money they could, while transferring as much responsibility as possible, a classic situation of moral hazard.

In 1993, two indigent mothers filed a lawsuit in the U.S. District Court on behalf of their children, and on behalf of all persons under 21 who were eligible for the Early Periodic Screening Diagnosis and Treatment plans (EPSDT). The program provided periodic screening and other health maintenance benefits for children, and included dentistry. The suit alleged inadequate outreach by the program, among other deficiencies that resulted in indigent children not having access to preventive healthcare.[13]

The court ruled for the plaintiffs, which started a series of corrective actions by the state of Texas to comply with the court rulings. The legislation, originally Frew versus Trailer, eventually resulted in legislative action by Texas in 2007 to increase the Medicaid rates paid to dentists by 50 percent.

In 2007, "Texas decided to pump $1.4 billion into dental services for indigent children. That decision followed a U.S. Supreme Court ruling that faulted the state for a lack of adequate dental care to that group."[14]

A serious problem of overtreatment developed, which resulted in not only wasted money but also grave threats to the health of children. By 2012, dental overtreatment of children had drawn the attention of the U.S. Senate. "We're finding that these dental practices, under pressure from owners who are not licensed dentists, have been providing services with the highest Medicaid reimbursement levels more often than less expensive, arguably more appropriate services," Senator Chuck Grassley said. "There are legitimate concerns that children are receiving unnecessary care, sometimes in a traumatic way, and taxpayers are paying for it."[15]

The June 2013 report, "Joint Staff Report on the Corporate Practice of Dentistry in the Medicaid Program,"[16] authored by the Senate staffs of Chuck Grassley and Max Baucus, concluded that "Despite state laws against the corporate practice of dentistry, numerous states have allowed

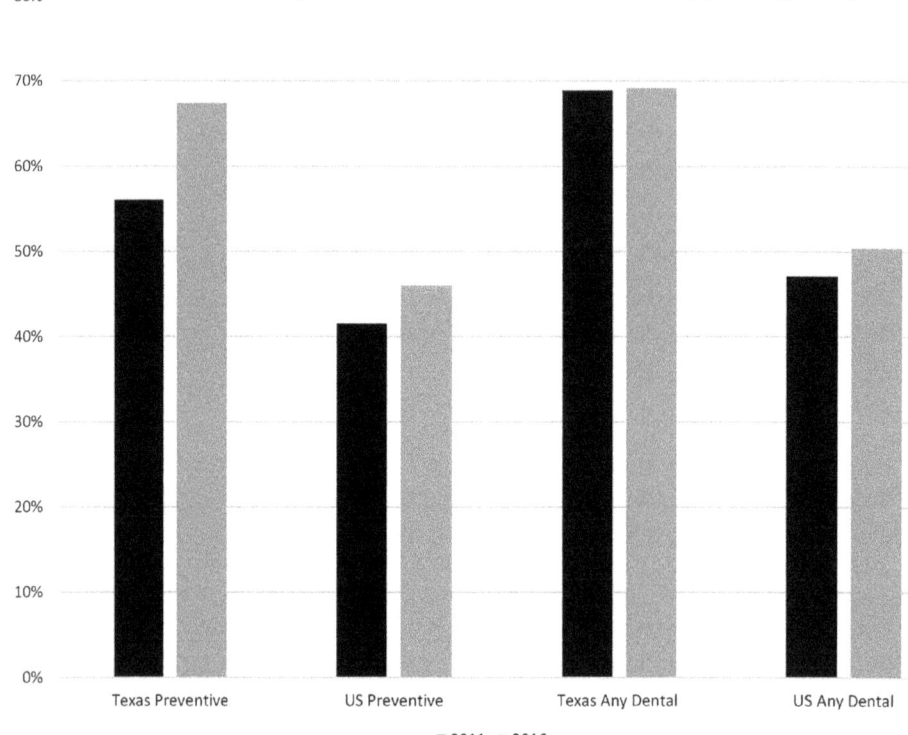

Chart 34. Dental Care Use 2011 and 2016

companies ... to operate dental clinics under the guise of management services agreements. These practices appear contrary to the purpose of state law requiring clinics to be owned and operated by licensed dentists. The result is poor quality of care, billing Medicaid for unnecessary treatment, and disturbing consumer complaints."

"We're finding that the business model has led to abuses because dentists are under pressure to perform as many high reimbursement services on the maximum number of children on Medicaid as possible," Grassley said. "You have dentists under pressure to perform more services than may be necessary—giving a child a crown instead of a filling, for example—because of a bonus payment structure that creates the wrong incentives."

Overall rates for children covered under Medicaid or CHIP have been higher than private insurance plans since 2009.

Texas ranks among the five highest rates of preventive dental care and dental use in 2016.

Chapter 13. Scams with Teeth, Regulations without Teeth   163

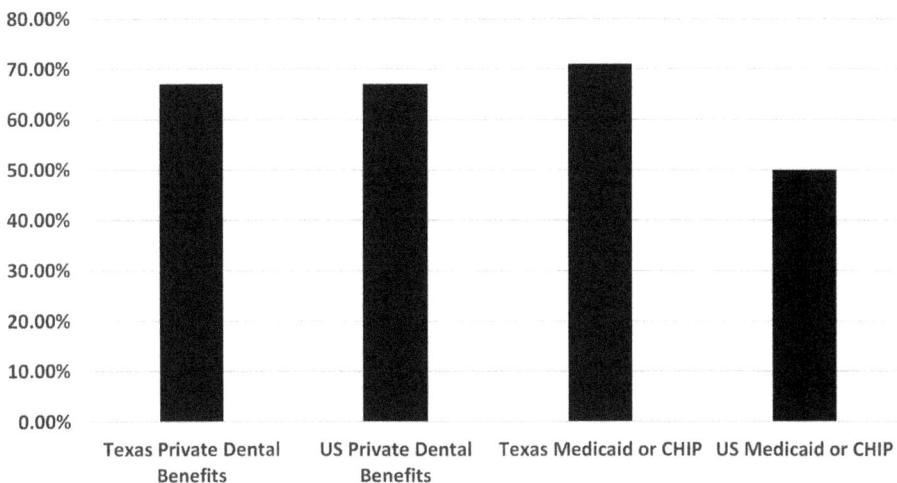

Chart 35. Dental Care Utilization 2016

Ninety-six percent of publicly insured children live within 15 minutes of a Medicaid dentist.

Texas averages less than 500 children per Medicaid dentist and less than 2,500 individuals per dentist for the state's population.

Newspapers around the country began reporting on cases of overtreatment in Medicaid dentistry. In 2013 in Ohio, a mother took her three-year-old son to a dental office for his first checkup, expecting a routine cleaning. She was shocked when the dentist told her that the child needed seven root canals. Two weeks later, in May 2013, the dentist put the child under sedation and drilled his teeth. The Medicaid bill came to $1,273—compared to the $61 that Medicaid would have paid for a checkup and cleaning.[17]

It turned out that the dental office was part of North American Dental Group, a chain backed by private-equity investors. At least a year earlier, the company had told dentists to meet revenue targets or risk expulsion from the chain. Those targets created pressure to overtreat patients.

An investigation found that pressure on North American Dental's offices to meet daily revenue targets led to allegations of overtreatment. Patients complained they were diagnosed with a mouthful of cavities only to later discover that nothing was wrong with their teeth. Employees said they felt uncomfortable with what they witnessed.

"I have watched them drilling perfectly healthy teeth multiple times a day every day," dental assistant Ashley Hughes said in an interview. She worked for two years at a North American Dental office in Austintown, Ohio, not far from where the three-year-old was treated.[18]

In 2015 in Florida, reports surfaced of questionable claims for dentistry in the elderly population. The Florida attorney general focused upon the practice of two dentists whom investigators suspected of billing Medicaid for dentures and extractions that frail and elderly patients may not have needed—or even received. "One alleged patient, now 99, has dementia, cannot communicate, has long been restricted to a liquid diet because of difficulty chewing and swallowing would have no need for false teeth."[19]

In 2017 in former Houston dentist was formally charged with failing to properly treat a four-year-old patient who was left with permanent brain damage in what should have been a routine procedure. The girl was sedated for treatment of tooth decay at the Diamond Dental office about 8:30 a.m. January 7, 2016, prosecutors said in a statement. Three hours later she suffered a seizure, and her oxygen level and temperature fell dramatically. Prosecutors say it took more than four hours before anyone called for medical assistance.[20]

The article noted that "Medicaid dental claims in Texas quintupled between 2005 and 2015 to $1 billion a year after the state doubled reimbursement rates in 2007," and that "The reimbursement system rewards dentists who perform multiple procedures, leading to allegations that clinics rush children through serious treatments to claim more government money."

Other disturbing stories of patient sedation came to light. On December 30, 2013, two parents took their only child to his only meeting with a Dallas-area dentist.[21] The dentist said that sedation was necessary, saying the boy was too young to cooperate with treatment otherwise. One of his aides sold them on a $100 December-only sedation "special," the mother recalled. "That's one of the things she said insurance does not cover."

The parents were told that their four-year-old child needed 12 stainless steel crowns—three times the number identified by their regular dentist. The parents agreed to have the work done in two installments, with the first costing $2,400.

On December 30, 2013, around noon, after not being allowed to eat or drink all morning, the child got a cocktail in a cup. It contained the narcotic painkiller Demerol and two anti-anxiety drugs: Valium and hydroxyzine.

Dental records say the triple cocktail aimed to induce conscious sedation—a drowsy state, defined by the state as moderate sedation, in which they would respond to commands and breathe normally. But dosages listed in the records were twice what Texas's three dental schools approve for moderately sedating preschoolers, an investigation found.

Treatment records called the sedation "semi-effective." Ten minutes into the procedure, the child's heart was beating twice as fast as at the beginning. He cried much of the time. Mucus had to be suctioned from the back of his throat.

The treatment team saw that a sensor had come off the child's right index finger, one that measured oxygen in his blood. And when the assistant in the room reattached it, dental records say, "no oxygen saturation or pulse registered." The boy was limp. His lower lip was turning blue.

"On Day 2, the parents learned that their child would never walk again. On Day 3—New Year's Day of 2014—they watched helplessly as he suffered seizures. And on Day 4 he died."[22]

An investigation brought out the fact that sedation dentistry safeguards were too often lax. In one message that came to light in a state investigation, Dr. Tammy Gough reported hearing that the Dallas dentist "used WAY above recommended dosages." Gough, a pediatric specialist in Collin County, served on the Texas State Board of Dental Examiners then. Her email went to the executive director of the board, which was investigating the child's death. She also passed along an email from a dentist on the children's hospital board, Dr. Robert E. Morgan. It said his medical colleagues were "frustrated with the number [of] dental patients they are seeing in the ICU" and "surprised that in dentistry, we are allowed to be our own 'anesthetists.'"[23]

Sedation dentistry is a logical outgrowth of the pressure to make profits. Patients can be treated more quickly and in greater numbers when they are sedated. But the practice obviously has its perils.

On March 29, 2016, a child "suffered complications from anesthesia while undergoing a procedure at an Austin dental office."

"Daisy went to Austin Children's Dentistry on March 29 to have two cavities filled and was placed under general anesthesia. A short time later she went into cardiac arrest and was rushed to a hospital where she died."

A forensic dental examiner who reviewed the patient's records at the request of the medical examiner's office raised questions about whether the child even needed treatment in the first place.

"One can only speculate as to why any treatment was performed considering no indication of dental disease or pathology," Dr. Robert G. Williams wrote in his review. The forensic examiner determined that that records from a previous dental visit also did not show any decay.[24]

Dental Support Organizations and Overtreatment

Do all these horror stories mean that dentists are especially unethical, or that sedation dentistry is not sometimes needed or necessary? Not at all. It is just that dentistry has become big business. In the excellent

July 2012 article "Unethical Private-Equity-Owned Dental Clinics Receive Well Deserved Attention," authors Charles Siegel and Jim Moriarty state that "It's been a bad few weeks in the limelight for private equity investors masquerading on the down-low as charity dentists when what they're really after is making millions by performing unnecessary dental work on poor kids and then getting Medicaid to pay for it."[25]

The extent to which private equity firms, devoted to making profits for shareholders, took over the practice of dentistry actually did not get enough attention. This phenomenon is at the root of the hurry-up and overtreatment that caused the tragedies briefly noted here. Dental sedation in the context of the private equity firms seems like just another assembly-line methodology to speed up production.

One reason for the corporate takeover of dentistry is to avoid oversight. Dental boards have the ability to take action against the licenses of dentists, not corporations or businesses. The regulations related to dentists are really a mirage when the decision makers are the corporate entities over which the dental boards have no jurisdiction.[26]

Dentists become employees of the private equity firms, dental support organizations (DSOs), that employ them. "Those who wind up working for private-equity-owned dental chains, however, often feel as though they are little more than indentured servants. When they sign on, they are forced to enter into employment contracts with non-compete clauses that forbid them from practicing anywhere else within a short distance of any dental clinic owned by the private equity firm. If the new dentists receive a signing bonus, they are required to give it back should they leave within the first year. And many contracts include provisions requiring the dentists to pay a $500-a-day penalty if they fail to give 90 days' notice when they do leave."[27]

Dentists who are employees of DSOs are subjected to quotas and other pressures, much like a car salesman. "Some clinics establish quotas requiring their dentist-employees to perform a given number of procedures each day, or to bill a minimum of, for example, $5,000 each day. Often, the quotas are not established by a practicing dentist. The general production minimums are set back at the chain's corporate office and then enforced by the office manager, who is generally not a dentist. Adjustments to the targets are made at the individual branches. On a day when fewer patients are scheduled, for instance, the per-patient target goals will go up; when more patients are seen, the sheer volume will reduce the pressure to sell additional procedures. In private-equity-owned dental clinics, all of this is discussed in weekly or even daily office-wide meetings, run by office managers. The bean counters announce the day's target goals, ask dentists to explain why the previous day's quotas were not met and offer

Chapter 13. Scams with Teeth, Regulations without Teeth   167

refresher tips for everyone on how to persuade patients to concede to additional dental work—that very day, if possible, to avoid the risk of a future 'no-show' appointment." Dentists who do not meet production quotas are given bad performance reviews and eventually fired.[28]

One of the larger cases where a DSO was accused of overtreatment was that of Kool Smiles. The government in fact did successfully bring a suit against Kool Smiles. On February 18, 2018, Fox News reported:

"In the recent settlement, Kool Smiles, which operates six El Paso locations, agreed to pay nearly $24 million to the federal government and 17 states for allegedly submitting false claims to state Medicaid programs." The DOJ claimed that "between January 2009 and December 2011 Kool Smiles knowingly submitted false claims for unnecessary baby root canals, tooth extractions and stainless-steel crowns." The government also alleged Kool Smiles billed Medicaid for baby root canals that were never performed, and that the clinics "routinely pressured and incentivized dentists to meet production goals by disciplining 'unproductive' dentists and awarded 'productive' dentists with substantial cash bonuses based on the revenue generated by the procedures they performed."

Kool Smiles agreed to pay $23.9 million to settle the claims.[29] They included a statement that "The companies are disappointed that reasonable disagreement between dentists can become a FCA case. The investigation largely focused on professional disagreements between qualified dentists in determining the appropriate level of cost and care." In a masterpiece of corporate double-talk, the company spokesman noted, "For perspective, the government disagreed with the care provided in less than one percent of the procedures billed during the reviewed period."

The company also said in their settlement statement, "Kool Smiles dentists have provided more than $128 million in uncompensated dental care to treat patients and families who did not have access to Medicaid dental benefits or other dental insurance; and could not afford to pay. The companies will continue to work towards expanding access to quality dental care for all families."[30]

And so they did. Kool Smiles still operates profitably to this day, under the new name Sunnybrook Dentistry.[31]

The scams in dentistry continue. Once in a while, prosecution of one of the more egregious examples come to light. In a recent case, "The filed complaint included a myriad of alleged violations, including that the pair (a) offered kickbacks to patients to utilize their services—including offering free dental services to parents of children who received services; (b) performed unnecessary procedures (including drilling healthy molars in order to fill them); (c) submitted claims for more advanced procedures than performed, and (d) submitted claims representing that other providers had performed the procedures."[32]

The complaint was particularly egregious because of the aggressive way that services were marketed, and the way that children were used to bill for unnecessary services. The complaint also alleged that the defendants offered a $10-per-head "bounty" to marketers for recruiting patients enrolled in Medicaid, and incentivized their employed dentists to see more patients than should be clinically permitted in a day by offering bonus compensation equal to 30 percent of billings generated. While many of the alleged behaviors are somewhat typical areas of fraud in the healthcare sphere, this case demonstrates a fraud unique to pediatric dentistry, which is the furnishing of unnecessary procedures, often on "baby teeth" which are by definition temporary and may therefore not always require extensive intervention.[33]

In this chapter we have "bitten off," so to speak, the realm of dentistry to describe various cases that drew media attention. In the next chapter we will tackle the much larger subject of hospital costs.

Chapter 14

Solutions for Unauditable Hospital Costs

> "**Abandon all hope, ye who enter here.**"
> Inscription on the gate of Hell in Dante's Inferno

We cite Dante's directive more in relation to trying to understand hospital costs than as a warning against going to the hospital. There are dangers in a hospital related to medical accidents, infections, and other aspects of care. However, we are focusing on costs and billing. Because the topic of hospital overbilling could fill several volumes, we can only present the highlights in this chapter, along with some possible remedies.

Total healthcare spending in America exceeded $4 trillion in 2020, and more than 30 percent of that—or about $1.24 trillion—was spent on hospital services.[1]

In America we believe in markets and charging what the market will bear. But the free-market philosophy presumes equal bargaining power and does not account for the artificially high cost of healthcare, which has been driven up in part by government subsidies. As Steven Brill points out in his excellent *Time* magazine article, the U.S. healthcare system is not a free market. "Put simply," he says of hospital bills, "the bills tell us that this is not about interfering in a free market. It's about facing the reality that our largest consumer product by far—one-fifth of our economy—does not operate in a free market."[2]

What bargaining power does someone who finds him or herself at the hospital have? "You have a bullet in your head," says the hospital administrator to the dying man. "If you want us to take it out, please sign here." Right from the start, hospitals are clearly in a dominant negotiating position. If the patient lives, or even if they die, the bill will have to be paid because they *agreed* to it. Some bills that are not paid by the patient are often reimbursed by the state or federal government.

During the COVID-19 pandemic, one of the most frightening things for the uninsured was the prospect of being hospitalized. The average cost of hospital care for a case of COVID-19 ranges from $51,000 to $78,000.[3] The median salary in the United States is $45,000 among those with jobs.[4] So, a bout of COVID would cost more than a year's salary.

Of course, it is worse for those with no salary. Unemployment rose to 12 percent in the second quarter of 2020,[5] which increased the ranks of the uninsured. For the year 2020, 27.4 million nonelderly people were uninsured, and the percentage of uninsured Americans was 10.2 percent.[6]

For uninsured Americans and those with high deductibles, the COVID-19 pandemic meant fear not only of sickness and death, but also of financial ruin. Hospitals are aggressive in pursuing debtors. "Two dozen hospitals sued up to hundreds of their patients over unpaid medical bills in 2020. Even before the pandemic, aggressive practices to recover medical debt have pushed many Americans into bankruptcy. Medical bankruptcies represent 66.5% of all personal bankruptcies, and 48% of those who filed for medical bankruptcy say their largest expense was the hospital bill."[7]

Corporate entities that drive hospital costs include hospital corporations like Hospital Corporation of America (HCA), large health insurance companies like UnitedHealth Group and Cigna, and a newer type of entity called Contract Management Groups (CMGs). If the hospitals are nonprofit, the excess payments wind up as executive compensation, bonuses, and fees for consultants who teach hospitals such things as how to maximize revenues. "In most cities, the highest-paid nonprofit executive by far runs the local hospital. In 2012 Jeffrey Romoff of the University of Pittsburgh Medical Center earned almost $6.1 million, far more than the university's president. Total cash compensation for hospital CEOs grew an average of 24.2 percent from 2011 to 2012 alone, which increasingly includes bonuses as well."[8]

There might be a presumption that insurance companies act as a control on hospital costs, since the insurance companies have to pay the hospitals. However, it is more often the case that the hospitals and insurance companies are "thick as thieves" when it comes to maintaining high costs.[9]

How and why do insurance companies and hospitals both benefit from rising healthcare costs? There is an illusory control of costs referred to as the "Medical Loss Ratio" (MLR), whereby insurance companies have to spend 80–85 percent of revenues on health claims. For the 15–20 percent they live off, it behooves them for the hospitals to spend high amounts, because 15 percent of $2 million is clearly preferable to 15 percent of $1 million. Then the insurance companies use the increased costs to raise insurance rates. So the hospitals can gouge the consumer, under the illusory promise that the insurance companies are there to keep costs down. This

Chapter 14. Solutions for Unauditable Hospital Costs

is another example of how moral hazard contributes to escalating costs. As long as the costs can be passed to someone who either does not understand them or is in no position to do anything about them, the costs will continue to skyrocket.

In a previous chapter we introduced the concept of rate-setting and the basic calculations that go into it. The Medicare rate-setting methodology is straightforward, transparent, and can allow for salaries, profits, inflation, and all the other financial goodies that are part of the capitalist system. The problem with hospitals and private insurance is that the lack of transparency allows for price-gouging.

"Private insurance payment rates were between 1.6 and 2.5 times higher than Medicare rates, with some variation among the ten DRGs included in our analysis."[10] Private insurers willingly pay more than Medicare because they can pass it along to the policy holders and earn a 15–20 percent "commission." Americans have been conditioned to think that this makes private insurance "better" than Medicare. In fact, the healthcare providers and the healthcare would be the same. The difference is that Medicare has an established and understandable methodology, with budget parameters, whereas private insurers are incentivized to pay more in total costs, in order to maximize the 15–20 percent of total cost that they can earn.

This creates a dynamic where the hospitals are like the character in *Brewster's Millions*, who has to spend as much money as fast as he can or lose out on a fortune. This causes outrageously inflated charges for simple items.[11]

First there are the charges for everyday supplies:

Tylenol: Charge to patient: $15 per individual pill, for a total of $345 during average patient stay

Patient belonging bag: Like a grocery bag, to hold your personal items. Charge to patient: $8

Box of tissues: Sometimes listed as "mucus recovery system," a single tissue box in a hospital costs $8. Charge to patient: $8

Gloves: Charge to patient: $53 per non-sterile pair (sterile are higher), for a total of $5,141 during average patient stay.

Cup medicine: Cost is for the plastic cup used to administer medicine, not the actual medicine inside it. Charge to patient, per cup: $10, for a total of $440 during average patient stay.

Marking pen, to mark the body for surgery: Charge to patient: $17.50

Blood-pressure cuff, adult: Use of blood pressure cuff in a hospital costs about $20. Charge to patient: $20

Oral administration fee: Charge for a nurse to hand you medicine taken by mouth. Charge to patient: $6.25 per instance, for a total of $87.50 during average patient stay.
Headlight: Cost of use of the overhead light in an operating room. Charge to patient: $93.50
Swabs, alcohol: Charge to patient: $23 per swab, for a total of $322 during average patient stay.[12]

These examples of overcharging for small items are just the tip of the iceberg. As Elisabeth Rosenthal writes in *An American Sickness*, "There is a lot of leeway in the pricing of something as nebulous as two hours in the endoscopy suite (some fees are billed in fifteen-minute increments). What's more, facility fees provided great incentive to stop performing any and all procedures in doctor's offices and instead use a surgi-center or a hospital outpatient department."[13]

"Facility fees are a unique construct of American healthcare and its business model. When you buy anything—a watch, a car, even groceries—you pay a single price for the goods. The Walgreens down the street doesn't add a separate charge to cover its rent, utilities, or the cost of refrigeration units."[14]

The practice of "upcoding," charging for a more expensive procedure than what is performed, is so much a part of the system that there is software to facilitate it. Treatments are assigned levels from 1 to 5. "A simple level 2 may yield $60, level 3, $120, level 4, $210."[15] One doctor said, "It's like a candy store—all you have to do is check the right boxes. We had software for dictation, and it would even say, 'You need to check two more boxes for level four.'"[16]

In their book, *Big Med: Megaproviders and the High Cost of Health Care in America*, David Dranove and Lawton R. Burns attribute much of the high cost of healthcare to mega providers and lack of competition. "Emboldened by ineffective antitrust enforcement, integrated systems continue to grow, becoming today's large mega providers. The takeover was complete. Despite their lofty compensation, health care executives have not figured out how to make systems work for patients or physicians. They have figured out how to wield their ever-increasing market power."[17]

Hospital overbilling has become so routine that it is out of control. "Broadly speaking medical overbilling began more than 30 years ago and not originally for the purpose of deceiving patients."[18]

"Hospitals had 'list' charges that were a little more than what they needed to collect to break even." Hospitals started to reverse the idea of a discount. "Rather than decreasing the payment they would accept, they

Chapter 14. Solutions for Unauditable Hospital Costs

started increasing the list price they charge. Then, whenever someone paid their inflated bill in full, they could pick up at least some of the lost revenues" from non-paying patients.[19]

High hospital and healthcare costs spill over into the economy and suppress wages. Shannon Brownlee notes that since the 1980s "private insurers could quietly pass on the rising cost to employers, who covered increasing insurance premiums by cutting back on wage increases that might otherwise have gone to employees."[20]

Dr. Robert Yoho, in his book *Butchered by Healthcare*, describes hospital billing: "Hospitals compute their bills using their charge master, a list of the highest prices for thousands of services. A Tylenol is $10, a gas pad is $60, and an alcohol pad is $8. Chest x-rays might be $289 but Medicare only pays $32. Blood drawing charges, which Medicare ignores, are often $36. All this adds up if services are performed daily for weeks. After a month, if you are partly in intensive care and have had a surgery or two, the bill might be nearly a million dollars."[21]

Dr. William E. Ackerman in his book *Healthcare Fraud: A Prescription for Disaster*,[22] provides an excellent summary of how hospitals may overcharge: "The types of improper behaviors that some hospitals may engage in include: fraudulent coding procedures, such as upcoding or unbundling, paying kickbacks to physicians or other health care organizations in order to induce patient referrals. Performing and billing for medically unnecessary procedures, billing for services not actually performed, reporting higher than actual costs, entering into or having existing financial relationships with health care providers who refer patients, paying recruiters to deliver homeless Medicare or Medicaid beneficiaries by ambulance to the hospital for medically unnecessary treatments in order to bilk the government."

Upcoding and unbundling account for a large proportion of hospital overcharges. Upcoding is charging for a worse condition than is justified by the patient's symptoms. Unbundling is similar to Thenardier, the innkeeper in the musical *Les Miserables*: "Charge 'em for the mice, extra for the lice, 2 percent for looking in the mirror twice...."

Upcoding was particularly pronounced in for-profit hospitals. Hospitals shifted some diagnostic work to outpatient facilities and discharged patients early under the care of hospital owned or affiliated home health agencies and skilled nursing facilities.[23]

Why do the American people allow "Big Med" to wield so much power? Elisabeth Rosenthal writes, "A report this year from researchers at Yale and other universities found that hospital prices increased a whopping 42% from 2007 to 2014 for inpatient care and 25% for outpatient care, compared with 18% and 6% for physicians. So why have politicians on both the left and right let hospitals off scot-free? Because a web of ties binds politicians to the health care system. Every senator, virtually every congressman and every mayor of every large city has a powerful hospital system in his or her district. And those hospitals are as politically untouchable as soybean growers in Iowa or oil producers in Texas."[24]

A recent entrant into the arena of healthcare profiteering is the Contract Management Group (CMG): "Some estimate that half of the nation's emergency departments are currently staffed by CMGs. Their priority is not to provide quality patient care. It is to generate profit. Some CMGs were traded on the New York stock exchange. Others have private equity firms investing in them. One CMG even sues patients who cannot pay. A study done by economists at Yale delved further into how CMGs used their power to exploit patients for profit. CMGs now staff half of the nation's emergency departments."[25]

So, what can be done about hospital costs?

"I think I can do it, sir!"

Where does all the money go? Can costs be monitored and controlled? Those are questions I (MS) have been occupied with for decades now. Before I became an auditor, I worked in corporate accounting.

I had my first major encounter with auditors when I worked in finance and wrote a memo about letters of credit. It was years before Enron and the phenomenon of whistleblowers. I had no thoughts of whistleblowing. In fact, I was just tired of having to manage foreign accounts receivable with no leverage.

The salesmen where I worked wanted to get credit for "sales" to foreign companies even though a lot of the time they were in effect giving away the product, which consisted of movies delivered by satellite, or "master tapes," as they were called during that time period.

I wanted letters of credit for the sales, but the salesmen prevented this because they didn't want to "annoy" the clients.

The auditors did notice the large and delinquent receivables. They asked some pro-forma questions about the larger balances. "So, you're pretty confident all those will be paid?"

I said "No." Apparently, they then talked to the salesmen or CEO, who gave them the answers they wanted.

Then the auditors started asking about whether all the travel that the company staff did was completely for business purposes. Because if not, "it might need to be added to someone's compensation." All of the staff were able to state confidently that we worked at least 10-hour days and that the

Chapter 14. Solutions for Unauditable Hospital Costs   175

trips were no fun at all. The auditors were happy and stopped asking questions. Auditors of financial statements in corporate America get paid very well by the corporations they audit and want to keep on getting paid very well.

I marveled at how skillfully the auditors asked meaningless questions so seriously, while ignoring the mostly fictitious sales that drove the company's stock price. I could never do that, I thought.

Yet, when one weekend some friends were talking about restaurants, bars, and the people who audited them, and that the auditors never had to work past four o'clock in the afternoon, auditing started to sound like a viable career path.

I said, "Do they have to vouch for financial statements or deal with the Securities and Exchange Commission?"

"No, it's all for the state regulators, they find tax cheats and money laundering stuff."

"The auditors aren't the big audit firms?"

"No, they work for the state. They're always looking for people who can figure out the frauds."

Not long after that conversation I was at the field office for the Texas Alcoholic Beverage Commission (TABC), asking about a job. I mentioned that I knew something about moving accounts around and that I might be able to figure out their complicated audits.

The gentleman said, "Yes, we are having some trouble tracking cash on the general ledger systems that the big places started using. We think they are hiding cash and falsifying the accounts. If I show you some printouts, do you think you could track them?"

I could hardly believe my luck. "Let's see them," I said.

I looked over the spreadsheets and saw that the company had turned the cash and revenue accounts over for review, but not the entire general ledger. I said, "They're putting the cash in the 1000 series, the revenue in the 4000 series, but they stop at 5300. They probably balance a cash entry with credits in the miscellaneous accounts with higher series numbers, and they just didn't give you those accounts and that part of the general ledger." I knew well enough how to offset cash transactions (or at least how it was done).

He said, "So that's how they make the general ledger match the registers without showing revenue?"

I said, "Yes, they can print it to sort of make it look complete. If they want to lower their taxes—"

He said, "The gross receipts tax rate is 14 percent."

"Well," I said, "If you can get hold of the complete general ledger you'll probably see the rest of the offset entries for the cash."

We chatted for a while longer and then he said he would get back to me.

A few days later he called me back and said I was right about the cash, and wanted to know if there was any way I could go to the TABC headquarters to interview for an auditor job.

"Sure," I said.

I had an interview with one of the top officials of the agency. He looked at me and said, "How did you figger out so fast about the clubs' door charges? You ain't never been arrested, have you? I mean other than a traffic ticket?"

I said, "No."

"Well, we run a check on you anyway. I'll need you to go talk to the human resources fella."

A while later the head of HR was explaining to me how the health insurance worked. I had heard the state's plan was great, and from what he was telling me it was "all that" indeed. He got around to the ethics policy. We would get badges but weren't supposed to use them to get into gentlemen's clubs for free.

"I can refrain from doing that, sir."

He said that I would be offered a lot of free stuff, and I was expected to show good judgment.

I said, "Do you mean lunches? Things like that?"

"Mark, when you're out there in the field, at a licensed establishment, they're gonna offer you lunch, maybe lap dances. What we expect you to do every time is, you gotta ask yourself, 'Will this lunch or other perk affect my judgment?' If the answer is 'no,' you can graciously accept." After a long pause loaded with import he added, "But we expect you to ask yourself that question every time."

I said, "I think I can do it, sir!"

So it was a piece of luck that landed me in the audit profession. The sale of liquor is mainly a cash business, and cash transactions are notoriously hard to audit. Add in door charges, "perks," money laundering, and what could be called disdain for regulation, and it would seem like the liquor business would be nearly impossible to audit. Yet we could nail down the reported and actual numbers within a high certainty rate with audit techniques that were basic math and statistics.

I subsequently learned to audit a wide variety of topics, including many aspects of healthcare. As noted in Chapter 3, even pharmaceuticals, with the industry's secretive formularies, were auditable. If there's a will, there's a way. So why not hospitals? Why are their costs so hard to audit and contain?

A primary obstacle is the concerted efforts by the healthcare industry

Chapter 14. Solutions for Unauditable Hospital Costs 177

to prevent transparency in pricing. In order to make any process auditable, there have to be established criteria. Then the audit process is a constant process of comparing "what is," or the condition, to what "should be," or the criteria. The audit profession documents five elements of an audit finding: condition, cause, criteria, effect, and recommendation. If I dare ask, "Can even hospitals be audited this way?" I would answer, "They can." Over the years I have found that almost any business process can be audited and controlled.

To audit any process or business, established benchmarks such as prices, quantities, and other basic factors must be established, so that there are criteria against which to measure and compare. The healthcare industry has been very diligent in creating confusion over price norms. As noted in Chapter 3, the pharmaceutical industry made a game of making sure that "AWP," which supposedly stood for "Average Wholesale Price," in reality represented "Ain't What's Paid."

Steven Brill followed up his excellent article for *Time* magazine in 2013 with his 2015 book *America's Bitter Pill*. In both works he describes the hospital practice of using a "chargemaster" that contains outrageously high "list prices" for hospital services and products, which are "discounted" for good customers. The uninsured and those with poor coverage must often pay the list prices. Brill writes of his own experience at the hospital: "My big bill had included $20,992 for use of the operating room during my six-and-a-half-hour operation."[26]

For decades the healthcare industry has deftly managed affairs so that the will to rein in costs has remained weak. Brill writes of healthcare costs, "How much taming can be done when the healthcare industry spends four times as much on lobbying as the number two Beltway spender, the much-feared military-industrial complex?"[27]

In the hospital business there are established chargemasters that list what are in effect highly inflated prices for virtually all hospital products and services. For insurance companies who can take advantage of standard discounts, the chargemaster also represents "Ain't What's Paid," and the real prices paid are much lower. The uninsured and underinsured with coverage gaps are often stuck paying the inflated list prices.

Brill cites an example of a truck driver, Emilia Gilbert, who suffered when a hospital's chargemaster and her coverage gaps converged to leave her holding the bag for overpriced services resulting from a simple fall in her back yard.

"Yale New Haven's Bridgeport unit applied its list prices to Gilbert's bill, the way most hospitals do before Medicare or insurance company discounts kick in. In the hospital business, these list prices are derived from what is called the hospital's chargemaster. In Gilbert's case, insurance-related discounts off the chargemaster prices didn't kick in, because of what she soon learned were the severe limits on her insurance coverage. The CT scan bills alone were $6,538."[28]

As we discussed in an earlier chapter, Medicare has established rates that are sometimes used as benchmarks. Brill writes that "Medicare, which pays hospitals based on their costs, plus overhead and a small profit margin, for providing each service, would have paid about $825 for all three tests. Also on Emilia Gilbert's bill were items that neither Medicare nor any insurance company would pay anything at all for: basic instruments, bandages, and even the tubing for an IV setup. Under Medicare regulations and the terms of most insurance contracts, these are supposed to be part of the hospital's facility charge, which in this case was $908 for the emergency room."[29]

Brill describes the effect of the billing on Emilia Gilbert. "When I got the bill, I almost had to go back to the hospital," she told Brill. "I was hyperventilating." Contributing to her shock was the fact that although her employer supplied insurance from Cigna, one of the country's leading health insurers, Gilbert's policy was from a Cigna subsidiary that insured mostly low-wage earners. The policy covered just $2,500 of Gilbert's bill, leaving her on the hook for about $7,000. That made Gilbert one of the millions who are woefully underinsured. They are routinely categorized as having health insurance but don't have anything approaching meaningful coverage. After the hospital sued Gilbert for the full $7,000, a judge ruled that Gilbert, who represented herself in court because she could not afford a lawyer, had to pay all but about $500 of the original charges. The judge put her on a payment schedule of $20 a week. In describing the forces that impelled the push for healthcare reform, *Harvard Business Review* would later cite a 2007 study reporting that medical bills "had become a factor in 62 per cent of personal bankruptcies, an increase from just 8 per cent in 1981." If Gilbert had been forced to pay her bill from Yale New Haven Health System in one lump sum, she would likely have been one of those, all for a fall in her backyard and a few hours in the emergency room. "As the candidates took to the Las Vegas stage that night in 2007, Yale New Haven, which has a tax exemption as a nonprofit institution, was on its way to recording operating income of more than $125 million. Its chief executive would earn a salary of more than $2.5 million, roughly 70 percent more than that of the president of Yale University."[30]

The hospital chargemasters' prices are known to be extremely inflated. They could be subjected to an audit process, much like the one I (MS) utilized when auditing the Vendor Drug Program in Texas, as noted in Chapter 3 of this book. Maybe nobody could force hospitals to undergo a financial audit. Well, you can't force a corporation to undergo an audit, *unless* they want to sell stock to the public. If there's a will there's a way, and a certification process for hospitals based on audited chargemaster data is well within the realm of possibility. Surely some inducement involving access to government funds could be used to encourage a system for auditing healthcare costs.

The Single Audit Act of 1984

For decades the accounting and auditing professions have analyzed and opined on costs from a huge variety of industries. Additionally, government has found ways to audit a wide variety of dissimilar programs. An interesting case in point was the establishment of the Single Audit Act, which created a way to audit all federal programs under a uniform or "single" audit.

By the 1970s, the costs associated with government programs in the United States had become a critical issue in American political and economic discussions. Ronald Reagan was able to successfully run a presidential campaign, one of the pillars of which was that "government is the problem, not the solution." One major problem was trying to account for and audit funds that went to state and local governments, and to nonprofit entities. Such entities might receive funds directly from the federal government, funds passed through by a state agency, funds passed through a city, and other configurations of pass-throughs. The entity also might receive funds from all levels of government from agencies tasked with transportation, healthcare, public safety, education, and so forth.

Anecdotes started to emerge during the sixties and seventies whereby various entities would double and triple dip, and more, on expenses. This was made possible by the uncoordinated auditing efforts of the funding agencies. The state transportation agency auditor would go out to audit the state's road project, and the city would show the auditor a box of legitimate payroll and other expense receipts. Then the federal government health auditor would go audit the health program, and the city would show *the same box of receipts*. The people whose payroll receipts they showed were working there, after all.

In 1984 Congress passed the Single Audit Act to solve numerous auditability issues related to federal funds, not the least of which was the widespread double-dipping. All of the programs had to be audited based on a consistent fiscal year. The auditors were required to audit all of the federal programs and issue opinions on not just the basic financial statements but also on the schedules of federal financial assistance. They also had to opine that the statements of federal assistance were prepared in a manner consistent with, "in relation to," the basic financial statements. In other words, the auditors had to attest that the entities receiving federal funds were not keeping two sets of books.

The Single Audit Act has been very successful in helping to manage federal assistance to states. The framework established cost principles, rules governing financial management, rules for distribution of audit reports, and a wide array of management tools that have been very effective in the management of government programs. When the 2009 American Recovery Act funds were distributed, auditors and financial managers with experience knew that it was not really a matter of starting a new economy of grant funds. Rather, it was more analogous to the federal government wanting to improve the fishing prospects for existing entities, not by creating new rivers and lakes from which to fish, but rather by restocking the existing rivers and lakes with a plethora of fish. Part of the reason the stimulus was workable was the Single Audit Act, and the framework for federal funds it had established.

Let me (MS) propose here that there might be useful parallels between the runaway costs of government programs in the 1960s and '70s and the runaway costs that now plague the healthcare system.

There are sophisticated administrative processes established for gathering cost data, reporting cost data, auditing cost date, and certifying cost data. Implementation of a robust system for auditing the chargemasters used by hospitals is operationally within easy reach of the auditing profession if there is a will to do so. Since healthcare costs are such an enormous drain on the American economy, the need to rein in costs is critical. This can only be achieved if there is more transparency of costs and the ability to audit them in a standardized way.

One of the opinions included in the audit reporting package could be that the prices are established based upon certain standards of reasonableness. Accountants and auditors evaluate financial data for reasonableness every hour of every day in every industry—why should healthcare be exempt? The way the required audit reports are worded would determine the types of testing the auditors would have to do. There are existing standard reports for reporting that costs charged to federal programs are determined in a standard and consistent way.

There have been recent efforts by both the Trump and Biden administrations to improve transparency regarding hospital costs. These have been resisted in the time-honored way of entrenched interests. Of the battle of Waterloo, the Duke of Wellington remarked that "The French army came forward in the same old way; and they were repulsed in the same old way." Actually, the problem was that the artillery, cavalry, and infantry attacks were not coordinated in their attempts to get through the entrenched British army.

In order to deal with the entrenched interests that drain the American economy by systematically overcharging for healthcare, a coordinated approach will be necessary. Requirements relating to posted prices will have to be followed up by a system of auditing.

The cost of a surgery should not be more complicated than the cost of an airplane. A model for a system of cost principles, cost transparency, and auditing is readily available.

The Code of Federal Regulations (CFR) 200 is easily adaptable to hospital costs. CFR 200 has detailed guidance for cost principles and audits, and the administration of both, that could readily adapted, if the political will is there.

Recent Moves Toward Increased Cost Transparency

A move toward better accountability and control of healthcare costs has been attempted recently, though without great success. On June 24, 2019, the Trump administration issued an executive order that established rules relating to hospital transparency. The order directed the federal Health and Human Services Department to develop a rule that would require hospitals to disclose prices that reflect what insurers and patients pay for common items and services.

Starting January 1, 2021, the Centers for Medicare and Medicaid Services required U.S. hospitals to provide "clear accessible pricing information online."[31]

Implementation of the new transparency rule has proven difficult. According to a July 2021 study by Patient Rights Advocate.org,[32] only 5.6 percent of hospitals nationwide are fully following it. Hospitals routinely refused to post prices by insurance payor as required. "They hide pricing information from consumers and search engines. And they violate the spirit if not the letter of the law by posting largely meaningless cost estimates in lieu of real prices."[33]

A former OR nurse had shared screenshots of a facility's electronic health record system with the press. The screenshots show price hikes ranging from 575 percent to 675 percent automatically generated by the hospital software. With such price hikes, it is clear why most hospitals do not look favorably on price transparency.

A *Los Angeles Times* report on the implementation of the rule noted that "to see price hikes of as much as 675% be imposed in real time, automatically, by a hospital's billing system still takes your breath away."[34]

So how can this problem of hospital costs be addressed? There are already methods in place in other areas of the economy that can be adapted to healthcare. There are prodigious volumes written on how to conduct cost accounting for airplanes, buildings, and highways. Corporate America requires that costs be identified and accounted for in order to accurately compute profits.

Costs charged to federal programs have been identified, specified, and audited for decades. There is no reason that hospital costs should not be brought under control in the same way as corporate and government costs outside of the healthcare industry.

Proper accounting and accountability for costs is generally accepted as a worthwhile goal by both liberals and conservatives. The power of the healthcare industry and their lobbyists has succeeded over recent decades in reducing the general political will to contain healthcare costs. But as we have seen, there is a way to do it.

15

Unnecessary Surgeries and Tests

> "Doctors will have more lives to answer for in the next world than even we generals."—Napoleon Bonaparte

When Napoleon made his remark about doctors in the early 19th century, he was referring to the fact that most battlefield deaths were from infections, which the doctors either contributed to by use of unsanitary instruments or were not able to cure. Napoleon made his comment out of frustration or spite. However, he gave a famous voice to the public's skepticism about the medical profession.

Because of the highly technical nature of medical prognoses and treatments, how much can the public rely on the medical profession to follow the Hippocratic oath to "First, do no harm"? In this chapter we will visit some well-publicized cases of unnecessary treatments that not only are a waste of money but can endanger patients in some cases.

Fraud You Can Feel in Your Bones

Orthopedic surgery fraud is widespread. One physician "defrauded insurance companies out of $150 million. Nearly two dozen patients were told that this doctor would perform surgery on them, only to have his physician's assistant who had not attended medical school operate once they were under anesthesia. The doctor wasn't even present for the surgeries. All 21 patients sustained lasting scars and many required additional surgeries and suffered physical and psychological trauma as a result of their experiences with this clinic."[1]

Another orthopedic doctor, Spyros Panos, performed prodigious acts of fraud. In 2013 reports started to surface that he "scheduled as many as 22 surgeries *per day*, whereas most orthopedic surgeons in the United States perform no more than 32 surgeries *per month*."[2]

That doctor was called out in a medical malpractice journal, which raised the obvious question of how he was able to commit such large-scale fraud.

"Twenty-two surgeries per day? How did this singular fact not raise concerns and result in a *timely investigation* of Dr. Panos by the medical practice that employed him, by the hospital(s) where he performed surgeries, by the various operating room personnel where allegedly 'phantom' surgeries were performed, by the billing personnel at both his employer and the hospital(s) where Dr. Panos' billings were so much greater than all of the other surgeons, or result in much earlier disciplinary action by state medical authorities that could have saved many of Dr. Panos' patients from the egregious results of his misconduct?"[3]

"We refrain from applauding the OPMC and the BPMC in the *Panos* disciplinary matter unless and until we learn of additional facts that they acted *timely and appropriately to protect the public*. ('The mission of the Office of Professional Medical Conduct [OPMC] is to *protect the public* by investigating professional discipline issues involving physicians, physician assistants, and specialist assistants.')"[4]

That doctor was convicted of fraud, sentenced to prison, and then released in 2017. In 2019, he pleaded guilty to new fraud charges.

"He was accused of stealing another physician's identity to bill more than $860,000 for workers' compensation case reviews that he was not licensed to perform—after his previous arrest and while serving a federal prison sentence for another healthcare fraud, according to the State Inspector General's Office and the Attorney's Office."[5]

A recently uncovered kickback scheme shows how device manufacturers work with doctors to push sales at the expense of patients' health.[6]

"Dr. Kingsley R. Chin was little more than a decade out of Harvard Medical School when sales of his spine surgical implants took off."

"Chin has patented more than 40 pieces of such hardware, including doughnut-shaped plastic cages, titanium screws and other products used to repair spines—generating $100 million for his company SpineFrontier, according to government officials."[7]

In March 2020, the Department of Justice accused Chin and Spine Frontier of illegally funneling more than $8 million to nearly three dozen spine surgeons through "sham consulting fees" that paid them handsomely for doing little or no work.[8]

Illegal kickbacks from device makers to orthopedic surgeons have become a major area of fraud in recent years. "Every year, a torrent of cash and other compensation flows to these surgeons from manufacturers of hardware for spinal implants, artificial knees and hip joints—totaling more than $3.1 billion from August 2013 through the end of 2019, a KHN analysis of government data found. These bone specialists make up a quarter of U.S. doctors who have accepted at least $100,000 or more, and two-thirds of those who raked in $1 million or more, from the medical device and drug industries last year, the data shows."[9]

This fraud is particularly pernicious because surgical devices are permanently implanted in the body and often replace native bone that has been removed. Referrals and kickbacks are rampant in the field of orthopedics.[10] The most blatant examples make the headlines. The financial incentives to the healthcare providers are so great that patients' health and the financial health of the healthcare system are both at constant risk.

The Unkindest Cuts

It is a great trauma to have to decide whether to have a major surgery like a hysterectomy when there is a pall of doom hanging over one's head, thinking that the surgery may be necessary to prevent cancer. However, it might not be necessary at all.

It would be agonizing enough if we were in a world where doctors could be trusted to have the best interest of patients as their guiding principle. But the prevalence of incentives to perform unneeded surgery and the actual cases make this doubtful. A recent example of particularly egregious conduct made headlines in 2021.

"A Virginia obstetrician and gynecologist was sentenced Tuesday to 59 years in prison after being convicted on federal charges of performing medically unnecessary surgeries including hysterectomies and improper sterilizations on scores of patients over nearly a decade, prosecutors said.

"In November 2020, a federal jury also convicted the doctor, Javaid Perwaiz, of Chesapeake, of 52 counts of health care fraud and false statements for procedures he performed from 2010 through 2019, according to the U.S. attorney in the Eastern District of Virginia.

"Prosecutors said the procedures had cost insurance programs more than $20 million in losses. The government seized assets including more than $2 million, a Bentley, two properties in Chesapeake and medical equipment after Dr. Perwaiz's conviction, according to court records."[11]

The Air That You Breathe

The vast majority of unnecessary surgery is more borderline and does not result in prosecutions.

"Overuse, or medical care that provides no benefit to the patient, is rampant in our health care system. At least 20% of the money we spend on health care is wasted—more than $700 billion dollars a year—and unnecessary care is a major contributor to this waste."[12]

"Endoscopic sinus surgery quickly became a big moneymaker for doctors, industry, and institutions. Physicians (and hospitals) could get reimbursed thousands of dollars for each surgery, instead of a small amount for antibiotics. Companies that sold instruments for sinus surgery gave courses and would loan instruments to surgeons to get them started. The procedure was advertised as being extremely safe, with famous surgeons making claims such as, 'More than 2500 endoscopic ethmoidectomies have been carried out ... without any serious complications.'"[13]

According to Arthur W. Curtis, endoscopic ethmoidectomies (ESS) were rendered unnecessary by less invasive procedures. "A few years into the ESS boom, otolaryngologists like myself learned to treat difficult sinus infections with antibiotics targeted against anaerobic bacteria. Shortly after that, we learned to open up the sinus passages pharmacologically with a short course of a high dose of an oral glucocorticosteroid such as prednisone. By 1995, with these two new tools, almost no one needed surgery for sinus infections."[14]

Dr. Curtis says that in order to justify continued use of ESS, doctors made up a new health condition, "chronic sinusitis" (CRS). Eventually, 10 to 15 percent of the population suffered from CRS. Curtis concludes that "Endoscopic sinus surgery has been done unnecessarily on millions of patients and wasted tens of billions of dollars."[15]

In 2021, the Lown Institute issued a first of its kind report on hospitals that performed the most unnecessary surgeries.[16]

"Hendry Regional in Clewiston, Florida, is at the bottom of the list with the most instances of overuse. For example, of beneficiaries who came to Hendry because they had fainted with no other risk factors, 23% underwent carotid artery imaging and 75% of them got a head CT or MRI.

"Nationally, the rate of hospitals that performed carotid imaging for patients with that presentation was 7% and for head imaging, was 23%."[17]

A detailed and comprehensive review of practicing doctors found that the majority thought unnecessary healthcare services were common. "An analysis of their answers revealed that a majority of them—64.7 percent—believe that at least 15 percent to 30 percent of medical care is not needed. On average, the response from physicians was that 20.6 percent of overall medical care is unnecessary, including 24.9 percent of tests, 22 percent of prescription medications and 11.1 percent of procedures.[18]

"The top three reasons the physicians cited for overtreatment was fear of malpractice (84.7 percent), pressure from patients (59 percent) and difficulty accessing the prior medical records of patients (38.2 percent). Other reasons cited included inadequate time spent with patients, pressure from colleagues and medical institutions or management, as well as concerns about 'looking good' in performance evaluations."[19]

The study's authors pointed out that fear of malpractice may be overblown: "perceptions of the prevalence of malpractice suits … may be greater than the reality of the problem.

"Only 2–3% of patients harmed by negligence pursue litigation, of whom about half receive compensation," they explain. "Paid claims have declined by nearly 50% in the last decade, and it has been suggested that honest disclosure and an offer of an apology by the physician can further mitigate litigation."[20]

The cost of malpractice and the defensive measures taken to protect healthcare providers against malpractice claims is hard to pin down. A 2010 study found that "The total cost of medical malpractice-related costs to the health care system, including defensive medicine, is about $55.6 billion per year, or about 2.4 percent of annual health care spending. Defensive medicine is about 80 percent of that total, the researchers found."[21]

Proposals and discussions about lawsuit reform often seem steeped in agendas. "What strikes me about these current proposals is that they really represent the agenda of medical professionals, which is all about limiting liability," said Michelle Mello, a Stanford University law professor and health researcher. "To take any malpractice reform seriously, it has to offer something to improve the situation of patients and lead to safer outcomes."[22]

In 2017 "researchers estimated that medical errors claim more than 250,000 lives annually, which would make it the nation's third leading cause of death behind heart disease and cancer."[23]

Unnecessary Testing

A CNN article emphasized that not only were needless medical tests costly, but they could also be dangerous. "At least $200 billion is wasted annually on excessive testing and treatment, according to an estimate by the Institute of Medicine, now called the National Academy of Medicine. This overly aggressive care also can harm patients, generating mistakes and injuries that are thought to cause 30,000 deaths each year.

"Galen Gunther, a 59-year-old from Oakland, said that during treatment for colorectal cancer a decade ago, he was subjected needlessly to repeated blood draws, often because the doctors couldn't get their hands on earlier results. Later, he said, he was overexposed to radiation, leaving him permanently scarred."

A mixture of financial incentives and taking the path of least resistance leads to over testing. "At Cedars-Sinai Medical Center in Los Angeles, officials said that economic incentives still drive hospitals to think more is better."

"'We have excellent patient outcomes, but it's at a very high cost,' said Dr. Harry Sax, executive vice chairman for surgery at Cedars-Sinai. 'There is still a continued financial incentive to do that test, do that procedure and do something more.'"

"In addition to financial motives, Sax said, 'many physicians still practice defensive medicine out of fear of malpractice litigation. Also, some patients and their families expect antibiotics to be prescribed for a sore throat or a CT scan for a bump on the head.'"[24]

Given the incentives to overtreat, the question arises as to what checks and balances would deter healthcare professionals from engaging in unnecessary procedures just to increase their incomes. We have seen in previous chapters that there are holes in the regulatory systems. In the following chapter we will discuss the ethical standards prescribed for healthcare practitioners that can serve as a check on the ever present factor of greed.

Chapter 16

Ethics in Healthcare Billing

This book has focused on overbilling and other aspects of the U.S. healthcare system that have led to its being the most expensive one in the world. In some instances, it seems almost as if a comedy of errors has created this bloated system. But to what extent do ethical and even fraud considerations need to be addressed?

The Florida Department of Health reported in September 2019: "Growth incorporation and profitization in medicine, insurance company payment rules, and government regulation have fed natural proclivities even among physicians to optimize profits and reimbursement."[1] The same publication notes that a recent healthcare fraud and abuse control program annual report indicated a managed care company "pressured incentivized dentists in the same way they referred to physicians." The report noted that the system of payment disciplined "unproductive dentists" but awarded those dentists who increased revenues for a procedure which, according to this publication, which constituted many allegedly medically unnecessary services for which payment should have been denied.[2]

The Centers for Medicare and Medicaid Services spent $1.1 trillion on healthcare services in 2016.[3] The Federal Bureau of Investigation estimates that fraudulent billing can constitute 3 to 10 percent of total spending, contributing to inefficiency, high care cost, and waste.[4] Due to the ongoing issues and the ongoing loss of monies related to waste, fraud, and abuse—and, perhaps, to incentivization and/or natural proclivities to benefit from government regulations, insurance company rate rules and increase profits—Congress attempted to address some of these issues legislatively. Physician issues are reviewed in the OIG's "Roadmap for New Physicians."[5]

An article published by the AMA's *Journal of Ethics*, March 2020, poses the question: "Whether physicians are being trained or encouraged to commit fraud within corporatized organization cultures through contractual incentives (or mandates) to optimize billing and process more patients is unknown. What is known is that upcoding and misrepresentation of clinical information (fraud) costs more than $100 billion dollars a year and can result in unnecessary procedures and prescription."[6]

The emphasis of the quoted publication focuses on physicians, but they are not the only licensed professional providers in healthcare. There are non-physician practitioners who follow the same rules as physicians. We have focused on the professional who is individually or group enrolled in insurance plans, public or private, who bills based on their professional credentials rather than as part of services provided by an institution. When reviewing these comments, it should be remembered that healthcare is a large continuum of care, and overutilization and any other type of optimized billing patterns are not exclusive to physicians or non-physician practitioners.

A 2012 CMS guidebook acknowledges that most physicians strive to work ethically, render high-quality medical care, and submit proper claims for payment. The published guidebook acknowledges that society places enormous trust in a physician who will not only treat patients appropriately, but also bill for their services appropriately. This federal publication indicated that it, too, places enormous trust in physicians and that the federal programs, Medicare, Medicaid, and others, rely on physicians' medical judgment to treat beneficiaries with appropriate services and to submit accurate and truthful claims information. It does note that the publication was necessary as there are "some dishonest healthcare providers who exploit the healthcare system for illegal personal gain," therefore creating the need for laws that combat fraud and abuse and ensure appropriate quality medical care. Congress created several laws to address federal fraud and abuse. The CMS guideline reviewed the five most important of these laws.

False Claims Act (31 U.S.C. §§ 3729–3733)

The False Claims Act attempts to protect the government and its funds from being charged or sold goods or services that are of poor quality. The Claims Act declares that the submission for payment to Medicare and Medicaid services "that you know or should know are false or fraudulent" is illegal. The Claims Act indicates "knowing" includes not only knowledge of the false claim but also claims that reflect deliberate ignorance or reckless disregard of the truth or falsity of the information carried in the claim. The act carries criminal penalties for submitting false claims, including imprisonment and fines.

The Anti-Kickback Statute (42 U.S.C. § 1320a-7[b])

The Anti-Kickback Statute prohibits the knowing and willful payment of remuneration, whether in goods or cash, to induce patient referrals or generate business involving any item or service for which the federal government healthcare plans would pay. Examples of these services or goods include drugs, supplies, or healthcare services. The definition of rewards includes free rent, expensive hotel stays and meals, and extensive compensation for medical directorships or consultancies.[7] This is a criminal statute; paying for referrals is considered a crime. The law addresses both the payers of kickbacks, those who offer rewards, and the recipients of kickbacks, those who receive the rewards. Therefore, criminal charges are not only focused on half of a kickback arrangement. This is a criminal law and therefore includes sanctions in violating it, including fines, jail terms, and exclusion from participation in federal healthcare programs. Some "safe harbors" exist. Safe harbors are those services and goods that are exempted under certain conditions. Physicians are a particularly attractive targets for kickback schemes, as their role in healthcare is pivotal.

The Anti-Kickback Statute was to address overutilization, increases in program costs, corruption in medical decision-making, patient steering, and unfair competition.

The Anti-Kickback Statute also addresses those referrals and incentives that are more subtle. For instance, it prohibits a healthcare provider from advertising that they will forgive copayments (which reduces the cost to the patient and incentivizes them to use your service rather than one for which they would have to pay the copayment). The law does not prohibit one from providing free or discounted service to the uninsured. However, healthcare professions generally must present a standard criterion for who is eligible for these services, i.e., a hardship criterion that is applied consistently to all their patients.

This statute also addresses the issue of taking money or gifts from a drug or a device company or a durable medical equipment supplier, even if the physician or non-physician practitioner would have recommended use of these supplies, DME or drugs.

The Physician Self-Referral Law (42 U.P.S.P.C.P § 1395nn)

The Physician Self-Referral Law, often referred to as the Stark Law, prohibits physicians from entering into certain conflicts of interest including referring patients to "designated healthcare services payable by Medicare, Medicaid, and other publicly-funded health services or to entities from which they derive profit unless an exception applies." Financial relationships include ownership/investment interest and compensation arrangements. The law prohibits a physician from referring patients to the facility.

Designated healthcare services include:

- clinical laboratory services
- physical therapy, occupational therapy, and outpatient speech and language pathology services
- radiology and certain other imaging services
- radiation therapy services and supplies
- DME and supplies
- prostheses, orthotics, and prosthetic devices and supplies
- home health services
- outpatient prescription drugs
- inpatient/outpatient hospital services

While the Anti-Kickback Statute is a criminal law, the Stark Law is a liability statute. This means that proof of specific intent to violate the law is required.

Exclusion Statute (42 U.S.C. § 1320a-7)

This is a statute that mandates that the Office of Inspector General is "legally required to exclude from participation all federal healthcare programs, individuals and entities convicted of criminal offences for

- Medicare and Medicaid fraud as well as any other offences related to the delivery of items or services under Medicare and Medicaid.
- Patient abuse or neglect.
- Felony convictions on any other healthcare related fraud, theft, or other financial misconduct, and
- Felony conviction for unlawful manufacture, distribution, prescription, or dispensing of cold controlled substances.

The OIG also has the right to exclude individuals or entities on other civil grounds including:

- Misdemeanor convictions related to healthcare fraud.
- Other Medicare or Medicaid fraud or misdemeanor conviction in connection with unlawful manufacture, distribution, prescription, or dispensing of controlled substances.
- Suspension, revocation, or surrender of license to provide

healthcare services for reasons bearing on professional competence, professional performance, or financial integrity, provision of unnecessary or substandard services.
- Submission of false or fraudulent claims, engaging in unlawful kick-back arrangements, and defaulting on health or education loan or scholarship obligations."

This statute extends beyond the Medicaid and Medicare program. If the OIG excludes an individual or entity from participation in Medicare or Medicaid, the entity or individual is also excluded from other federal programs, including TRICARE and the Veterans' Health Department. Any professional excluded from the Medicare and Medicaid programs may not directly bill for their services, nor can they indirectly bill for their services as an individually licensed professional, nor can they bill indirectly through an employer or group practice. If you are an excluded professional with prescriptive authority, even if you see the patient on a private-pay basis, the prescription that may follow from this consultation or visit is excluded from payment by the Medicare and Medicaid program, as the prescriber is an excluded professional.

The statute also mandates that healthcare providers and entities must ensure that they do not employ or contract with excluded individuals or entities. The statute requires screening of all current and prospective employees and contractors against the list of excluded individuals and entities published by the OIG.

Civil Monetary Penalties Law (42 U.S.C. § 1320a-7)

This law emboldens the Office of Inspector General to seek civil monetary penalties ranging from $10,000 to $50,000 for violation. This statute also allows for the exclusion of a wide variety of conduct. Violations of the Civil Monetary Penalties Law (CMPL) may include:

- Presenting a claim that the person knows, or should know, is for an item or service that was not provided or claimed or is false or fraudulent;
- Presenting a claim the person knows or should have known is for an item or service for which payment may not be made;
- Violating the Anti-Kickback Statute;
- Violating Medicare assignment provisions;
- Violating Medicare physician agreement;
- Providing false or misleading information expected to influence a decision or discharge;

- Failing to provide an adequate medical screening examination for patients who present to a hospital emergency room department with an emergency medical condition or in labor.

The Physician Payment Sunshine Act was signed into law as part of the Patient Protection and Affordable Healthcare Act of 2009 (HR 3590 § 6002) in 2010.[8] The purpose of this legislation was to "regulate or control the amount of funding that flows from pharmaceutical companies and medical manufacturers to doctors." The act requires disclosure of the amount of funding. It also requires disclosure of specificity in detail of the amount of funding that flows between the entities.

Medical manufacturers and pharmaceutical manufacturers were to begin reporting all their payments to doctors as of March 2013.

An *AMA Journal of Ethics* publication in 2020 stated that in 2016, CMS indicated that $95 billion of the $1.1 trillion spent on healthcare was connected to fraud or abuse. There are estimates suggesting that program integrity issues constitute 3–10 percent of total healthcare spending and contributes to inefficiency and high healthcare cost and waste. CMS indicated that program integrity issues are divided into four categories:

- Mistakes resulting in administrative errors such as incorrect billing;
- Inefficiency causing waste such as ordering excessive diagnostic tests;
- Bending and abuse of rules such as coding;
- Intentional deceptive fraud such as billing for services or tests not provided, not rendered, or of questionable medical necessity.

The article stated that some of the root causes of these issues are practice site–induced, including:

- Optimizing volume;
- Focusing on reimbursable and profitable services;
- Restructuring clinical staffing to include extended use of medical assistants and clerical personnel to perform some patient care–related functions that might be constituted as unlicensed practice.

Based on the AMA's concerns, let us return to our example from the Texas Medicaid program and the curious case of CPT 92507. The Texas Health and Human Services Investigator General, in its report of October 2, 2017, IG Report No. INS-16-002, indicated it conducted a review of medical necessity for speech therapy services due to concerns regarding the possible overutilization of speech therapy services in the Texas Medicaid Children's Program. This report concluded that medical

Chapter 16. Ethics in Healthcare Billing

necessity was established for the need of therapy, through initial evaluation. However, the agency expressed concerns regarding the provision of therapy. In particular, the report noted that in its review of services reimbursed by MCOs, a significant number of the services were provided by speech-language therapy assistants. The inspection team of the IG stated that "MCOs engage in variable levels of oversight to verify the deliveries of service. Aside from concerns of recipient attendance, it is also possible that providers failed to meet scheduled appointments and could bill when services were not rendered. Additionally noted, after a record review of providers associated with 10 identified MCOs, providers almost exclusively utilized speech language assistants to provide therapy to MCO members. Speech language assistants are only authorized to provide therapeutic service if they are appropriately supervised by a fully licensed speech language pathologist. On-site interviews with the MCOs revealed and emphasized that this practice is not currently monitored."

The 2002 publication of the *AMA Journal of Ethics* suggests that artificial intelligence–based systems can be used to identify waste, fraud, and abuse. The required fields for electronic claims is reviewed in the coding and billing chapter of this book. CMS currently uses the fraud prevention system, which uses data analytics and "big data" to monitor and analyze claims and payments. With the use of this data collection, the Office of Inspector General should be able to compare:

- Patient volume for similar professional claims to identify abnormally high reimbursement submissions;
- Unnatural practice growth patterns;
- Unusually high numbers of procedures based on specialty and practice size, which may highlight excessive numbers of patients seen by an individual within a 24-hour window and other patient visit anomalies.

In the case of 92507, the data analytics as proposed by the above AMA article would require the use and NPI of the individual professional rendering the service.

As described in Chapter 7 of this book, three provider types provide CPT 92507 to the Texas Medicaid program:

- Home health agencies including Medicare-certified home health agencies and at-home service providers, often referred to as licensed at-home, therapy-only agencies;
- Comprehensive outpatient rehabilitation facilities/outpatient rehabilitation facilities; (CORF/ORF)
- Individually enrolled speech-language pathologist and/or physicians.

See the chart on page 81, "HHSC Consolidated Budget, Fiscal Years," which shows growth in use of services over several years.

The use of data analytics and algorithms is very difficult to analyze, given the way the payment structures and filing requirements were established for the Texas Medicaid Children's Program. The NPI number is the key to determining which professional provided the service. CORFs/ORFs and at-home service agencies and Medicare-certified home health agencies were not required to provide the NPI of the rendering provider/therapist for outpatient services; they only had to use their institutional NPI. Only the independently enrolled therapists and physicians were required to use the individual NPI. Additionally, until 2017, speech therapy services billed as CPT 92507 did not carry a modifier indicating whether a fully licensed speech-language pathologist or a speech pathology assistant rendered this service. Before that time, the services were treated the same and paid at the same rate.

The state did introduce the use of modifiers to indicate the level of qualifications of the provider in 2017. Even though that modifier was required, if the individual NPI of the rendering professional was not provided, it is impossible to use "big data" to analyze who provided the services and under what context, because the rendering provider who would be the supervising and treating speech-language pathologist was not required to provide their individual NPI on these institutional claims.

For many years, the difficulty with the issue of waste, fraud, and abuse has been of significant concern. Government and insurance plans have instituted regulations and policies to curb the tide, but with little success.

Referencing our example of CPT 92507 in the Texas Medicaid Children's Program, many services are provided in the home. Until 2017, when provided in the home, these therapy services were paid at different rates depending on the provider type. Place of service can be used in data analysis. Due to the exponential increase in the cost of at-home therapy services, the sole Texas Medicaid agency, Texas Health and Human Services, required that services be provided in the home only when it was medically necessary. One would have hoped that analytics and algorithms could recognize major shifts in volume provided by provider types and/or place of service. Unfortunately, this policy did not curb the growth in utilization and was not enforced.

While data analytics and big data can be used to review claims and determine trends and patterns, claims data does not indicate whether or not services provided by speech-language assistants were provided in accordance with state law with supervision requirements. This can only be assessed at the beneficiary, clinical record level.

"Restructuring clinical staffing to include extended use of medical assistance ... to perform some patient care related to function that can be constituted as unlicensed practice."[9]

The Texas IG report indicated a high usage of speech-language pathology assistants and expressed concern that there was not a monitoring system used by MCOs to provide oversight of assistants relative to the state's licensing act.

Congress has attempted many legislative cures to reduce the burden of cost-associated waste, fraud, and abuse. The amount of money that constitutes improper payments, waste, fraud, and abuse continues to grow and has not been abated over the years by standard transactional codes, data analytics, or "big data." The use of data analytics can only be of any significant value if the data is used in comparison to standardized information and required fields are designed to extract specific data.

We ask again, where does the money go? In 2016, Texas HHSC stated that it had identified "where the money went," but did not assess critical elements contributing to the overpayment, including the fee schedule. The report simply ignored abnormal increases in patient volume, unnatural practice growths, and unusually high numbers of procedures provided in one place of service. All data points were available in claims reviewed.

Reinstatement of Disparate Rates Despite HHSC and CMS Investigations

While telehealth is relatively new, it offers the ability to receive services from a specialist without excessive travel. This is a godsend for individuals in rural communities as well as for those in metropolitan areas. Specialty providers often have more than one brick-and-mortar facility. Only large group providers and hospital-based services can put satellite brick-and-mortar facilities in multiple communities within a large metropolitan area. Someone living in a metropolitan area can spend up to two hours or more going to and from a healthcare facility. Some metropolitan areas in Texas are more than 60 miles wide. Prior to the COVID pandemic, telehealth practice in the state of Texas required the individual to be seen by the practitioner face to face for the initial encounter. Subsequent treatment services for therapy could be provided via interactive audio and visual conferencing. While permitted by state law, insurance companies generally did not cover telehealth services, with the exception of the 11 percent of health plans governed by the Texas Department of Insurance. As of 2019, the Texas Medicaid program opted to expand telehealth services to therapies. All state licensing requirements must be adhered to, but the provision of therapy was allowed as this would allow for more patients to have more access to specialty facilities.

With the pandemic, many of the telehealth requirements in a state, if they had any, were waived due to the high level of possible infection in traveling to a facility, particularly before vaccines were available. This was important, most especially in the Medicare and disabled populations, who were more vulnerable to severe effects of the virus.

Pre-pandemic, multiple provider types, including home health and independently enrolled therapists in the Texas Medicaid program, were allowed to provide services in the home, making the place of service a significant issue. As of 2010, under the Texas Medicaid Children's Program, licensed therapy professionals, whether employed by an institutional provider or in private practice, could provide services in the home, and were paid more for at-home services than services provided in an office setting. As you recall from the curious case of CPT 92507, if the rates were consistent with Medicare rate-setting as required by federal policy, all these outpatient services would be provided at the same rate. The Medicare site-neutral rates for outpatient therapy provided in the home have been in place for many years. Site-neutral rates for hospital-based services were reimbursed differently, but recently CMS has required that all outpatient service reimbursements be site neutral. While hospitals and other providers of therapy services will be reimbursed at the same rate by Medicare, Medicaid program payments are governed by the state, and in Texas, the Medicaid program pays more for services rendered in the home.

If site-neutral payments were implemented throughout healthcare, the decrease in expenditures could total as much as $672 billion over a decade.[10]

Re-establishment of the rate disparities means that telehealth services, presumably at the same cost to each provider type, was paid at two different rates.

See chart on page 138, Texas HHSC Rates CPT 92507, 2019 Fee For Service, Chapter 11.

See chart on page 148, HHSC Adopted Rates Effective 09/01/2019 Comparing Licensed Assistant Rates to Medicare Rate for Fully Licensed SLP, Chapter 11.

If the services were billed to an MCO, the disparity is of even greater significance.

This is one example in one discipline for one service.

How many times is this pattern repeated? To determine the answer, a review of healthcare services requires both a macro and micro perspective. Our review continues.

Chapter 17

Adding Up the Costs

Uncompensated care costs for the nation's uninsured averaged $42.4 billion per year in the 2015–2017 time period.[1] Although healthcare providers incur substantial cost in caring for the uninsured, the bulk of their costs are compensated through a web of complicated funding streams, financed largely with public funds from the federal government, states and localities.[2]

One of the costs of fraud, waste, and abuse in healthcare is that so many Americans have to go without healthcare. Despite spending the most of any country in the world, the United States rates 34th in percentage of citizens covered by health insurance, below Slovakia, Chile, Estonia, and Poland.

The rate of uninsured Americans hovers perpetually around 10 percent, while a larger percentage have some type of insurance but still live in constant fear of illness because of high copays, fear of job loss, and insurance that covers only a small percentage of health issues. This is part of the cost of the exorbitant amount of money misspent on healthcare in the United States.

Some Americans with insurance are so squeezed by high deductibles and copays that they avoid seeking care whenever possible. Healthcare has become so expensive that it is in effect rationed.

In 2009 the *American Journal of Public Health* reported on a Harvard Medical School study that concluded that 45,000 Americans die every year because they lack health insurance and access to healthcare.[3] In 2020, "US health insurance decreased significantly ... the number of uninsured Americans increased by roughly 2.3 million between 2016 and 2019—resulting in as many as 25,180 deaths before the COVID-19 pandemic hit the country."[4]

For some insured Americans, high deductibles, preexisting condition restrictions, and other restrictions on their healthcare policies leave them almost as vulnerable as the uninsured.

"Pour Encourager les Autres"

What is the psychology behind allowing the citizens of a rich nation to go without healthcare? The eighteenth-century Anglo-Dutch philosopher Bernard Mandeville wrote that "One of the reasons why so few people understand themselves is that most writers are always teaching them what they should be, and hardly ever trouble their heads with telling them what they really are."[5]

Mandeville's French contemporary, Voltaire, makes fun of the English in his satirical book *Candide*. Candide is perplexed by the British, who from time to time execute an admiral *"pour encourager les autres"*[6] (to encourage the others) to work harder and be more disciplined. This expression has carried down through the ages to refer to an action carried out as a warning to others. During World War I on the Western front, executions of deserters were numerous, *pour encourager les autres*.

In *Uninsured in America: Life and Death in the Land of Opportunity*, authors Susan Starr Sered and Rushika Fernandopulle describe a de facto caste system in America, whereby there is a permanent underclass of people who are unemployed or in prison, without healthcare. They serve as a warning, and a constant prod to others to keep their noses to the grindstone.

Sociologist Herbert Gans argues that the existence of an underclass serves as a warning that keeps mainstream Americans in line. "Stigmatization of poverty, unemployment and marginal employment help serve as a warning to abide by normative values standards and life practices in order to avoid such a fate. Homeless shelters and prisons provide a powerful encouragement to stay in line with society's norms. This observation is used to help explain why American society is doing so little to combat the process of caste formation. Inasmuch as the association between employment and health coverage conjoins core American beliefs in the merit of work and the virtue of health, the possibility that unemployment can serve as a punishment for poor health and poor health can serve as punishment for unemployment is compelling indeed."[7]

In this light, systematic lack of healthcare for some is part of the societal framework, playing a role like that of enforced illiteracy in the antebellum South. People who are constantly worried about their health have less time to compete for better jobs or participate in political activities that might level the playing field in economic competition.

Some may say this is a political argument or denigrate the logic as "liberal" or use some other label. However, there is a basic economic argument for curbing waste and improving the prospects of getting all Americans covered by health insurance. The uninsured are up to four times less likely to have a regular source of healthcare. The uninsured

Chapter 17. Adding Up the Costs

tend to look for healthcare in the emergency room, the most expensive setting.

The wasted healthcare dollars delineated in this book could have insured millions of Americans who are without healthcare. "In 2020, the average national cost for health insurance is $456 for an individual and $1,152 for a family per month."[8] The $630 million for a biennium in overpayments for one therapy code, identified in the curious case of CPT 92507, could have insured 22,786 American families for two years.

In this book we have provided specific and known examples of systematic waste. They are just the tip of the iceberg. The fact that overcharging is so common, and the machinations involved in scamming the public are so well developed, might even be amusing but for the enormous financial and human cost of the broken healthcare system. Every year lack of healthcare increases the rift between haves and have-nots. The overcharging and waste constitute huge drains on our economy and economic competitiveness.

Overcharging is a problem for which there are known solutions. Pharmaceutical costs can be lowered by eliminating the "spreads" we described in Chapter 3 and removing ridiculous rules such as the "non-interference clause" that enshrine exorbitant profits. Information systems can help identify and correct overpricing, but effort is required by regulators in order to understand and utilize the available information.

The sophisticated coding and billing systems for healthcare can be used for analysis that would have prevented the overpayments of over $600 million for speech therapy in one biennium, if the administrators of the information systems had been paying better attention. As noted in the curious case of CPT 92507, information systems today are sophisticated enough to spot trends that indicate overspending and waste, but the willingness to analyze and use the data must be present.

We noted in Chapter 11 of this book that in March 2021, a publication of the Healthcare Finance Management Association stated, "If site-neutral payments were implemented throughout healthcare, the decrease in expenditures could total as much as $672 billion dollars over a decade."

We also noted in Chapter 11 that in 2011, the U.S. Department of Health and Human Services and the Office of Inspector General estimated the potential savings to state and federal Medicaid programs from third party liability to be $13.6 billion. Recovery of third party liability amounts remains a challenge a decade later.

We demonstrated how accounting trickery and lack of transparency plagues healthcare and facilitates overcharging. Improvements in accounting for healthcare pricing, especially in hospitals, can do much to make healthcare more affordable and available.

The field of dentistry grows more corporatized every year. Dental

Maintenance Organizations have created a situation where dentists are employees of venture capitalists, and they are pushed to perform unnecessary procedures in order to profit the DMOs.

We have described how seemingly un-auditable hospital costs can in fact be audited, and the costs can be contained with a more systematic approach to accounting and auditing for the healthcare industry.

The waste, fraud and abuse activities described in this book constitute only a small sample of the fraud that plagues the healthcare industry. "Three percent, or $60 billion, of all health care spending is lost to fraud. The National Health Care Anti-Fraud Association (NHCAA) conservatively estimates that 3 percent of all health care spending, or $60 billion, is lost to health care fraud. Other estimates place this number closer to $200 billion. The Federal Bureau of Investigation (FBI) has estimated fraudulent billings to health care programs, both public and private, at between 3 percent and 10 percent of total health care expenditures."[9]

The 3 percent lost to outright fraud is dwarfed by the amounts lost to waste. "Waste accounts for one-quarter of healthcare spending." One study broke down waste in the healthcare industry:

- "Failure of care delivery: $102.4 billion to $165.7 billion
- Failure of care coordination: $27.2 billion to $78.2 billion
- Overtreatment or low-value care: $75.7 billion to $101.2 billion
- Pricing failure: $230.7 billion to $240.5 billion
- Fraud and abuse: $58.5 billion to $83.9 billion
- Administrative complexity: $265.6 billion."[10]

Overcharging falls somewhere between waste and fraud. The practices are deliberate but not necessarily criminal. Also, the risk of being caught, whether for fraud or overcharging, is diluted or made nonexistent by the complexity of the system and the ability of healthcare administrators to transfer risks, thus creating moral hazard.

Profits are part of a healthy capitalist system. However, the profits that are made from healthcare often cross the line into profiteering. Every year MCOs, hospitals, and pharmaceutical companies get richer as healthcare premiums soar. As we discussed in Chapter 5, healthcare corporations charge, by increasing premiums, for not only all administrative costs, including huge salaries and bonuses for executives, but also for their "required profits."

Contracts for "cost plus a percentage of costs" were prohibited by the federal government in the mid-20th century in *Muschany et al. v. United States; Andrews et al. v. Same* (February 5, 1945) because they incentivize high costs, yet they are in effect the norm today among MCO providers in the Medicaid program, in the way that MCOs are paid. The methodologies for tracking and charging for healthcare costs are so murky that the general public and many regulators do not understand them. Transparency and a willingness to analyze costs are needed if healthcare costs are to be brought under control.

We discuss numerous examples in this book of the ways that "managed care" and MCOs fail to contain costs, and actually lead to higher costs. CMS established a new approach for conducting managed care audits beginning in 2016. However, only a few audits were ever conducted because of impediments identified by states, such as the lack of some provisions in MCO contracts. CMS did update the standards for state capitation rates for MCOs; however, overpayments to providers by MCOs are not consistently accounted for in determining future state payments to MCOs, which can result in the payments being too high.

GAO identified six types of payment risks associated with managed care, including four related to payments that state Medicaid agencies make to MCOs and two related to payments that MCOs make to providers. These two have a higher level of risk:

- Incorrect fee-for-service payments from MCOs
- Inaccurate state payments to MCOs

A 2019 review in the *Journal of the American Medical Association (JAMA)* published a study: "based on 6 previously identified domains of health care waste, the estimated cost of waste in the US health care system ranged from $760 billion to $935 billion, accounting for approximately 25% of total health care spending, and the projected potential savings from interventions that reduce waste, excluding savings from administrative complexity, ranged from $191 billion to $286 billion, representing a potential 25% reduction in the total cost of waste. Implementation of effective measures to eliminate waste represents an opportunity reduce the continued increases in US health care expenditures."[11]

As we have described in this book, methods of numerous cost-saving measures are known but often are not implemented because of political pressure and moral hazard. Measures taken to favor industry at the expense of the public, such as the "non-interference clause" protecting Medicare drug suppliers from having to negotiate prices, are kept in place by industry lobbyists and politicians who are dependent on industry campaign contributions.

The healthcare industry should not be allowed to proselytize about the benefits of free markets, and demonize governmental regulations, while systematically avoiding the basic accounting and accountability that make free markets thrive. The waste and profiteering in healthcare must be addressed in order to make Americans and their healthcare system healthy.

Chapter Notes

Chapter 1

1. Robin Marantz Henig, *A Dancing Matrix: How Science Confronts Emerging Viruses* (Vintage Books, 1994), 166.
2. ArLuther Lee, "Obama Warned of Pandemic Threat in 2014, but Republicans Blocked Funding," *Atlanta Journal-Constitution*, April 15, 2020.
3. Matthew Mosk, "George W. Bush in 2005: 'If We Wait for a Pandemic to Appear, It Will Be Too Late to Prepare,'" ABC News, April 5, 2020.
4. Walt Willet, "Public Health & the U.S. Economy," Harvard T.H. Chan School of Public Health, Fall 2012.
5. Laurie Garrett, *The Coming Plague: Newly Emerging Diseases in a World Out of Balance* (Penguin Books, 1994), 153.
6. Garrett, *The Coming Plague*, 167.
7. Garrett, *The Coming Plague*, 5.
8. Edward T. O'Donnell, *Turning Points in American History* (The Teaching Company, 2011), 4.
9. Colleen Aycock and Mark Scott, *Joe Gans: A Biography of the First African American World Boxing Champion* (McFarland, 2008), 180.
10. Aycock and Scott, *Joe Gans*, 181.
11. John M. Barry, *The Great Influenza: The Story of the Deadliest Pandemic in History* (Penguin Books, 2004), 105.
12. Richard Preston, *The Hot Zone* (Anchor Books, 1995), 15.
13. Helen Thomson, "Children with Long Covid," National Library of Medicine, March 3, 2021, doi: 10.1016/S0262-4079(21)00303-1.
14. Preston, *The Hot Zone*, 103.
15. Preston, *The Hot Zone*, 15.
16. Henig, *A Dancing Matrix*, 162.
17. Henig, *A Dancing Matrix*, 164.
18. Marisa Taylor, "Exclusive: U.S. Slashed CDC Staff Inside China Prior to Coronavirus Outbreak," Reuters, March 25, 2020.
19. Soumya Karlamangla, Anita Chabria, and Emily Baumgaertner, "Despite Promises of More Masks, Doctors and Nurses Have to Reuse N95s," *Los Angeles Times*, April 14, 2020.
20. Mark Dornauer, "Why Was America So Unprepared for the COVID-19 Pandemic?" FREOPP.org, August 5, 2020, https://freopp.org/why-was-america-so-unprepared-for-the-covid-19-pandemic-8c0602a971ec.
21. Saskia Miller, "The Secret to Germany's Covid-19 Success: Angela Merkel Is a Scientist," *The Atlantic*, April 20, 2020.
22. "40 Times Trump Said the Coronavirus Would Go Away," *The Washington Post*, November 2, 2020.
23. Eliza Relman, "Rep. Louie Gohmert Says He May Have Contracted the Coronavirus Because He Wore a Mask, Despite the Fact That He Regularly Refused to Wear Masks," *Business Insider*, July 29, 2020.
24. "Coronavirus Denier Says She Won't Wear a Mask or Underwear Because 'Things Gotta Breathe,'" Mollie Mansfield, *The U.S. Sun*, June 25, 2020.
25. Soo Kim, "Arizona Activates Emergency Plan to Ration Dwindling Healthcare Resources," *Newsweek*, July 1, 2020.
26. Sarah R. Champagne, "As Texas Morgues Fill Up, Refrigerator Trucks Are on the Way in Several Counties," *The Texas Tribune*, July 10, 2020.
27. Annalisa Boscolo, et al., "Outcomes of COVID-19 Patients Intubated

After Failure of Non-invasive Ventilation: A Multicenter Observational Study," PubMed, September 6, 2021, doi: 10.1038/s41598-021-96762-1.

28. Brian Bennett and Tessa Berenson, "'Our Big War': As Coronavirus Spreads, Trump Refashions Himself as a Wartime President," *Time* Magazine, March 19, 2020.

29. Winston Churchill, *The World Crisis* (Charles Scribner's Sons, 1927).

30. Christian Paz, "All of Trump's Lies About the Coronavirus," *The Atlantic*, July 13, 2020.

31. Paz, "All of Trump's Lies."

32. Michael Marshall "The Lasting Misery of Coronavirus Long-haulers," *Nature Journal*, September 1, 2020.

33. Wendy Dean and Simon G. Talbot, "Beyond Burnout: This Surge of Covid-19 Is Bringing Burnover," *STAT*, December 14, 2020.

34. Bob Woodward and Robert Costa, *Peril* (Simon and Schuster, 2021), 128–130.

35. Laurel Wamsley, "As U.S. Reaches 250,000 Deaths from COVID-19, a Long Winter Is Coming," NPR, November 18, 2020.

36. Steven H. Woolf, Derek A. Chapman, and Jong Hyung Lee, "COVID-19 as the Leading Cause of Death in the United States," *Journal of the American Medical Association*, December 17, 2020.

37. Heather E. Quinlan, *Plagues, Pandemics and Viruses from the Plague of Athens to COVID-19* (Visible Ink Press, 2020).

38. Quinlan, Plagues, Pandemics and Viruses.

Chapter 2

1. Kagan, Julia, "Medicaid," Investopedia, updated July 14, 2020, https://www.investopedia.com/terms/m/medicaid.asp.

2. U.S. Department of Health & Human Services, Office of the Assistant Secretary for Planning and Evaluation, "Using Medicaid to Support Working Age Adults with Serious Mental Illnesses in the Community: A Handbook. a Brief History of Medicaid," January 24, 2005.

3. U.S. Government Accountability Office, "Medicaid Managed Care. Improvements Needed to Better Oversee Payment Risks," Report to Congressional Requestors, July 2018, https://www.gao.gov/assets/700/693418.pdf.

4. Jon Coss, "Managed Care Fraud," Pondera, January 9, 2017, https://www.ponderasolutions.com/managed-care-fraud/.

5. Olivia Levada, "Texas Has the Highest Uninsured Rate in the Nation for the Second Year in a Row," KXXV.com, September 12, 2019.

6. Kristin Allen, "Texas 2020–21 Biennium Budget Overview," HealthManagement.com, June 6, 2019. https://www.healthmanagement.com/blog/texas-2020-21-biennium-budget-overview/.

7. Texas Health and Human Services Commission 2020, *Texas Medicaid and Chip Reference Guide*, 13th ed., https://hhs.texas.gov/sites/default/files/documents/laws-regulations/reports-presentations/2020/medicaid-chip-perspective-13th-edition/13th-edition-complete.pdf.

8. Robin Rudowitz, Rachel Garfield, and Elizabeth Hinton, "10 Things to Know About Medicaid: Setting the Facts Straight," Kaiser Family Foundation (kff.org), March 6, 2019.

9. Spencer Grubbs and Bruce Wright, "Uninsured Texans. Many More Lose Coverage in Pandemic," January 13, 2021, Comptroller.texas.gov/economy/fiscalnotes/2020/oct/uninsured.php.

10. Sean Price, "Texas' High Rate of Uninsured Hurting the Economy, Study Says," Texas Medical Association, January 13, 2021, https://www.texmed.org/TexasMedicineDetail.aspx?id=49562.

11. Kimberly Amadeo, "U.S. Inflation Rate by Year from 1929 to 2023," The Balance, December 14, 2022, https://www.thebalance.com/u-s-inflation-rate-history-by-year-and-forecast-3306093.

12. Texas Health and Human Services, *Frew Et Al V. Phillips Et Al*, lawsuit documents, https://hhs.texas.gov/sites/default/files/documents/laws-regulations/legal-information/feb-20-1996.pdf.

13. "U.S. Congress Looks at Medicaid Funds Spent on Texas Orthodontics," Waters Kraus, August 28, 2012, https://www.waterskraus.com/u-s-congress-looks-medicaid-funds-spent-texas-orthodontics/.

14. "Dental Chain Sued by State of Texas for Medicaid Fraud," Waters Kraus, June 29, 2012, https://www.waterskraus.com/

dental-chain-sued-state-texas-medicaid-fraud/.

15. "Xerox/Conduent Settling Its $2 Billion Dental Medicaid Fraud Case with Texas?" Texas Dentists For Medicaid Reform, February 7, 2019.

Chapter 3

1. Tom Kertscher, "20% of Health Costs Are Prescription Drugs? Presidential Candidate Amy Klobuchar's Claim Is Close," PolitiFact, February 22, 2019.
2. United States Code. Title 42. Chapter 7. Subchapter XIX. State plans for medical assistance. 42 U.S.C. 1396a (a) (30)(A) and 42 CFR § 447.
3. Andrew W. Mulcahy, et al., "Prescription Drug Prices in the United States Are 2.56 Times Those in Other Countries," Rand Corporation, January 28, 2021.
4. Matej Mikulic, "U.S. Total Medicine Spending 2002–2021," Statista, June 8, 2022.
5. Texas Department of Health, "Internal Audit," April 23, 2001.
6. Augustus Caesar's lament after hearing of the annihilation of three Roman legions at the Battle of Teutoburg Forest.
7. Robert Langreth, David Ingold, and Jackie Gu, "The Secret Drug Pricing System Middlemen Use to Rake in Millions," Bloomberg, September 11, 2018.
8. Rachel Dolan, "Understanding the Medicaid Prescription Drug Rebate Program," Kaiser Family Foundation (kff.org), November 12, 2019.
9. "How PBM Mail-Service Pharmacies Help Patients, The Value of PBMs" Stitcher.com, October 10, 2021.
10. United States Code. Title 42. Chapter 7. Subchapter XI. Part A. Criminal penalties for acts involving federal health care programs. 42 U.S.C. § 1320a-7b
11. Exceptions to criminal penalties to United States Code. Title 42. 42 C.F.R. § 1001.952(h).
12. "Drug Rebates Impact Rising Prescription Drug Spending and Continue to Increase for High Cost Drugs Like Brand and Specialty," Center for Improving Value in Health Care, August 13, 2021.
13. David Belk and Paul Belk, *The Great American Healthcare Scam: How Kickbacks, Collusion and Propaganda Have Exploded Healthcare Costs in the United States*, (Self-published, 2020), 224.
14. Steven M. Lieberman, Paul B. Ginsburg, and Erin Trish, "Sharing Drug Rebates with Medicare Part D Patients: Why and How," Health Affairs, September 14, 2020.
15. Larry Husten, "Drug Ads: Why Consumers Tune Out the Side Effect List—Long Recitation Actually Dilutes Perception of Risk," CardioBrief, October 11, 2017.
16. Husten, "Drug Ads."
17. Husten, "Drug Ads."
18. "Do Not Get Sold on Drug Advertising," Harvard Health Publishing, Harvard Medical School, February 14, 2017.
19. Jeffrey K. Aronson and A. Richard Green, "Me-too Pharmaceutical Products: History, Definitions, Examples, and Relevance to Drug Shortages and Essential Medicines Lists," *British Journal of Clinical Pharmacology* 86(6) (May 2020), DOI:10.1111/bcp.14327.
20. John LaMattina, "Impact of 'Me-Too' Drugs on Health Care Costs," Forbes.com, January 19, 2015.
21. Marcia Angell, *The Truth About the Drug Companies: How They Deceive Us and What to Do About It* (Random House, 2005), 75.
22. Angell, *The Truth About Drug Companies*, 75.
23. Robert Yoho, *Butchered by "Healthcare"* (Self-published, 2020), 48.
24. Juliette Cubanski, Tricia Neuman, and Meredith Freed, "What's the Latest on Medicare Drug Price Negotiations?" Kaiser Family Foundation (kff.org), July 23, 2021.
25. Gerald Posner, *Pharma: Greed, Lies, and the Poisoning of America* (Avid Reader Press, 2020), 495.
26. House Committee on Oversight and Reform, "Cummings and Welch Propose Medicare Drug Negotiation Bill in Meeting with President," press release, March 8, 2017.

Chapter 4

1. Ken Gross, *Ross Perot: The Man Behind the Myth* (Random House 1992), 74.
2. Gross, *Ross Perot*, 75.
3. Gross, *Ross Perot*, 76.

4. WH6404.12 Tape 3125. Lyndon B. Johnson Tapes
5. Steve Anderson, "A Brief History of Medicare in America," Medicareresources.org.
6. LinkedIn, Electronic Data Systems company profile.
7. Social Security Amendments of 1965, 42 U.S.C. §§ 1396 et seq.
8. Terri Langford, "The HHSC-21CT Contract Investigations: How Did It Get to This Point?" *The Texas Tribune*, February 5, 2015.
9. Texas Government Code Section 2261.256.
10. U.S. Government Accountability Office, "Medicaid Information Technology: Effective CMS Oversight and States' Sharing of Claims Processing and Information Retrieval Systems Can Reduce Costs," GAO-20-179, September 9, 2020.
11. "Medicaid Management Information System," Medicaid.gov.

Chapter 5

1. "Medicaid Margin Assumptions—Opening the Black Box," Society of Actuaries, Session #091, June 25, 2019.
2. Adam Hayes, "Cost of Capital," Investopedia, updated June 13, 2022.
3. Beatrix Hoffman, *Health Care for Some: Rights and Rationing in the United States Since 1930* (University of Chicago Press, 2013), xiii.
4. "Weighted Average Cost of Capital (WACC) for Grocery Outlet Holding Corp; GO Grocery Outlet Holding Corp Price: $27.76 USD Avg. Volume: 1,103,490. United States." Food & Staples Retailing, November 17, 2021.
5. Jeff Campbell, "Is Owning a Grocery Store Profitable?" *The Grocery Store Guy*, November 13, 2021.
6. "Energy Valuations Insight," August 2, 2016, PV-X: WACCs for E&P Companies
7. "Centene Market Cap 2006–2021 | CNC," Macrotrends, November 14, 2021.
8. U.S. Government Accountability Office, "Medicare: Changes to HMO Rate Setting Method Are Needed to Reduce Program Costs," HEHS 94-119, September 2, 1994, 2.
9. U.S. Government Accountability Office, "Medicaid: Methods for Setting Nursing Home Rates Should Be Improved," HRD 86-26, 3.
10. Medicaid and CHIP Payment and Access Commission, "Provider Payment Under Fee for Service," MACPAC website.
11. Medicaid and CHIP Payment and Access Commission, "Factors Affecting the Development of Medicaid Hospital Payment Policies," MACPAC website.
12. Medicaid and CHIP Payment and Access Commission, "Provider Payment Under Fee for Service," MACPAC website.
13. Medicaid and CHIP Payment and Access Commission, "Managed Care Rate Setting," MACPAC website.
14. Texas State Auditor's Office Report, report number 18-015, January 2018.
15. Christine Vestal, "Managed Care Explained: Why a Medicaid Innovation Is Spreading," PEW Stateline, May 31, 2011.
16. Andy Schneider and Allie Corcoran, "Medicaid Managed Care: 2020 Results for the 'Big Five,'" Georgetown University Health Policy Institute Center for Children and Families, February 23, 2021.

Chapter 6

1. June 2, 2014 letter to Mr. Bill Brooks, Associate Regional Director, Centers for Medicare and Medicaid Services, published in the *Austin American-Statesman*, December 2014.
2. UCLA Department of Epidemiology. "Introduction to Applied Epidemiology and Biostatistics." *Old News* 16(8), 8–10 May & June 2005. cdc.gov/csels/dsepd/ss1978/lesson1/section2.html.
3. "Health Insurance Coverage of the Total Population: Medicaid in Texas Oct 2019." Henry J. Kaiser Family Foundation. https://www.kff.org/other/state-indicator/total-population/?dataView=0&currentTimeframe=1&selectedDistributions=medicaid&selectedRows=%7B%22states%22:%7B%22texas%22:%7B%7D%7D%7D&sortModel=%7B%22colId%22:%22Location%22,%22sort%22:%22asc%22%7D. Accessed March 23, 2023.
4. Kaiser Family Foundation, "Medicaid in Texas," fact sheet, https://files.kff.org/attachment/fact-sheet-medicaid-state-TX.
5. Kaiser Family Foundation, "Medicaid

Expenditures as a Percent of Total State Expenditures by Fund," SFY 2019, https://www.kff.org/medicaid/state-indicator/medicaid-expenditures-as-a-percent-of-total-state-expenditures-by-fund/.

6. Texas Health and Human Services Commission, Office of Inspector General, "Texas Medicaid Speech Therapy, Informational Report on Payment Trends and Service Delivery," IG Report No. IG-17–00, February 28, 2017, 10.

7. Centers for Medicare & Medicaid Services, "Billing and Coding: Speech Language Pathology (SLP) Services: Communication Disorders," https://www.cms.gov/medicare-coverage-database/view/article.aspx?articleID=54111.

8. Texas Medicaid & Healthcare Partnership, "TPI Number Removed from Medicaid Prior Authorization Forms, Instructions, and Consent Forms: Transition Period Ending November 30, 2021," TMHP.com, November 12, 2021, https://www.tmhp.com/news/2021-09-01-tpi-number-removed-medicaid-prior-authorization-forms-instructions-and-consent.

9. Centers for Medicare & Medicaid Services, "HCPCS Coding Questions," cms.gov/Medicare/Coding/MedHCPCSGenInfo/HCPCS_Coding_Questions.

10. Medicare Learning Network, "How to Use the Medicare National Correct Coding Initiative (NCCI) Tools," January 2021, https://www.cms.gov/outreach-and-education/medicare-learning-network-mln/mlnproducts/downloads/how-to-use-ncci-tools.pdf.

11. U.S. Attorney's Office Northern District of Texas, "Fort Worth Man Arrested on $25 Million Health Care Fraud Scheme," press release, October 13, 2017.

12. June 2, 2014, letter to Mr. Bill Brooks, Associate Regional Director, Centers for Medicare and Medicaid Services, published in the Austin American-Statesman, December 2014.

Chapter 7

1. David Vachon, "Part One. Doctor John Snow Blames Water Pollution for Cholera Epidemic," UCLA Department of Epidemiology, *Old News* 16(8), 8–10 May & June 2005.

2. October 3, 2017 letter from CMS to Texas Medicaid Director. Source is from the attachment to the letter. https://www.hhs.texas.gov/sites/default/files/documents/services/health/medicaid-chip/state-plan/spa-17-0018-non-emer-med-transport.pdf Accessed March 23, 2023.

3. In 2015, the Texas Legislature directed HHSC to adjust these rates to be consistent with industry standards, policies, and utilization for acute care therapy services while considering stakeholder input and access to care and that in SFY 2016 and SFY 2017 at least $50 million in General Revenue Funds savings should be achieved each fiscal year through rate reductions. See 2016–2017 General Appropriations Act (House Bill 1, 84th Leg. R.S., art. II, Ride 50, at 11–96 to 11–98 (Health and Human Services section, Health and Human Services)), Page 4 of Attachment 1.

4. Texas Medicaid Speech Therapy, "Informal Report of Payment Trends and Service Delivery." IG Report No. IG-17–010

5. CPT codes, including CPT 92507, are copyrighted by the American Medical Association.

6. Adam Graham, "How Much Does It Cost to Build a Hospital?" https://www.fixr.com/costs/build-hospital.

7. State Plans for Medical Assistance. Section 1902 of the Social Security Act(a)(30) (A). https://www.ssa.gov/OP_Home/ssact/title19/1902.htm. Accessed March 23, 2023.

8. June 2, 2014 letter to Mr. Bill Brooks, Associate Regional Director, Centers for Medicare and Medicaid Services, published in the *Austin American-Statesman*, December 2014. Texas State Medicaid Director Letter, SMDL 13–003.

9. Partial Settlement Agreement, *Alberto N. Et Al V. Dona a Gilbert Et Al.*, 5 and 6.

10. June 2, 2014 letter to Mr. Bill Brooks, Associate Regional Director, Centers for Medicare and Medicaid Services, published in the *Austin American-Statesman*, December 2014. State Medicaid Director Letter, SMDL 13–003.

11. Section 6. Claims Filing Section of the Texas Provider and Procedures Manual. Volume 1. November 2015.

12. Blue Cross and Blue Shield of Texas, "Proper Speech Therapy Billing," https://www.bcbstx.com/provider/claims/claims-eligibility/submit/speech-therapy-billing.
13. October 3, 2017 letter from CMS to Texas Medicaid Director. Source is from the attachment to the letter. https://www.hhs.texas.gov/sites/default/files/documents/services/health/medicaid-chip/state-plan/spa-17-0018-non-emer-med-transport.pdf Accessed March 23, 2023.
14. American Speech-Language-Hearing Association, "Calculating Medicare Fee Schedule Rates," https://www.asha.org/Practice/reimbursement/medicare/Calculating-Medicare-Fee-Schedule-Rates/.

Chapter 8

1. State Plans for Medical Assistance. Section 1902 of the Social Security Act(a)(30) (A). https://www.ssa.gov/OP_Home/ssact/title19/1902.htm. Accessed March 23, 2023.
2. "Health Insurance Coverage of the Total Population: Medicaid in Texas Oct 2019." Henry J. Kaiser Family Foundation. https://www.kff.org/other/state-indicator/total-population/?dataView=0&currentTimeframe=1&selectedDistributions=medicaid&selectedRows=%7B%22states%22:%7B%22texas%22:%7B%7D%7D%7D&sortModel=%7B%22colId%22:%22Location%22,%22sort%22:%22asc%22%7D. Accessed March 23, 2023.
3. June 2, 2014 letter to Mr. Bill Brooks, Associate Regional Director, Centers for Medicare and Medicaid Services, published in the Austin American-Statesman, December 2014.
4. June 2, 2014 letter to Mr. Bill Brooks, Associate Regional Director, Centers for Medicare and Medicaid Services, published in the Austin American-Statesman, December 2014.
5. June 2, 2014 letter to Mr. Bill Brooks, Associate Regional Director, Centers for Medicare and Medicaid Services, published in the Austin American-Statesman, December 2014.
6. Texas Medicaid Children Services Handbook, Volume 2.
7. Texas Medicaid Provider Enrollment Application. 2016
8. HHSC Chief Counsel Letter. Dated July 19, 2012.
9. Review of Texas Medicaid Acute Care Therapy Programs. Interim Report. Research Questions 1-4. Texas A&M University. February 2015.
10. Attachment 1 to Attachment to Block 7 of CMS Form 179 incorporating results from HHSC Strategic Decision Support, April 9, 2015.
11. Texas Medicaid Provider Enrollment Application. 2016
12. Nick Hut, "Site-neutral Payments Could Reduce Healthcare Spending by at Least $350 Billion Over 10 Years, Report Finds," Healthcare Financial Management Association, March 22, 2021.
13. Katherine Drabiak and Jay Wolfston, "What Should Health Care Organizations Do to Reduce Billing Fraud and Abuse?" *AMA Journal of Ethics*, March 2020.

Chapter 9

1. Kaiser Family Foundation, "Medicaid MCO Enrollment by Plan and Parent Firm, 2019," State Health Facts.
2. Texas Health and Human Services Commission 2020, *Texas Medicaid and Chip Reference Guide*, 13th ed., https://hhs.texas.gov/sites/default/files/documents/laws-regulations/reports-presentations/2020/medicaid-chip-perspective-13th-edition/13th-edition-complete.pdf.
3. October 3, 2017 letter from CMS to Texas Medicaid Director. Source is from the attachment to the letter. pp. 11-12. https://www.hhs.texas.gov/sites/default/files/documents/services/health/medicaid-chip/state-plan/spa-17-0018-non-emer-med-transport.pdf Accessed March 23, 2023.
4. October 3, 2017 letter from CMS to Texas Medicaid Director. Source is from the attachment to the letter. pp 11-12. https://www.hhs.texas.gov/sites/default/files/documents/services/health/medicaid-chip/state-plan/spa-17-0018-non-emer-med-transport.pdf. Accessed March 23, 2023.
5. Texas Office of Inspector General (TX OIG) Report No. INS-16-002.

6. Edgar Walters, "Court Tosses Lawsuit Over Medicaid Cuts to Therapy Services," *Texas Tribune*, April 21, 2016, https://www.texastribune.org/2016/04/21/court-tosses-lawsuit-over-medicaid-cuts-therapy/.

7. "Informal Report of Payment Trends and Service Delivery," Office of Inspector General, Texas Health and Human Services Commission. Texas Medicaid Speech Therapy. IG Report No. IG-17-010. February 28, 2017, p. 12.

8. Texas Medicaid and CHIP Uniform Managed Care Manual. Chapter 1. November 2015. Version 2.1.

9. "Acute Care Services" include physician, inpatient, outpatient, pharmacy, lab, and X-ray services.

10. "Long-term Services and Supports" include home and community-based services, nursing facility services, and services provided in intermediate care facilities for individuals with an intellectual disability or related conditions.

11. Until August 31, 2016, Medicaid LTSS providers billed for services delivered to Medicaid recipients in FFS programs through the Texas Department of Aging and Disability Services (DADS) Claims Management System. Effective September 1, 2016, responsibility of LTSS programs was transferred to HHSC by legislative mandate.

12. "Capitation Payments" are monthly prospective payments HHSC makes to MCOs for the provision of covered services. HHSC makes capitation payments to MCOs at fixed per-member, per-month rates based on members' associated risk groups. These capitation payments include federal and state funds and both medical and pharmacy payments.

13. MCOs refer to enrollees as "members." An "enrollee" is an individual who is eligible for Medicaid or CHIP services and is enrolled in an MCO either as a subscriber or as a dependent.

14. Medicaid, "Home & Community-Based Services 1915(c)," https://www.medicaid.gov/medicaid/hcbs/authorities/1915-c/index.html

15. Social Security, "Part E—Miscellaneous Provisions," https://www.ssa.gov/OP_Home/ssact/title18/1861.htm

16. Texas Medicaid Provider Procedures Manual. Volumes 1 and 2. December 2018. Page vi. https://www.tmhp.com/sites/default/files/file-library/resources/provider-manuals/tmppm/archives/2018-12-TMPPM.pdf. Accessed March 23, 2023.

17. Texas Medicaid Provider Procedures Manual. Volumes 1 and 2. March 2023. Section 1.1. https://www.tmhp.com/sites/default/files/file-library/resources/provider-manuals/tmppm/archives/2023-03-TMPPM.pdf Accessed March 23, 2023.

18. Texas Medicaid Provider Procedures Manual. Volume 2. Physical Therapy, Occupational Therapy, and Speech Therapy Services Handbook. January 2021. Section 5. https://www.tmhp.com/sites/default/files/file-library/resources/provider-manuals/tmppm/pdf-chapters/2021/2021-01-jan/2_PT_OT_ST_Srvs.pdf. Accessed March 23, 2023.

19. American Speech-Language-Hearing Association, "Code of Ethics," March 1, 2016, https://www.asha.org/code-of-ethics/

20. Texas Speech-Language-Hearing Association, "Code of Ethics," http://www.txsha.org/code_of_ethics.

21. Texas Health and Human Services Commission Inspector General, "Speech Therapy Inspection. Managed Care Organization Controls for Prior Authorization, Medical Necessity Determination, and Utilization Processes." October 2, 2017. IG Report No. INS-12-002. Page 4. https://oig.hhs.texas.gov/sites/default/files/documents/reports/IG-Inspections-Division-Report-Speech-Therapy_10092017.pdf.

22. American Speech Language and Hearing Association. "Documentation in Healthcare." https://www.asha.org/practice-portal/professional-issues/documentation-in-health-care/ Accessed March 23, 2023.

23. Centers for Medicare & Medicaid Services, "Physical, Occupational, and Speech Therapy Services," PowerPoint presentation, slide 7, September 5, 2012, https://www.cms.gov/Research-Statistics-Data-and-Systems/Monitoring-Programs/Medical-Review/Downloads/TherapyCapSlidesv10_09052012.pdf.

24. Partial Settlement Agreement, https://www.hhs.texas.gov/sites/default/files/documents/laws-regulations/legal-information/alberto-n-settlement-agreement.pdf

Chapter 10

1. Shao-Chee Sim, et al., "Building Community-Oriented Medicaid Managed Care in Texas and Beyond," Health Affairs Forefront, January 11, 2022.
2. Jack Charles Shoenholtz, *The Managed Health Care Industry: A Market Failure* (Self-published, CreateSpace, 2012), xvii.
3. 2018 Texas State Auditor's Office Report, 18-015.
4. 2018 Texas State Auditor's Office Report, 18-015.
5. GAO Report (18-528). July 2018.
6. Robert S. Kaplan and Michael E. Porter "The Big Idea: How to Solve the Cost Crisis in Health Care," *Harvard Business Review*, September 2011.
7. "2020 Estimated Improper Payment Rates for Centers for Medicare & Medicaid Services (CMS) Programs," November 16, 2020, https://www.cms.gov/newsroom/fact-sheets/2020-estimated-improper-payment-rates-centers-medicare-medicaid-services-cms-programs.
8. "2020 Estimated Improper Payment Rates."
9. "2020 Estimated Improper Payment Rates."

Chapter 11

1. Hut, "Site-neutral Payments Could Reduce Healthcare Spending."
2. "Blue Cross Blue Shield Home Health Criteria." https://www.bcbstx.com/docs/provider/tx/network/credentialing/home-health-cred-checklist.pdf Accessed March 23, 2023.

Chapter 12

1. "Health Care Cost Shift," Rocky Mountain Health Plans, https://www.rmhp.org/blog/2012/june/who-pays-the-bill-cost-shifting-from-the-public-to-the-private-sector
2. Mark Green, "'Cost Shifting' Is a Major Contributor to the Healthcare Crisis Today," *The Tennessee Star*, October 16, 2018.
3. Wendell Potter, "The Enduring Myth of Cost Shifting," The Center For Public Integrity, March 30, 2015, https://publicintegrity.org/health/the-enduring-myth-of-cost-shifting/.
4. Potter, "The Enduring Myth of Cost Shifting."
5. Potter, "The Enduring Myth of Cost Shifting."
6. Potter, "The Enduring Myth of Cost Shifting."
7. Sherry Glied, "Covid-19 Overturned the Theory of Medical Cost Shifting by Hospitals," JAMA Forum, June 24, 2021.
8. Glied, "Covid-19 Overturned the Theory of Medical Cost Shifting by Hospitals."

Chapter 13

1. Centers for Medicare & Medicaid Services, "Dental Services Increased—National Expenditures 2019 Highlights," https://www.cms.gov/newsroom/press-releases/cms-office-actuary-releases-2019-national-health-expenditures:
2. "The Challenge of Health Care Fraud." National Health Care Anti-Fraud Association. https://www.nhcaa.org/tools-insights/about-health-care-fraud/the-challenge-of-health-care-fraud/ Accessed March 23, 2023.
3. Daryl Austin, "Why Your Dentist Might Seem Pushy," Kaiser Health News, May 19, 2021.
4. U.S. Department of Health and Human Services. Office of Inspector General. https://oig.hhs.gov/fraud/enforcement/court-awards-165-million-to-texans-in-medicaid-fraud-lawsuit/. August 11, 2020. Accessed March 23, 2023.
5. Supreme Court of the United States. Frew, on behalf of her daughter, Frew et al. v. Hawkins, Commissioner, Texas Health and Human Services Commission et al. 540 US 431 No. 02628 (January 24, 2003) Argued October 7, 2003. https://www.law.cornell.edu/supremecourt/text/540/431. Accessed March 23, 2023.
6. Texas Health and Human Services Commission, Inspector General, "Dental Service Organizations Informational Report," OIG Report No. AUD-17-013, May 31, 2017, 26.
7. "Oral Health: The Silent Epidemic." Public Health Rep 2010 March-April; 125(2): 158-159; PMCID: PMC2821841, National Library of Medicine.

8. "12-year-old Deamonte Driver Dies." Child Watch Column. March 4, 2011.
9. Mary Otto, *Teeth: The Story of Beauty, Inequality, and the Struggle for Oral Health in America* (The New Press, 2017).
10. Congressional Round—Senate Volume 160. March 14, 2014.
11. Mary Otto, *Teeth: The Story of Beauty, Inequality, and the Struggle for Oral Health in America* (The New Press, 2017), 217.
12. Otto, *Teeth*, 218.
13. Ellyn Sternfield. "Texas: A Cautionary Tale for Medicaid Management and Managed Care Organizations." Published July 8, 2018. https://www.mintz.com/insights-center/viewpoints/2018-07-08-texas-cautionary-tale-medicaid-management-and-managed-care. Accessed March 21, 2021.
14. "All Smiles Dental Centers Turning Away Young Medicaid Patients, Closing Clinics." *The Dallas Morning News*. July 26, 2012.
15. Jim Moriarty and Charles S. Siegel, "Unethical Private-Equity-Owned Dental Clinics Receive Well Deserved Attention." Waterskraus.com, July 9, 2012.
16. Staffs of Senators Chuck Grassley and Max Baucus, "Joint Staff Report on the Corporate Practice of Dentistry in the Medicaid Program," U.S. Senate Committee on Finance, June 2013.
17. David Heath, Mark Greenblatt, and Aysha Bagchi. "Dentists Under Pressure to Drill 'Healthy Teeth' for Profit, Former Insiders Allege." *USA Today*, March 19, 2020.
18. Heath, Greenblatt, and Bagchi. "Dentists Under Pressure."
19. Mary Otto, "New Fla. Case Alleges Medicaid Dental Fraud Targeting Frail, Elderly." Association of Health Care Journalists, September 17, 2015, https://healthjournalism.org/blog/2015/09/new-fla-case-alleges-medicaid-dental-fraud-targeting-frail-elderly/.
20. Andrew Kragie, "Houston Dentist Indicted on Charges of Causing 4-year-old's Brain Damage." *Houston Chronicle*, July 24, 2017.
21. Brooks Egerton, "Junior's Story: Drugged to Death, in a Dallas Dental Chair." *Dallas Morning News*, December 9, 2015.
22. Egerton, "Junior's Story."
23. Egerton, "Junior's Story."
24. Mary Otto, "Texas Child's Death During Dental Surgery Reawakens 'Deadly Dentistry' Debate." Association of Health Care Journalists, July 29, 2016, https://healthjournalism.org/blog/2016/07/texas-childs-death-during-dental-surgery-reawakens-deadly-dentistry-debate/.
25. Moriarty and Siegel, "Unethical Private-Equity-Owned Dental Clinics."
26. Moriarty and Siegel, "Unethical Private-Equity-Owned Dental Clinics."
27. Moriarty and Siegel, "Unethical Private-Equity-Owned Dental Clinics."
28. Moriarty and Siegel, "Unethical Private-Equity-Owned Dental Clinics."
29. David, Michael W. "Kool Smiles Dental Quietly Changes the Names of Its Clinics." Dentistry Today. May 6, 2019. https://www.dentistrytoday.com/kool-smiles-dental-quietly-changes-the-names-of-its-clinics/ Accessed March 21, 2021.
30. Baum Hedlund Aristei & Goldman PC, "Kool Smiles Fraud Allegations Result in $24 Million Settlement." Baum Hedlund Law, January 16, 2018.
31. Michael W. David, "Kool Smiles Dental Quietly Changes the Names of Its Clinics." *Dentistry Today*, May 6, 2019.
32. Kendra E. Pannitti and Theresa M. DiGuglielmo, "Fraudulent Pediatric Dentistry Claims Result in $3.1 Million Settlement." Frier Levitt website, June 15, 2021.
33. Pannitti and DiGuglielmo, "Fraudulent Pediatric Dentistry Claims."

Chapter 14

1. Bill Fay, "Hospital and Surgery Costs." October 12, 2021. https://www.debt.org/medical/hospital-surgery-costs/. Accessed March 23, 2023.
2. Steven Brill, "The U.S. Healthcare System Is Not a Free Market," *Time*, March 4, 2013, 54.
3. "Average Cost of Hospital Care Cost for Covid Treatment Ranges from $51,000 to $78,000 based on age," Healthcare Finance News, November 5, 2020. https://www.healthcarefinancenews.com/news/average-cost-hospital-care-covid-19-ranges-51000-78000-based-age. Accessed October 17, 2021.
4. "Income percentile calculator for the

United States." Don't Quit Your Day Job. https://dqydj.com/income-percentile-calculator/ Accessed March 24, 2021.

5. "Unemployment Rises in 2020, as the Country Battles the COVID-19 Pandemic," U.S. Bureau of Labor Statistics, Monthly Labor Review, June 2021.

6. Jennifer Tolbert, Kendal Orgera, and Anthony Damico, "What Does the CPS Tell Us About Health Insurance Coverage in 2020?" Kaiser Family Foundation website, September 23, 2021.

7. Christo Petrov, "25+ Medical Bankruptcy Statistics to Know in 2021." SpendMeNot (blog), May 17, 2022.

8. Belk and Belk, *The Great American Healthcare Scam*, 67.

9. Belk and Belk, *The Great American Healthcare Scam*, 62.

10. Eric Lopez et al. "Comparing Private Payer and Medicare Payment Rates for Select Inpatient Hospital Services." Kaiser Family Foundation. Published July 7, 2020. https://www.kff.org/medicare/issue-brief/comparing-private-payer-and-medicare-payment-rates-for-select-inpatient-hospital-services/. Accessed March 25, 2021.

11. Lauren Gelman, "10 Wildly Overinflated Hospital Costs You Didn't Know About," The Healthy, updated March 30, 2022, https://www.thehealthy.com/healthcare/health-insurance/wildly-overinflated-hospital-costs/.

12. Eric Lopez, et al., "Comparing Private Payer and Medicare Payment Rates for Select Inpatient Hospital Services," Kaiser Family Foundation, July 7, 2020.

13. Elisabeth Rosenthal, *An American Sickness: How Healthcare Became Big Business and How You Can Take It Back* (Penguin Books, 2017), 38.

14. Rosenthal, *An American Sickness*, 39.

15. Rosenthal, *An American Sickness*, 39.

16. David Dranove and Lawton R. Burns, *Big Med: Megaproviders and the High Cost of Health Care in America* (University of Chicago Press, 2021), 8.

17. Belk and Belk, *The Great American Healthcare Scam*, 54.

18. T. R. Reid, *The Healing of America: A Global Quest for Better, Cheaper and Fairer Healthcare* (Penguin Books, 2010), 113.

19. Shannon Brownlee, *Overtreated: Why Too Much Medicine Is Making Us Sicker and Poorer* (Bloomsbury, 2007), 83.

20. Yoho, *Butchered by "Healthcare,"* 287.

21. William E. Ackerman, *Health Care Fraud: A Prescription for Disaster* (Self-published, CreateSpace, 2017), 33.

22. Dranove and Burns, *Big Med*.

23. Uwe E. Reinhardt, *Priced Out: The Economic and Ethical Costs of American Health Care* (Princeton University Press, 2019), 20.

24. Elisabeth Rosenthal, "Analysis: How Your Beloved Hospital Helps to Drive Up Health Care Costs," Kaiser Health News, September 5, 2019.

25. Steven Brill, *America's Bitter Pill: Money, Politics, Backroom Deals, and the Fight to Fix Our Broken Healthcare System* (Random House, Kindle Edition), 428.

26. Brill, *America's Bitter Pill*, 8.

27. Brill, *America's Bitter Pill*.

28. Brill, *America's Bitter Pill*.

29. Brill, *America's Bitter Pill*, 34–36.

30. Brill, *America's Bitter Pill*, 34–36.

31. CMS, "Hospital Transparency." https://www.cms.gov/outreach-and-educationoutreachffsprovpartprogproviderpartnership-email-archive/2020-12-18-mlnc-se. Accessed March 23, 2023.

32. "New Detailed Report Shows Only 5.6% of Hospitals Examined Are Compliant with Hospital Price Transparency Rule," Patient Rights Advocate, July 16, 2021.

33. New Detailed Report Shows only 5.6% of Hospitals."

34. David Lazarus, "Leaked SoCal Hospital Records Reveal Huge, Automated Markups for Healthcare," *Los Angeles Times*, December 10, 2021.

Chapter 15

1. Ackerman, *Health Care Fraud*, p. 279

2. "Dr. Spyros Panos: How Did One Surgeon Cause So Much Harm?" Medical Malpractice Lawyers, September 27, 2013.

3. Ryan Santistevan, "Spyros Panos: Ex-Surgeon Admits to Health Care and Wire Fraud, Identity Theft," *Poughkeepsie Journal*, October 30, 2020.

4. Santistevan, "Spyros Panos: Ex-Surgeon Admits."

5. Santistevan, "Spyros Panos: Ex-Surgeon Admits."
6. Fred Schulte and Elizabeth Lucas "Device Makers Have Funneled Billions to Orthopedic Surgeons Who Use Their Products," Kaiser Health News, June 17, 2021.
7. Schulte and Lucas, "Device Makers Have Funneled Billions."
8. Schulte and Lucas, "Device Makers Have Funneled Billions."
9. Schulte and Lucas, "Device Makers Have Funneled Billions."
10. U.S. Attorney's Office, Central District of California, "Orthopedic Surgeon Sentenced to 2½ Years in Federal Prison for Receiving Kickbacks in Massive Healthcare Fraud," press release, November 22, 2019.
11. Azi Paybarah, "Virginia Doctor Gets 59 Years for Unneeded Surgery and Improper Sterilizations," *New York Times*, May 18, 2021.
12. Arthur W. Curtis, "Endoscopic Sinus Surgery: A Tale of Overuse," Right Care Alliance, February 2022.
13. Curtis, "Endoscopic Sinus Surgery."
14. Curtis, "Endoscopic Sinus Surgery."
15. Curtis, "Endoscopic Sinus Surgery."
16. Cheryl Clark, "Report: Worst Hospitals for Unnecessary Procedures," MedPage Today, May 12, 2021.
17. Clark, "Report: Worst Hospitals."
18. Susan Perry, "U.S. Physicians Say Up to 30 Percent of Medical Services Are Unnecessary," MinnPost, September 12, 2017
19. Perry, "U.S. Physicians Say Up to 30 Percent."
20. Perry, "U.S. Physicians Say Up to 30 Percent."
21. Julie Rovner, "Study: Malpractice Costs Just a Tiny Fraction of Health Spending," NPR News, September 7, 2010.
22. Chad Terhune, "Top Republicans Say There's a Medical Malpractice Crisis. Experts Say There Isn't," Kaiser Health News, *Washington Post*, December 30, 2016.
23. Terhune, "Top Republicans Say There's a Medical Malpractice Crisis."
24. Chad Terhune, "Needless Medical Tests Not Only Cost $200 Billion, They Can Do Harm," Kaiser Health News, CNN Money, May 20, 2017.

Chapter 16

1. Florida Department of Health. Oral Communication. September 2019.
2. Drabiak and Wolfson, "What Should Health Care Organizations Do to Reduce Billing Fraud and Abuse?"
3. Centers for Medicare and Medicaid Services, "CMS Office of the Actuary Releases 2016 National Health Expenditures," press release, December 6, 2017.
4. John S. Darden, "Health Care Fraud: Criminal Prosecution Necessary but Not Sufficient," *The Hill*, September 20, 2016.
5. U.S. Department of Health and Human Services, Office of Inspector General, "A Roadmap for New Physicians," https://oig.hhs.gov/compliance/physician-education/.
6. Drabiak and Wolfson, "What Should Health Care Organizations Do to Reduce Billing Fraud and Abuse?"
7. "How to Avoid Stark Law and Anti-Kickback Statute Penalties," Symplr, January 28, 2022.
8. Elizabeth Richardson, "The Physician Payments Sunshine Act," HealthAffairs.org, October 2, 2014.
9. Drabiak and Wolfson, "What Should Health Care Organizations Do to Reduce Billing Fraud and Abuse?"
10. Hut, "Site-neutral Payments Could Reduce Healthcare Spending."

Chapter 17

1. David Cecere, "New Study Finds 45,000 Deaths Annually Linked to Lack of Health Coverage," *The Harvard Gazette*, September 17, 2009.
2. "Decrease in U.S. health insurance coverage led to 25,180 deaths," Open Access Government, October 29, 2020.
3. Cecere, "New Study Finds 45,000 Deaths."
4. Jennifer Tolbert, Kendal Orgera, and Anthony Damico, "Key Facts About the Uninsured Population," Kaiser Family Foundation (kff.org), November 6, 2020.
5. Bernard Mandeville, *The Fable of the Bees, or Private Vices, Publick Benefits* (1806), 1.
6. Voltaire, *Candide* (1759), 88.
7. Susan Starr Sered and Rushika Fernandopulle, *Uninsured in America: Life*

and Death in the Land of Opportunity (University of California Press, 2007), 165.

8. Anna Porretta, "How Much Does Individual Health Insurance Cost?" eHealthInsurance, updated on November 05, 2021.

9. Darden, "Health Care Fraud: Criminal Prosecution Necessary but Not Sufficient."

10. Dagny Taggart, "The U.S. Healthcare System Is Hemorrhaging: It Is Bleeding Close to $1 TRILLION a Year," NexusNewsfeed.com, October 16, 2019.

11. Christopher Cheney, "Wasteful Spending in U.S. Healthcare Estimated at $760 Billion to $935 Billion," HealthLeaders.com, October 7, 2019.

Bibliography

Alexander, Brian. *The Hospital: Life, Death and Dollars in a Small American Town.* St. Martin's Press, 2021.
Angell, Marcia. *The Truth About the Drug Companies: How They Deceive Us and What to Do About It.* Random House, 2005.
Ashton, Jerry, Robert E. Goff, and Craig Antico. *End Medical Debt: Curing America's Healthcare Crisis.* Hoku House, 2021.
Barr, Donald A. *Health Disparities in the United States: Social Class, Race, Ethnicity, and the Social Determinants of Health.* John S. Hopkins University Press, 2019.
Bezalel, A. *The True Cost of Healthcare Today: A View from Behind the Curtain in a Massachusetts Hospital.* Self-published, 2019.
Bragg, Stephen N. *Healthcare Accounting.* Publisher Accounting Tools, 2017.
Brownlee, Shannon. *Overtreated: Why Too Much Medicine Is Making Us Sicker and Poorer.* Bloomsbury USA, 2010.
Day, Philip. *Health Wars.* Credence Publications, 2002.
Dixon, Marlene, and Thomas Bodenheimer, eds. *Health Care in Crisis: Essays on Health Services Under Capitalism.* Synthesis Publications. 1980.
Finkler, Stephen A., and Thad D. Calabrese and David M. Ward. *Accounting Fundamentals for Health Care Management.* Jones & Bartlett Learning, 2019.
Geyman, John, MD. *Profiteering, Corruption and Fraud in U.S. Health Care.* Copernicus Healthcare, 2020.
Goff, Robert E., and Jerry Ashton. *The Patient, the Doctor and the Bill Collector: A Medical Debt Survival Guide.* Hoku House, 2016.
Grelsamer, Ronald P. *A Patient's Guide to Unnecessary Knee Surgery: How to Avoid the Pitfalls of Hasty Medical Advice.* Skyhorse Publishing, 2017.
Hoerig, Barry G. *Affordable Medicare for All: American Health Care Is the Problem and Medicare for All Americans Is the Solution.* Archway Publishing, 2021.
Hoffman, Beatrix. *Healthcare for Some: Rights and Rationing in the United States Since 1930.* University of Chicago Press, 2012.
Hofmann, Peter. *Dentistry Xposed: Protecting You, Your Smile, and Your Wallet.* Self-published, 2019.
Holland, Stephen. *Public Health Ethics.* Polity Press, 2015.
Huggins, Hal A., and Thomas E. Levy. *Uninformed Consent: The Hidden Dangers of Dental Care.* Hampton Roads Publishing Company, 1999.
Jones, Douglas B. *Medicare for the Lazy Man: Simplest and Easiest Guide Ever!* Self-published, 2021.
Joscow, Paul L. *Controlling Hospital Costs: The Role of Government Regulation.* MIT Press, 1984.
Label, Wayne A., and Weldon E. Havins. *Healthcare and Medical Office Accounting: Medical Practice Finance and Accounting Basics for Doctors, Medical Assistants and Bookkeeping Professionals.* 2nd ed. Solana Dreams Publishing Company, 2015.
Lee, Vivian S. *The Long Fix: Solving America's Health Care Crisis with Strategies That Work for Everyone.* W. W. Norton & Company, 2020.

Maag, Jeffie. *How to Start a Home Health Care Agency*. Xlibrius, 2015.
Makary, Marty. *Unaccountable: What Hospitals Won't Tell You and How Transparency Can Revolutionize Healthcare*. Bloomsbury Publishing, 2012.
Marmont, Michael. *The Health Gap: Improving Health in an Unequal World*. Bloomsbury Publishing PLC, 2016.
Matthew, Dana Bowen. *Just Medicine: A Cure for Racial Inequality in American Health Care*. New York University Press, 2018.
Melek, Stephen P., and Bruce S. Pyenson. *Capitation Handbook: Actuarially Determined Capitation Rates for Mental Health Benefits*. American Psychiatric Association, 1995.
Morrisey, Michael A. *Cost Shifting in Health Care: Separating Evidence from Rhetoric*. AEI Press, 1994.
Oshinsky, David M. *Polio: An American Story*. Oxford University Press, 2005.
Posner, Gerald D. *Pharma: Greed, Lies and the Poisoning of America*. Avid Reader Press, 2020.
Potter, Wendell, and Nick Penniman. *Nation on the Take: How Big Money Corrupts Our Democracy and What We Can Do About It*. Bloomsbury Press, 2016.
Quinlan, Heather E. *Plagues, Pandemics, and Viruses: From the Plague of Athens to COVID-19*. Visible Ink Press, 2020.
Reid, T. R. *The Healing of America: A Global Quest for Better, Cheaper and Fairer Healthcare*. Penguin Books, 2010.
Reinhardt, Uwe E. *Priced Out: The Economic and Ethical Costs of American Health Care*. Princeton University Press, 2019.
Renault, David, and Lawon R. Brunch. *Big Med: Megaproviders and the High Cost of Health Care in America*. University of Chicago Press, 2022.
Renee, Angela. *Healthcare Fraud?* 1st ed. Self-published, CreateSpace, 2013.
Sared, Susan Starr and Rushika Fernandopulle. *Uninsured in America: Life and Death in the Land of Opportunity*. University of California Press, 2006.
Schoenholtz, Jack Charles. *The Managed Healthcare Industry—A Market Failure*. 2nd ed. Self-published, CreateSpace, 2012.
Schwartz, Catherine. *Reinsuring Health: Why More Middle-Class People Are Uninsured and What Government Can Do*. Russel Sage Foundation, 2006.
Shilling, John W. *Undercover: How I Went from Company Man to FBI Spy—and Exposed the Worst Healthcare Fraud in U.S. History*. American Management Association, 2008.
Silver, Charles, and David A. Hyman. *Overcharged: Why Americans Pay Too Much for Health Care*. Cato Institute, 2018.
Singh, Harvey. *Why Is American Healthcare So Expensive? Solving the Puzzle of American Healthcare Costs to Build a Low-Cost System*. Self-published, CreateSpace, 2015.
Sloan, Mark. *The Cancer Industry: Crimes, Conspiracy and the Death of My Mother*. EndAllDisease Publishing, 2020.
Tong, Rosemarie. *New Perspectives in Healthcare Ethics: An Interdisciplinary and Cross-cultural Approach*. Pearson Prentice Hall, 2007.
Wagner, Karen A., Francis Wickham Lee, and John P. Glaser. *Health Care Information Systems: A Practical Approach for Healthcare Management*. John Wiley and Sons, 2013.
Welch, Gilbert H., Lisa M. Shorts, and Stephen Woloshin. *Overdiagnosed: Making People Sick in the Pursuit of Health*. Beacon Press, 2011.
Wen, Leana. *Lifelines: A Doctor's Journey in the Fight for Public Health*. Metropolitan Books, 2021.
Wynbrandt, James. *The Excruciating History of Dentistry: Toothsome Tales and Oral Oddities from Babylon to Braces*. St. Martin's Griffin, 1998.

Index

accounts receivable 20–21, 36, 174
Advance magazine 102
Affordable Care Act 16, 17, 58, 72, 111, 131
Alberto N. v Traylor 85, 116, 120, 124
All Smiles Dental 24, 156, 159
American Medical Association (AMA) 35, 64, 67, 76, 86
American Occupational Therapy Association (AOTA) 119
American Physical Therapy Association (APTA) 119
American Speech-Language-Hearing Association (ASHA) 119, 123
Anti-Kickback Statute 30, 191–193
at-home therapy 90, 96, 99–101, 104–105, 107, 113–115, 117, 119, 145, 195–196, 198

balance billing 143
beneficiary 72, 74, 89, 122, 132, 140–144, 197
Biden, Joe 180
Bipartisan Budget of 2015 136
Buffet, Warren 1
Bush, George W. 5, 37, 127

capitation payment; capitated rates 52, 57, 117, 203
Catalogue of Federal Domestic Assistance (CFDA) 18
Center for Public Integrity (CPI) 151
Centers for Medicaid and Medicare (CMS) 7, 16, 40, 57, 60, 64, 66–69, 72, 74, 77, 79, 84, 86–89, 91–92, 95, 98, 101, 104, 106, 112, 123–125, 131, 136–138, 190, 194–195, 197–198, 203
Children's Comprehensive Care Program (CCP) 97–101, 111, 119
Children's Health Insurance Program (CHIP) 19, 50, 54, 80, 111, 115, 131–132, 162
cholera 60–62, 77–78
Churchill, Winston 10, 11
Civil Monetary Penalties Law 193
clean claim 59
coinsurance 54–55, 143–144, 146
Comprehensive Outpatient Rehabilitation Facility (CORF) 88–89, 91, 95–96, 99, 102–106, 113–114, 119, 135, 137, 145–147, 195–196
consolidated budget 79, 81, 93, 196
Contract Management Groups (CMG) 170, 174
copayment 54–55, 121, 157, 191, 199
cost of goods sold 15
Covid-19 1–2, 5–13, 153, 169–170, 197, 199
CPT 92507 64, 75, 77–78, 80, 82–84, 88–89, 92, 102, 105–108, 111–115, 126, 134, 136, 138, 145–147, 194–196, 198, 201
crossover claims 143
Current Procedural Terminology (CPT) 64–65

data mapping 77
deductible 30, 55, 59, 140, 143–144, 146, 157, 170, 199
dental support organizations (DSO) 156–157, 165–166
Dr. Dave 73–74
drug rebate 29–30

Early and Periodic Screening, Diagnosis, and Treatment (EPSDT) 119, 133, 137, 161
electronic claims 59, 63–64, 195,
Electronic Data Systems (EDS) 34–36, 38–40, 127
elements of an audit finding 177
epidemiology 60–61, 76–77, 126
Exclusion Statute 192
exclusive provider 112, 114–116, 118–121, 123–124

False Claims Act 190
Famiglietti, Lisa 1, 4, 75, 144
Federal Acquisition Regulations (FAR) 38
fee-for-service (FFS) 16–17, 45, 48–49, 55, 57, 86–88, 105, 112–113, 115, 117–118, 128, 130, 145, 198, 203
flip and roll 150, 154
Fortune 500 52–53, 58
fraud, waste, and abuse 14, 27, 51, 96, 156, 199
Frew et al v. Phillips et al 23

219

Index

Frew v. Hawkins 157
Frew v Traylor 161

Generally Accepted Accounting Principles (GAAP) 153

HCFA 1500 63, 66, 72
Health Maintenance Organization (HMO) 54, 56, 70, 143
Healthcare Common Procedure Coding System (HCPCS) 64, 67–68, 107
Hippocratic oath 183
Home and Community Support Services Agency (HCSSA) 90–91, 96–101, 104–105, 116–118
Home Health Agency (HHA) 88, 91, 94–96, 99–102, 105–106, 108, 113–114, 119, 135–137
Hospital Corporation of America (HCA) 170
hospital cost audits 51
House Bill 2292 26, 51

ICD-10 64–66
independent therapists 91–92, 95, 113, 135, 145
Institute of Medicine (IOM) 122–123

Johnson, Lyndon B. 35
Journal of the American Medical Association (JAMA) 152–153, 203

Kaiser Family Foundation (KFF) 54, 57, 94, 96, 111

LBJ Great Society 154
Licensed and Certified Home Health (LCHH) 97
lobbyist 28, 32, 151, 182, 203
long-term services and supports (LTSS) 117

macro accounting 76, 126–127, 150, 198
managed care; managed care organization (MCO) 16–17, 41–43, 49–51, 54–58, 64–65, 72, 74, 85, 104, 107, 111–119, 121, 126, 128–130, 139, 141–142, 144–146, 159, 161, 189, 195, 197–198, 202–203
MaxROI 44, 108, 112–113, 115–125, 129
Medicaid and CHIP Payment and Access Commission (MACPAC) 50
Medical Loss Ratio (MLR) 57, 170
medical necessity 79, 86, 90, 116–117, 122–124, 139, 194
Medicare Conditions of Participation (CoPs) 100–101
Medicare Physician Fee Schedule 87, 91, 134, 136
modifiers 65, 68, 89, 147, 196
moral hazard 20, 22–25, 31, 36, 52, 156, 171, 202–203

National Correct Coding Initiative (NCCI) 65, 72, 93, 106, 112
National Health Care Anti-Fraud Association 202
National Heritage Insurance Company (NHIC) 35–36, 38–39, 127–128
National Provider Identifier (NPI) 21, 37, 64–65, 68–71, 73, 98–99, 104–105, 132, 195–196
non-Medicare-certified HCSSA 99–100

Obama, Barack, also Obamacare 5, 16, 18–19
occupational therapy 85, 89, 97–99, 102, 116, 120, 124–125, 139, 142, 192
Office of Inspector General (OIG; HHSC-OIG) 27, 51, 74–75, 102, 116–117, 123, 125, 140, 189, 192–193
Outpatient Rehabilitation Facility (ORF) 88–89, 91, 95–96, 102–106, 114, 119, 135, 137, 145–147, 195–196
overpayment 21, 37, 77, 80, 88, 92, 112, 129, 131, 197, 201, 203

payor of last resort 137, 139, 143
Perot, Ross 34–35, 39–40, 60
Personal Care Services (PCS) 98
personal protection equipment (PPE) 7–8, 12
Pharmacy Benefit Manager (PBM) 30–31
pharmacy price "spread" 22–23, 25–26, 29, 201
physical therapy 85, 89, 98, 116, 120, 124–125, 139, 142, 192
Physician Payment Sunshine Act 194
Physician Self-Referral Law 191
place of service (POS) 65–66, 75, 82, 85–86, 88, 107, 112, 115, 137, 142, 196–198
poverty level 16–17
Prefered Provider Organization (PPO) 54, 116, 120–121, 143
private practice 1, 91, 118–119, 137, 139, 146, 198

recoup 21, 31, 36–37, 133
Resource-Based Relative Value Scale (RBRV) 86–87
risk adjustment 44–45
Roosevelt's New Deal 154

Say's Law of Markets 102
Scott, Mark 1, 4, 14 20, 31, 35, 38, 43, 51, 129, 174, 178, 180
service delivery area 115, 118
Single Audit Act of 1984 154–155, 179–180
site neutral 82, 92, 135, 137, 139, 147, 149, 198
Snow, John 60, 62, 77–78
Social Security Act 35, 50, 58, 81–82, 88, 93, 100, 111, 120, 137, 139
speech therapy 63–64, 74–75, 77, 80, 88–91, 94–95, 99–100, 102, 108–109, 116–117, 119–120, 125, 137, 139, 147, 194, 196, 201

Index 221

speech therapy assistants 99, 101, 109, 148
speech-language pathologist (SLP) 1, 91, 98, 104–106, 108–109, 112, 116, 119, 124–125, 142, 147–148, 198; *see also* speech therapy
State Medicaid Director's Letter (SMDL) 87

Tax Identification Number (TIN) 21, 70
taxonomy 65, 69–71, 73, 98–99
Texas Alcoholic Beverage Commission (TABC) 175–176
Texas Department of Aging Disability Services (DADS) 96
Texas Health and Human Services Commission (HHSC) 63, 74, 84, 105, 113, 119, 129, 194, 196
Texas Health Department 21
Texas Medicaid Administrative Systems (TMAS) 39
Texas Medicaid Health Partnership (TMHP) 104, 117, 121
Texas Medicaid Provider Procedures Manual (TMPPM) 68, 89, 121–122, 125

Texas Provider Identifier (TPI) 21, 64, 99–100
Texas State Auditor's Office (SAO) 53, 129
Texas State Board of Dental Examiners 159, 165
third party liability 132–133, 139–142, 144, 201
Title XIX 16, 35, 97,-98
Trump, Donald 7–8, 10–12, 180–181
tuberculosis 6

UB 04 63
unbundling 173
US Government Accountability Office (GAO) 14, 16, 20, 44–45, 130, 141, 145, 203
US Supreme Court 24, 137, 161
upcoding 172–173, 189

Vendor Drug Program 22, 178

World Health Orgranization (WHO) 32, 65